MASTERFUL COACHING FIELDBOOK

MASTERFUL COACHING FIELDBOOK

*Grow Your Business,
Multiply Your Profits,
Win the Talent War!*

JOSSEY-BASS/PFEIFFER
A Wiley Company
www.pfeiffer.com

Copyright © 2000 by Jossey-Bass/Pfeiffer

ISBN: 0-7879-4755-5

Library of Congress Cataloging-in-Publication Data

Hargrove, Robert A.
    Masterful coaching fieldbook : grow your business, multiply your profits, win the talent war! /
Robert Hargrove.
       p.   cm.
    Includes bibliographical references and index.
    ISBN 0-7879-4755-5 (pbk. : alk. paper)
    1. Teams in the workplace. 2. Industrial efficiency. 3. Employee motivation. 4. Employees—Training
of. 5. Group relations training. I. Title.
HD66.H372   1999
658.3'124—dc21   99-37628
                                              CIP

Printed in the United States of America

Published by

350 Sansome Street, 5th Floor
San Francisco, California 94104-1342
(415) 433-1740; Fax (415) 433-0499
(800) 274-4434; Fax (800) 569-0443

Visit our website at: www.pfeiffer.com

Acquiring Editor: Matthew Holt
Director of Development: Kathleen Dolan Davies
Developmental Editor: Rachel Livsey
Editor: Rebecca Taff
Senior Production Editor: Dawn Kilgore
Manufacturing Supervisor: Becky Carreño
Interior Design: Yvo Reizebos
Cover Design: Jennifer Hines

Printing 10 9 8 7 6 5 4

This book is printed on acid-free, recycled stock that meets or exceeds the minimum GPO and EPA requirements for recycled paper.

CONTENTS

ACKNOWLEDGMENTS
& Dedication

I would like to dedicate this book to Sue and Eva, wife and daughter. During the time that I was writing this book, my daughter Eva was born. Sue not only took on the sometimes daunting responsibilities of new motherhood, but also contributed immeasurably to the book.

I would like to acknowledge Carl Kaestner, my colleague, for his friendship, tireless dedication to the production of this book, unflagging research, and careful editing. It was a true team effort that I have seldom experienced before.

I would like especially to acknowledge Matt Holt of Jossey-Bass, who has been my partner on this book (and the ensuing films, tools, and methods that come with it) from the very first. He is, in addition to being a great businessperson, wonderfully personal, positive, and caring in his approach.

I am extremely grateful to the people I interviewed for this book, some of whom became friends and business partners in the process—Jay Abraham, Chris Higgins, Tony Jimenez, Steve Johnson, Tom Kaiser, Bob Mason, J. Mays, Gary Peck, Phebe Farrow Port, Michel Renaud, Hubert Saint-Onge, Tom Sudman, Art Wilson, and Ben Zander.

Finally, I would like to acknowledge all the people who have called, written, or e-mailed to say they were genuinely inspired by the first *Masterful Coaching* book. Many of these calls came while I was writing this fieldbook, and I cannot express how personally inspiring and encouraging your thoughtfulness was for me.

Let's keep the connection!

INTRODUCTION
The Germination of This Book

One night I stood on top of a mountain in Vail, Colorado, talking about the future with my part-ner, Susan. It was a balmy spring night and the breeze seemed to clarify our thoughts. Coaching is a prerequisite whenever higher performance is required—in business, sports, the performing arts.

She said that, given the shift to the competitive, high-performance, high-velocity environment we are in, every Fortune 500 CEO and manager, every team leader, and every small business leader is going to have to become a coach and teacher. That conversation led to the flash of the obvious—a book on masterful coaching targeted at a broad spectrum of managers in America and the rest of the world today.

I had written *Masterful Coaching* in 1995 and been told by many how inspired they were by it, but frankly there were still many unanswered questions that needed to be addressed—questions we didn't have the answers to when we started out, such as, What is coaching? What is the busi-ness case for coaching? How do you introduce coaching into organizations in which coaching is nonexistent? What are the distinct roles that the coach plays? Is coaching for individuals or groups? Is there a simple, powerful, step-by-step model? How can I be more effective with coach-ing conversations?

I then talked to Matt Holt, an editor at Jossey-Bass, about a masterful coaching fieldbook. He solidly backed the idea and amplified it by suggesting masterful coaching courseware and other peripherals to go with it. We were suddenly off and running.

THE BOOK'S TEACHABLE POINT OF VIEW

I have written this book for leaders, managers, and business owners who are looking for a way to create a powerful new future for their companies and a way to catapult their careers forward. It is my view that great leaders of inspired, high-performance organizations are always, first and foremost, coaches and teachers.

I see coaching as everything you do as a manager to (1) win the war for the best talent; (2) maximize performance on demand in the face of change, complexity, and competition; and (3) ignite personal and team learning while building organizational capability. It is a masterful coach's ability to combine these three elements in his or her job with both *individuals* and *groups* that is powerful and dynamic.

Coaching is viewed here as something that lies at the heart of the manager's daily and weekly agenda, not at its periphery. It encompasses much more than annual reviews, team sessions, or abstract training programs that don't connect to the real work or to bottom-line results. It has been my observation that coaching is by far the most effective way to develop leaders, increase performance, improve problem solving, and foster creative collaboration.

The book is intended not as a "swipe" at your management expertise, but rather to complement and augment what you already know about managing by distinguishing the specific roles that masterful coaches play in today's "knowledge economy" to produce extraordinary and tangible results amid change and complexity—roles you may not be familiar with.

The focus of this book is specifically on coaching knowledge workers and knowledge work that involves creativity and innovation. I am speaking of new products, new services, finding faster, better, cheaper ways of doing things—not coaching in jobs that involve single tasks or repetitive transactions. As knowledge work is a social activity, the book is about both coaching individuals and coaching teams made up of far-flung collaborators. It will provide guidelines for coaching individuals and groups through multiple media, face-to-face, and by phone, e-mail, or groupware over the Web.

WHAT'S IN IT FOR YOU?

The book has a structure that is designed to help you become a masterful coach, as well as to introduce coaching into your organization.

PART I

Chapters One through Five provide a coaching mind-set as well as some basic coaching conversation skills. They show how to build a business case for coaching, they define what coaching is, and they will help you to establish a culture of coaches and coaching in your organization.

PART II

Chapters Six through Ten provide a powerful, concise, universally applicable five-step coaching model, which I call *Masterful Coaching—The Method*™. Be sure to read the introduction to Part II, which provides a synopsis of the model, so you will quickly be able to understand and put it to use.

PART III

Chapters Eleven through Sixteen provide interviews with masterful coaches who have specific domain expertise in a wide variety of areas—product design, project management, marketing, sales, e-coaching, and so on.

LET'S KEEP UP THE CONVERSATION

In the past, the limits of print technology kept the answers to the questions raised in books bound and carefully covered. Today, with the advent of digital technology, it is possible to write a perpetual book that allows both new questions and answers to evolve in conversation between author and readers—or among a community of people. This is especially needed today because by the time you have figured out the answers, most of the questions have changed.

I would like to share with you any new perspectives, methods, tools, and issues that I develop or that come into view in the years ahead. I am certain that as you try to apply the principles and tools in your business and job, you will have many insights that you would also like to pass on. For this purpose, I have created a Web site: *masterfulcoaching.com*. This will be a place for us to engage in dialogue about your coaching goals and challenges. It will be a place for you to have your questions answered. There will be coaching essays by various experts on leading-edge ideas, coaching tips, and techniques. Also, you will have the opportunity to find more information on masterful coaching educational products offered in collaboration with Jossey-Bass.

So, let's keep in touch. Keep up the conversation. Share the knowledge.

Robert Hargrove
September 1999

MASTERFUL COACHING FIELDBOOK

PART I

DEVELOPING A COACHING MIND-SET

After writing **Masterful Coaching** *in 1995, I received many phone calls and letters from company leaders and others about the book. These people would often invite me to come into their organizations and talk about coaching in various kinds of executive roundtables and gatherings.*

It was during these meetings that I became aware of the significant cultural obstacles that existed in many organizations to introducing coaching and a culture of coaching. I have a saying, "Everything you say reveals you." Eventually, if you keep talking long enough, you will reveal not just your goals and aspirations but also your underlying beliefs and assumptions. As I spoke to managers, I realized from what they said that most of them did not have a coaching mind-set, nor did their companies have a coaching culture.

For one thing, there was a great deal of confusion as to just what coaching is. Was it the leader's job, human resource professional's job, or outside consultant's job? Was it for top talent or for midrange people? Was it about performance or was it about development? One thing is certain: few people saw it as something that lay at the heart of management. Many saw it as a discreet activity to be tacked on at the end of the annual performance review.

Coaching was not showing up in these organizations in any meaningful way. It is my observation that the higher you raise the bar of excellence, the more you need coaching. It is interesting to me that most Olympic athletes are coached for four to five hours a day for four years. The same kind of coaching intensity applies to most people and groups in the performing arts. Yet if you ask most managers whether or not they have received any coaching lately, the answer will probably be no.

This has implications not only in terms of the performance standards that are set in organizations but also for the development standards. William James said something to the effect that the most intolerable state for a human being is the absence of acknowledgment. It is rare that I come across a talented person in an organization who has had a meaningful conversation with his or her leader about next developmental steps. In many cases, people consider this not only a lack of acknowledgment for their efforts, but also a reason to respond to the messages of search firms on their voice mail.

By contrast, those talented people who had a coach or mentor who understood their passions, goals, and aspirations and empowered and enabled them on both the performance and developmental side, looked at this as a strong reason not only to remain in a company but also to work with passion, commitment, and zeal.

What all of this told me was that it would be important in this book to establish a coaching mind-set before providing readers with a method. I personally believe that without a coaching mind-set, no technique, no matter how well-conceived or taught, is sustainable.

The first five chapters are intended to provide this mind-set, as well as some basic coaching conversation skills.

- Chapter One clarifies what *masterful coaching* is and will assist you in clarifying the roles that masterful coaches play in leading companies. It also creates the business case for coaching in almost any organization today.

- Chapter Two addresses the "four big myths" that represent a substantial barrier to creating coaches and a culture of coaching today in most organizations. Personally, it will assist you in developing the mind-set you need to become a masterful coach in your business with colleagues, amid change and complexity.

- Chapter Three supports you in looking at the individuals or groups you coach from a coach's perspective, as if for the first time, and in developing a personal coaching mission. It also provides guiding principles for coaching in today's knowledge economy.

- Chapter Four provides more than a dozen ideas you can use personally to get ready for coaching. For example, it is difficult to be a coach if you have never received any coaching yourself.

- Chapter Five provides you with the *six-cap coaching conversation system*. It shows you how to have powerful and profound coaching conversations by distinguishing six different kinds of coaching conversations, and provides cues for when to use each one.

EVERY MANAGER A COACH, EVERY PERSON A BUSINESSPERSON

Building the Business Case

This book is about you! This book is for leaders at all levels—CEOs, business unit managers, project leaders, small business owners. It is based on one elemental truth, the ignorance of which will make the difference between being a winning business organization and being just another "me too" competitor. That fundamental truth is that leadership is about coaching and teaching. If you are a leader, you are first and foremost a coach and a teacher.

It is only through coaching and teaching that you will be able to reframe people's paradigms and transform who they are—from "cop" to coach, from warring tribes to teams, from resignation to passion. It is only through coaching and teaching that you will be able to accomplish breakthroughs and solve complex problems in the face of change and complexity. It is through coaching and teaching that you will be able to spark learning and build the capabilities needed to succeed.

One of the fundamental insights I gained in researching this book is that the most admired CEOs all devote a great deal of time to coaching and teaching. It is this aspect of their leadership that seems to lead to high-performance organizations, evokes excellence in others, and at the same time outdistances the competition. Some well-known examples are Jack Welch of General Electric, Andy Grove of Intel, Roger Enrico of PepsiCo, and Leonard Lauder of Estée Lauder.

These people, and many others at other levels whom you will meet in this book, discovered the insight in building leading organizations that coaching (teaching) is the essential ingredient whenever high performance occurs—whether in sports, the performing arts, or business. They have translated this insight into personal and organizational success. And so can you!

A leader is the relentless architect of the possibility that others can be.

Benjamin Zander, Conductor of the Boston Philharmonic[2]

ORGANIZATIONS NEED COACHES AND A CULTURE OF COACHING MORE THAN EVER

Although a handful of CEOs and managers have embraced the importance of coaching and teaching, coaching is still not practiced in many organizations. This has to do with the way leadership is defined. It also has to do with the fact that until recently the level of performance required of most businesses simply was not high enough to require coaching. Today, the high-performance environment is not unlike standing in the Olympic tunnel before the games, at the base camp at Mt. Everest, or in the practice rooms at Carnegie Hall before a big concert. As a result, many business leaders are rethinking the way they look at leadership, to include coaching as well as a culture of coaching. The following are some examples of changes taking place in business today.

Talent Wars. McKinsey and Company reports that every business should prepare for a long and grueling war to attract, develop, and keep the best talent. It will take innovative hiring practices to recruit people, not search firms and worn-out personnel practices. For example, Robert Ford, a native South African who formerly held top-level posts in Intrinsa Corporation and Objectivity Incorporated, was being courted by two dozen companies in Silicon Valley. He was made a glowing offer to take charge of all product development at Extensity Inc. The commute, however, was a killer. The CEO (coach) decided to look at Ford as if he were an all-star athlete. The deal maker was a chauffeur-driven car to and from work.[3] Other companies are offering talented working mothers "home office" options and giving young MBAs fresh out of school hot projects, rather than mind-numbing, entry-level jobs.

Hypercompetition. Today, you may or may not be a global competitor operating in several different continents, yet you can be sure that you have global rivals, whether you are a major oil company, a software designer, or a local movie house. You probably have competitors conspiring twenty-four hours a day to corner your market and take your customers. For example, Shell Oil Company in France saw its market share cut it half in two years by oil companies in the European hypermarket it had never even heard of. A combination of aggressive coaching and collaborative teamwork turned Shell France around. In 1998 it recorded double-digit profitability and growth.[4]

Ever-Increasing Customer Expectations. In the battle for markets, almost every company strives to give customers exactly what they want, when they want it, at a price they can afford. The result is that customers have ever-increasing expectations. Priceline Inc., for example, has created a healthy business selling airline tickets on top airlines at the price customers ask for.

Today all businesses are faced with doing complex, difficult things for customers that traditional management is ill-equipped to handle. It will take coaches to bring a talented team together, create a value proposition, and package knowledge from whomever or whatever to meet ever-changing customer demands.

Impact of a Digital Economy. Today change is happening so fast that there is a blur between producers and consumers, products and services, high-tech (e-mail) and high-touch (relationships). The speed of providing marketing information, doing transactions, and providing customer service has accelerated dramatically.

As Kevin Kelly of *Wired* says, "If you are not responding to customers in real time, you are dead."[5] The flow of bread off the grocery store's shelf can be monitored in real time with digital tools so that the baking company can show up with a second order today, not tomorrow. Your company needs coaches to examine the speed of knowledge in your system and to bring it closer to real time so that your company can perform on demand.

Gap Between Performance Demands and Capability. As demand increases, the gap between performance expectations and organizational and personal capability grows. It takes coaching and mentoring to fill the gap in real time, whether it involves sending a high-potential leader on a stretch assignment, orchestrating an "outsourcing" alliance with another firm, or igniting a sense of curiosity and learning on a team with a tough performance goal.

Coaching is about continuously expanding your personal (organizational) capacity to perform and learn.

WHAT IS COACHING? THE NEW FACE OF LEADERSHIP

As Steve Miller, group managing director of Royal Dutch Shell, says, "In the past, the leader was the guy who told people what to do and had all the answers. Today, if you are going to have a successful company, you have to realize that no leader can possibly have all the answers. The leader may have a vision. But the actual solutions about how to best meet the challenges of the moment have to be made by the people closest to the action. . . . As they struggle with the details of this challenge, the leader becomes their coach, teacher, and facilitator. Change how you define leadership, and you change the way you run the company."[6]

I feel that it is important to offer business leaders a definition of coaching that is broader and deeper than the conventional one used in business today. Coaching is more than interacting one-to-one with people and giving them some advice or feedback. Coaching is more than acting as a facilitator at a team meeting. Coaching people to perform at peak levels and develop in their jobs in real time is different from sending them off to abstract training programs.

Coaching lies at the heart of management, not at the edges. Coaching is *everything* you do to produce extraordinary results in your business with colleagues amid change, complexity, and competition. (You don't need coaching for "ordinary results.") Coaching is *everything* you do to improve your strategic thinking about the business future you want to create. Coaching is *everything* you do to ignite personal and team learning in solving business problems while building the organizational capability you need to succeed. It is *everything* you do to give you and your entire organization an edge and advantage. Figure 1.1 illustrates this concept.

FIGURE 1.1 *What coaching is*

Business coaching is everything you do to

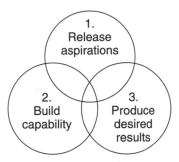

1.
Release
aspirations

2.
Build
capability

3.
Produce
desired
results

Admid change, complexity, competition

> *Coaching involves holding out a possibility in front of others while coaching them to move to the next level with relentless compassion.*

WHAT DOES COACHING LOOK LIKE?

Many leaders today who become involved in strategic issues, stakeholder issues, and legal issues lose touch with the people and customers who actually drive the business. Instead of preaching and teaching about the reality of what it will take to reach goals, they make polite conversation. Instead of saying, "These are *my* people; how can I further develop them on the job?" they look at people as abstractions on a human resource report to be shuttled off to developmental programs. This is not what coaching looks like.

A coach is less like the imperial CEO of the past and much more like a platoon leader with a mission to accomplish, a teachable point of view, and a camaraderie with people on the front lines.[7] Coaching may not always fit our pictures of the right way to coach people—hierarchal or collaborative, tough-minded or compassionate, challenging or supportive. It may not always be called coaching or teaching—even when it is that.

One of the best stories I've heard was about Coca-Cola's chief executive, Doug Ivester, whose mission is, "I want to buy the world a Coke" and whose teachable point of view is to make sure you can buy a Coke any time, anywhere in the world. He often touts something taught to him by former CEO Roberto Goizueta, "Think 'share of stomach' versus 'share of market.'"

Late one night Ivester, a burly man, was spotted storming down Nanjing Road in Shanghai with a small platoon of people from the local market area. He was looking for a place where he could buy a Coca-Cola. He went into one shop and the Coke fountain was turned off because they were waiting for spring and the warm weather. As he left the shop, he saw an old woman selling a drink made of tea-soaked eggs and soy sauce.

He asked her if she had any Coke. No sale. A few weeks later, he was talking to a group of young protégées back at the home office telling them this story. "Do you realize the significance of that lady with the tea-soaked eggs?" he asked. The group looked puzzled. "We are competing with that egg," he said, and then encouraged them to see what they could do about it.[8]

Coaching and teaching do not have to look a certain way. Ask yourself, Does what I'm doing unleash aspirations? Does it alter the paradigm people are operating from so they are able to recognize possibilities for personal and business success they did not see before? Does it build business performance? Does it build capability or ignite personal (team) learning?

YOUR COACHING ROAD MAP: BECOMING ORIENTED

There is often a need for a "coaching road map" to ground what might otherwise be an amorphous concept. The key is recognizing that although business performance is central, maximizing human performance—both individually and in teams—lies at the core. For decades now, companies have been concerned with "process," regardless of whether it was strategic planning, reengineering, or management development. Today's leaders are making a shift from process to results, or from inputs to outputs. That's part of why coaching can be defined as "everything you do to produce extraordinary results."

It is useful to understand how coaching varies according to your role in the organization, as well as to have a basic coaching road map. Ten strategic road markers map our journey to masterful coaching in business. Each one of these markers can have a significant impact on maximizing human performance. Figure 1.2 illustrates the coaching road map. The following paragraphs describe the steps along the road.

FIGURE 1.2 *The coaching road map*

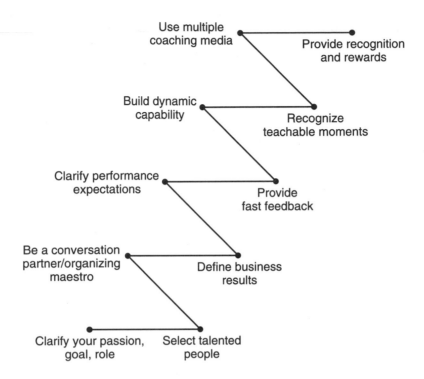

Use multiple coaching media

Provide recognition and rewards

Build dynamic capability

Recognize teachable moments

Clarify performance expectations

Provide fast feedback

Be a conversation partner/organizing maestro

Define business results

Clarify your passion, goal, role

Select talented people

1. *Clarify your passion, goal, and role in the company.* The way you approach coaching will vary according to the company's vision and values and your roles and responsibilities. An executive will have different coaching tasks than a local line manager or network member as their jobs carry different responsibilities.

2. *Select talented people and engage their passions.* This means being a connoisseur of talent who can attract people who may be powerful assets in accomplishing your goals and objectives. The key is not only selecting the best talent but also engaging people by offering them roles that are challenging and empowering and that speak to their emotional needs.

3. *Be a conversation partner and organizing maestro.* This means interacting with people to improve strategies and sculpt new patterns of relationships and interaction, including creating forums in which strategic conversations can take place and facilitating people in thinking and working better together.

4. *Define the business results.* Coaching needs to take place in the context of stretching business goals and communicating what needs to be achieved—reinventing the brand, developing product breakthroughs, smoothing operations, generating customers, or seeking greater sales and profits.

5. *Clarify performance expectations.* Once desired business results are defined, it's essential that a masterful coach collaborate to set goals that unleash personal and collective aspirations. Once these goals are set, a coach must be prepared to create a climate of accountability and breakthrough.

6. *Provide fast feedback.* In today's high-performance, high-velocity business world, even a quarterly review is often not enough. People need performance-related feedback that is FAST—*fast, accurate, straightforward,* and *timely.*[9] Make sure that feedback is both challenging and supportive as this can have a huge impact on results.

7. *Build dynamic capability.* As performance expectations increase dramatically, there is always a gap between performance and capability. On an individual level, this involves recognizing people with high potential and developing them as leaders. On a group level, it involves sculpting new patterns of relationships and interaction and improving the quality of conversations.

8. *Recognize teachable moments.* Coaching often involves recognizing small incidents that occur on the job and using them as "teachable moments." For example, if someone is struggling with a goal or problem and asks for help or if team members are pursuing their own agenda at a meeting rather than group initiatives, it's the perfect time to engage in discussion on the issue.

9. *Use multiple coaching media.* In a fast-paced global economy, face-to-face coaching is not always possible. An effective coach today needs to be able to make effective use of multiple media, not only the telephone and e-mail but also groupware.

I know many people who did very good work before and after they worked with him. Everyone I knew, however, did great work while they worked with him.

Ken Olsen on Edwin Land, founder of Polaroid[10]

10. *Provide recognition and rewards.* Masterful coaches imbue a generosity of spirit that allows them to have difficult conversations with others and, at the same time, to be generous in their acknowledgments. They look for numerous small ways to reward people.

COACHING IS A WAY TO GET THE MOST OUT OF WHAT YOU HAVE

What does this all mean for you? Whether you are a CEO of a Fortune 500 company, a division vice president, a front-line leader in charge of a project team, or a small business owner with just a few employees, you owe it to yourself and your business to obtain the maximum possible performance (results) with a minimum of cost and effort. Whether your goals include giving your career a boost, developing the next generation of leaders, growing your business exponentially, multiplying profits, or winning the talent war, reaching them starts with tapping the vast hidden reserves of resources at your disposal.

No doubt there are ways in which your company or business area is possibly underperforming: there may be manufacturing capacity you are not using, products and services that could be marketed more effectively, or customer relationships that could be more highly leveraged. And no doubt you have yet to tap the talent, performance potential, or skills of the people on your team either individually or collectively.

The question many business leaders are asking today is, "How do I make the most of what I have?" The answer to the question lies in masterful coaching. The moment you begin to develop coachable goals that are near and clear and a teachable point of view, you will begin to powerfully move your business from where it is to where you want it to be.

STARTING RIGHT NOW, BEGIN TO SEE YOURSELF DIFFERENTLY

I have observed in the process of coaching thousands of people over the years that if people see themselves in a new way, they will begin to act in a new way. If people start to think differently, they will act differently. One of the ways to alter people's frames of reference is to make distinctions between the *old way* and the *new way.* Starting right now, from this moment on, look at yourself differently.

- See yourself as a leader who has an impact on others' visions and values and enables them to create a new future, rather than just managing people on tasks.

- See yourself as a coach (intervener) who expands people's capacity to perform at higher levels by intervening in situations and providing what's missing, rather than being a supervisor or checker.

- See yourself as a teacher who transforms people's paradigms and shares practical know-how with others, rather than as just a function head.

- See yourself as a mentor who furthers people's professional development, rather than as someone who simply gets things done through other people.

REFLECTION ASSIGNMENT
Seeing Yourself as a Coach

Who we are, the way we think and interact, is shaped by an inner conversation that plays in the back of our minds. Old conversations (tapes) are those that lead to unintended results. New conversations allow us to see things differently and act differently.

1. Take a piece of paper. Write one sentence that sums up the way you see yourself as a manager today, for example: cop, checker, coach, thinking partner.

2. Notice whether that view in any way limits you as a coach. Reflect on it with a colleague or by yourself over the next few days.

3. Then write another sentence that represents a new conversation. Act on that conversation for the following week.

4. When the old thinking or behavior comes up or gets in the way, say to yourself, "I am not committed to that" and adjust your thinking and behavior accordingly.

NOW, BEGIN TO ACT DIFFERENTLY

How you coach depends on your role, purpose, and perspective. We said earlier that leaders' coaching involves everything you do as a manager to produce extraordinary results—in a high-performance, highly competitive, high-velocity environment. To be sure, coaches do some of the same things that managers do in every corporation—set higher goals, plan collaboratively, stick with fundamentals, and mobilize people. Yet there are distinct things that leaders or managers will do when they are coaching that pertain to their role, purpose, and perspective.

Executive Leader's Key Coaching Responsibilities. Coaching at the "C" level of management—CEO, COO, CIO, and so on—can have an enormous impact on maximizing human performance. It involves vision, values, strategies, being an organizing maestro, creating teamwork at the top, and mentoring. It is curious that so many managers at this level have told me they receive little or no coaching. Here are the key coaching responsibilities at this level:

- Fostering leadership and teamwork at the top with a teachable point of view

- Transforming a climate of resignation into a climate of opportunity

- Creating stretch goals, winning strategies, and tactics with others

- Building strategic capability—being a talent connoisseur, organizing genius (alliances), developing a learning organization

- Coaching local line leaders on their thinking, performance, development

- Connecting everyone through "relationships tech" so that virtual coaching of individuals and groups is possible

Local Line Leaders' Key Coaching Responsibilities. At this level of leadership, decision makers tend to be less concerned with the broad strategic and cultural issues and more concerned with producing specific results for the operations of the business. Here are the key coaching responsibilities at this level:

- Selecting the most talented people to get the job done

- Setting higher performance goals and standards for yourself and others

- Communicating these goals and providing performance feedback on operational issues

- Creating a development plan for each person in the group

- Expanding team capability through teaching collaboration skills

- Providing recognition and numerous small rewards

- Mentoring people from other areas

Network Members' Key Coaching Responsibilities. As Hubert Saint-Onge, head of strategic capability at the Mutual Group in Canada, says, "Coaching is the way to relate to people across the firm with the intent of causing their success, regardless of boundaries." It involves interacting with people you come into contact with in a way that inspires them to pursue their dreams or maximize performance and capability. It could also involve providing wisdom, compassion, and a sense of humor as it is required. Here are some of the responsibilities:

- Offering a teachable point of view on a business issue

- Sharing practical know-how with colleagues when asked

- Facilitating to further the purpose of the group at meetings

- Intervening when you anticipate an individual or group making a mistake

- Providing potentially embarrassing feedback needed for growth and learning

- Mentoring someone on his or her professional development

FOUR CATALYTIC ROLES FOR COACHES IN THE NEW ECONOMY

The network economy requires new skills for leaders. Wealth is created by creating knowledge needed for innovative products and services that meet customer needs. Coaches need not only to develop innovative leaders and coach for immediate performance results, but also to make knowledge workers more productive, both individually and collectively.

Coaching people to unleash their aspirations, move beyond what they already think and know, and maximize their results is one of the highest aspirations of what it is to be a human.

In researching over a hundred different organizations in forty different countries, I have discovered that there are four key roles that masterful coaches play in today's "knowledge economy." These are not the only roles that coaches play, of course, but they are the central ones. They are like major keys in a symphony on which all the other notes depend. Roles shape, limit, and define people's attitudes and behavior. The clearer people are about what their roles are (and are not), the more powerful, direct, and immediate their actions will be.

These roles are important, whether you are the president of your company, the head of a division, or a project leader or production team manager. Of course, the application of these roles will vary. The four roles are shown in Figure 1.3.

FIGURE 1.3 *Four roles of a masterful coach*

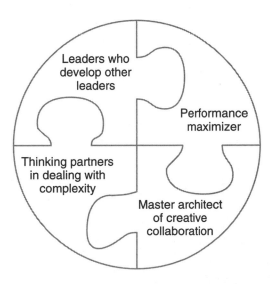

ROLE 1   BEING A LEADER WHO DEVELOPS OTHER LEADERS

Today, there is a growing gap in the supply of leadership, brought about by the proliferation of new businesses as new technologies emerge and customer choices proliferate. This gap is also being generated by new alliances in which no one is directly in charge, by the flattening of organizations, and by the fact that in today's knowledge economy everyone is a volunteer. Filling this leadership supply gap will be essential to building a successful business in the years ahead.

My research with dozens of leading firms shows that leaders developing others leaders, not sending people off to business schools or abstract training programs, is the most high-leverage way to fill the necessary slots. Developing other leaders usually involves presenting talented people with challenging work assignments intended to strengthen their professional development and have an impact on business performance simultaneously. It also involves providing ongoing coaching and mentoring of people in groups, in light of the extraordinary results desired. This approach usually transforms not only the participants but their sponsors as well.

LESSONS FROM GREAT COACHES—GRASSROOTS LEADERSHIP

Royal Dutch Shell is an organization with $128 billion in annual revenues, with a staff of over 101,000 employees in about 130 countries throughout the world. When Steve Miller, 52, became a group managing director, he realized that to grow Shell's business in his area he would have to generate entrepreneurial attitudes at the local level because efforts to transform the culture and bureaucracy of the organization had completely failed to have an impact.

The prior approach was based on transforming one layer of management at a time. The wonderful plans hatched by executives at the home office did not seem to have any impact at the "coal face," Shell's term for front-line activity. Miller realized that he was going to have to find a way to reach past the bureaucracy and get these people involved in the business, especially in the European hypermarkets, where loss of market share and slack growth were already present.

Miller saw that he was going to have to show a different type of leadership. Instead of telling people what to do or giving them the answers from three layers above, he would have to reach through the bureaucracy and act much more like a coach, teacher, and facilitator. Week after week he met with people from more than twenty-five different countries that represented more than 85 percent of Shell's retail sales volume—fifty thousand service stations. Each service station represented an entrepreneurial opportunity.

"We brought together a six- to eight-person team from a half a dozen operating companies worldwide into an intense retailing boot camp. One example, from Malaysia: In an effort to improve service station revenues along major highways, we brought in a cross-functional team that included a dealer, union trucker, and four or five marketing executives." They were taught leadership principles and given some tools for segmenting markets, and they created a value proposition that could apply to a business opportunity in their local areas, for example, to improve filling station performance in Malaysia or sell liquefied natural gas elsewhere in Asia.

Then those teams went home while another group came in. The first teams were asked to spend the next sixty days creating a business plan, then return to the boot camp for a peer review. These sessions took place in a "fishbowl" setting with Miller and others acting as coaches. The sessions were tense but productive learning experiences. At the end of the boot camp, the teams went home to translate their ideas into action. They returned later to report the "breakdowns and breakthroughs."

Miller felt personally challenged as a leader to shift from the role of a manager who figures it all out from the top to the role of coach and conductor. His vulnerabilities were exposed: "One day, all of a sudden, I found myself standing in front of seventy people talking about my transformation." The scariest thing for him was letting go of control, but then he realized that he gained control in a different way—by developing relationships and bringing out the best in people and groups. He also had to learn to be more authentic: "If a business team brings in a plan that is really a bunch of crap, I've got to say so. If I cover for people and praise everyone, what do I do when someone brings in an excellent plan?"

The boot camps worked remarkably well. In January of 1997, Miller received a note from the business team leader for France. Before the boot camp, the company had lost almost half its market share in less than two years to new aggressive competitors, and managers were concerned and did not know what to do. But now Shell in France had recorded double-digit profitability, exceeded its growth target, and achieved double-digit growth. More importantly, the people involved learned how to lead, how to coach, and how to create an organization of businesspeople.[11]

Today, you need to coach people for high-performance every day or you and your business will sink to the bottom of the pool.

PERFORMANCE MAXIMIZER

What does it mean to be a performance maximizer? In most organizations, it means the leader of a business unit adding up the sales, subtracting the losses, and then assigning different areas for improvement the following year. But being a performance maximizer is really about leaders intervening in their businesses as coaches with the intent of producing performance on demand. There is a story about Jack Welch, CEO of General Electric (GE), that illustrates both this and the fact that masterful coaches think and interact with people in ways that don't always fit our pictures.

LESSONS FROM GREAT COACHES

It started with a customer visit during which Welch found out his CAT-scan and X-ray tubes were good for only 25,000 scans, less than half that of the competition. Welch reached down two levels of management, found the person in charge, Marc Onetto, a general manager for service and maintenance in Europe, summoned him to GE headquarters and said, "I want 100,000 scans out of my tubes!" Onetto gasped at the number but was even more shocked by the fact that the chairman would take an interest in what is one of GE's smaller business units; so he went to work.

Onetto took it as a personal challenge. It was an opportunity to be coached by one of the most effective business leaders in the world. Every week for the next four years he faxed Welch progress reports. Welch faxed back in his own handwriting, sometimes cajoling and congratulating, at other times growling.

Onetto formed a team and was at first afraid they would never be able to achieve the goal. But Welch's relentlessness in pursuing the goal, and his belief that they could do it, caused the team to challenge its own methods of building tubes and led to a breakthrough. They began to view their interactions with Welch as not only challenging and supportive but also fun. Today, the division produces tubes that put out between 150,000 and 200,000 scans per tube.

Onetto reported that this was the single most powerful performance breakthrough of his life, as well as the single most powerful learning experience. He learned a tremendous amount about leadership, team collaboration, and achieving something that he and others did not really believe they were capable of.[12]

You can't manage knowledge workers.

Peter Drucker[13]

ROLE 3 **BEING A THINKING PARTNER**

Today, every business and function is trying to reach breakthrough goals and solve complex problems when the answers are not obvious and the solutions are unknown. The idea that leaders delegate a goal or project to a professional manager who then comes up with all the answers is out. Today leaders cannot afford to manage by objectives and action plans alone. They must learn to "manage by collaborative inquiry."

LESSONS FROM GREAT COACHES

As Tom Kaiser, president of Zurich-American International Accounts in Schaumburg, Illinois, told me, "There are only so many customer relationships and projects that you can personally drive as a manager. Being a thinking partner is the only way to manage in a world in which the people in your group are specialists who know much more about their jobs than you do. I cannot dictate their behavior or simply tell them the answers." Kaiser sees being a thinking partner as asking questions and listening in a way that helps people come to a clearer understanding of their own ideas. It could also mean challenging assumptions or making provocative statements that lead to new creative insights.

When Kaiser joined Zurich, the people on his team said, "We're a mature business in a tough market, not a growth business. How do we preserve our market share?" Kaiser's response was, "Let's reframe that; every business is a growth business. Now, what do we have to do to take on the world?" This led to brainstorming ideas that would maximize Zurich's underperforming possibilities, opportunities, and business assets. Sales went from $300 million to $700 million in the next three years.[14]

Being a thinking partner often involves helping people make the best decisions. You may discover that people are overly analytical and don't pay attention to their intuition or that they make intuitive decisions that have not been fully thought out.

Let's say you are coaching someone who is deciding which of two talented managers to hire. The person's intuition tells him to choose "A," but reasoning tells him to choose "B." Instead of coaching the person to choose "A" or "B," giving an answer, ask him or her to wait a while to gain insight into why his or her intuition and reason are in conflict.

What other skills are needed to be a thinking partner? I use the *triple loop learning model,* which has been enormously effective in my role as a thinking partner, both in impacting performance and solving complex problems. The typical scenario is that people have a goal, take action, and produce unintended results. I guide my thinking about what is needed by asking myself the following questions: (1) Does the person need to switch a way of being or role, perhaps becoming a leader instead of a manager? (2) Does the person have ways of thinking that are leading to an inability to solve the problem or to misfired actions? and (3) Does the person need a tip on how to do the same thing better? Figure 1.4 illustrates the triple loop learning model.

Coaching involves sculpting new patterns of relationships and interactions that result in creative and innovative solutions.

FIGURE 1.4 *Triple loop learning*

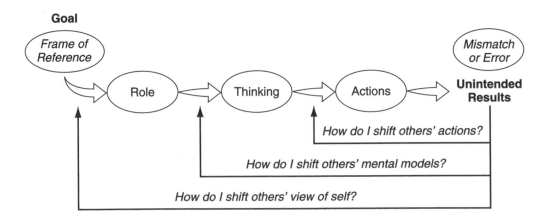

ROLE 4 BEING A MASTER ARCHITECT OF CREATIVE COLLABORATION

Today most companies have discovered that to succeed they have to focus on products and services within their circle of competence. At the same time, customer demand for complex products or difficult services is causing companies to expand their circles of competence through alliances and outsourcing at minimum cost and effort. In the first half of 1998 alone, there were over 10,700 such alliances formed worldwide. The Intelligence Unit of the *Economist* reported that the traditional corporation may cease to exist except as a legal contrivance—to be replaced by an "enterprise community."

At the same time, people in organizations are discovering that although solving complex problems requires teams, solving problems of the highest complexity requires creative collaboration among extraordinary combinations of people who represent different views and backgrounds. It has become increasingly clear that creative genius is not the result of individual efforts but rather collaborative in nature, whether it is happening in research and development, in marketing, or on the factory floor.

As Joan Holmes, executive director of the Hunger Project, pointed out to me, "Collaborations don't just happen. They take leadership."[15] One of the coaching roles that is essential today is what I call being a "master architect of creative collaboration," or what Warren Bennis refers to as an "organizing genius."[16] It takes a certain kind of coaching skill beyond normal team building to articulate goals that inspire collaboration, to create and bring together extraordinary combinations of people around a business problem, and to facilitate a focused dialogue that results in a collective work product.

One of the best examples I have ever seen of this is Douglas Dayton, the Boston director of IDEOS, an industrial design firm that helped come up with the Apple mouse, the stand-up Crest toothpaste tube, and the Motorola flip phone. Dayton considers himself a "horizontal engineer" when solving customer problems. He regularly brings together such motley groups as industrial designers, hardware engineers, fashion experts, venture capitalists, and end users in his brainstorming sessions. The idea behind this is that the more juxtapositions there are of talented people with different perspectives, the more innovation there will be.

It is important not only to bring unlikely collaborators together but also to ensure real dialogue. In Dayton's world, this often looks like a lot of people in one room shouting at each other, which is a sign that people have given up the need to be in agreement—the secret of real dialogue. Someone usually states a solution, someone else states a second solution, and then someone else comes up with a third solution that integrates the previous two but takes it to a whole new level.[17]

Granted, you may not be a member of an industrial design firm, but the next time you are dealing with a complex problem, what kind of extraordinary combination of people will you bring together to solve it? How will you create a dialogue in which people give up the need to be in agreement? How will you move people past a warring tribes syndrome and guild mentality?

REFLECTION ASSIGNMENT

Leadership Agility

Masterful coaches practice leadership agility. Rate yourself on a scale of 1 to 5 (1 is low and 5 is high) on your ability to play each one of these roles. Then decide what the results show about new roles you need to take on or capabilities you need to strengthen.

1. Foster a spirit of inquiry into the situation when appropriate.

2. Play a leadership development role when appropriate.

3. Play a coaching and teaching role when appropriate.

4. Play a demanding, driving execution role when appropriate.

5. Play a collaborative leadership role when appropriate.

6. Play a hands-off, fully delegating leadership role when appropriate.

7. Play a (supportive) encouraging leadership role when appropriate.

SIMPLE BUT POWERFUL WAYS TO GET INVOLVED IN COACHING

Transformational change starts with shifting your mind-set, seeing yourself differently; but it is sometimes useful to have a few guidelines for action. These can be like a flashlight in a dark room.

- Declare your intention to operate much more like a coach, teacher, people developer. Ask to co-lead a seminar.

- Set stretch goals that are near and clear, that raise the bar of excellence for everyone in your group and create conditions for performance on demand.

- Lead a coaching project in which you personally guide people to results and work on developing their expertise at the same time.

- Offer to act as a thinking partner with someone who has a complex problem.

- Invite people to co-lead a course or seminar.

- Bring together an extraordinary combination of people to solve a problem.

- Find someone who can act as your coach and mentor.

- If you are exceptional at something, such as making a budget presentation or sales call, have people from your team watch you.

- Brainstorm with your group more ways to get involved with coaching.

Up with business persons. Down with empowerment.

Tom Peters[18]

EVERY JOB HOLDER A BUSINESSPERSON

Business is a game. Masterful coaches have a passion for winning. At the same time, it is hard to win if the people you are playing with don't see themselves as players or understand how to have an impact on the things that influence the score. Today, many companies are seriously looking at the question of how to turn every employee into a business unit of one. To be sure, one of the most powerful forms of leadership—coaching and teaching—is the ability to alter people's perspectives and transform the paradigms that shape who they are.

It usually starts with one or more leaders at the executive level having a teachable point that they cascade down. According to Hubert Saint-Onge, director of strategic capability (formerly human resources) at the Mutual Group, "When I first joined the company, I told the top management group, 'I am a businessperson first, and second, I bring a particular perspective to bear on issues.' I see my role primarily as a business coach with a particular focus on making sure the company can meet its strategic goals by building capability and organization learning. This starts with speaking up honestly at business strategy meetings and giving my opinions, even when it includes challenging the orthodoxies of others around the table."[19]

What about middle management? Says Chris Turner of Xerox Business Systems (XBS), as quoted in Tom Peter's *Circle of Innovation,* "Our ultimate strategy is about creating an organization of 15,000 effective business people where everybody thinks about the future, everybody energizes customers, and everybody pays attention to the bottom line."[20] Xerox is one of many companies that is wrapping big service around a product. They are becoming the Electronic Data Systems of photocopying. Today, many big companies are outsourcing their entire document processing operation to XBS, whose people work on the customer's premises, far from any Xerox office.

XBS employees are expected to show strong entrepreneurial attitudes—to be their own marketers, reengineering freaks, and cost controllers. They are expected not just to make copies and fix machines but also to lead mini-seminars in their respective client organizations on how their staffs can better "share the knowledge" through documents and "keep up the conversation" needed for innovation and complex problem solving. At least 25 percent of people's salaries comes from the sales and profits they produce with these efforts.[21]

MASTERFUL COACHES GET EVERYONE INVOLVED
IN THE GREAT GAME OF BUSINESS

Jack Stack is the charismatic yet practical leader of Springfield Remanufacturing, a company that rebuilds bulldozer, truck, and car engines in a down-and-dirty plant. Stack was tired of how demoralized people were at the big industrial firm and wanted everyone to feel involved in the business—not in the sense of empowerment but in making every person a businessperson.

His amazing idea: Teach everyone to play the great game of business. Stack coaches everyone in the company on the four to five things they can do to have an impact on the profit-and-loss statement and the balance sheet and then measures and rewards them accordingly. He is often amazed at the commitment, passion, and zeal these people bring to their jobs. Since Jack and his team took over about ten years ago, the company's sales have increased 20,000 percent.

According to Stack, one of the key things is to set up specific, short-term business goals and tasks that are like a game in which managers are actively involved in coaching people to succeed. This may involve acknowledging people with numerous small rewards. The next week, it may have something to do with tinkering with the machines in the plant to produce a 15 percent productivity increase. The next week the game might have to do with cutting defective parts by 47 percent, and so on.[22]

Start right now. Get people in your group to see themselves as full-fledged businesspeople. Start with some simple steps, such as showing every job holder that whatever he or she does is significant in terms of the whole picture. For example, the receptionist who answers the phone in a company has an enormous impact on how people perceive the relative excellence of the organization and the products and services it offers.

It means giving people at all levels the opportunity to come into contact with clients, engage in dialogue, and scope out their real needs. (Chances are that satisfying customer needs will involve much more than the salespeople. It will require the support of the whole organization.) It means getting more people involved in projects on which they collaborate with clients.

GROUP COACHING ACTIVITY

Seeing Yourself as a Businessperson

This exercise is similar to the exercise you did earlier, except this time you will involve the people in your group. Only do this exercise if you have the courage and imagination to make changes.

1. Ask people to write one sentence that frames the way they see themselves as job holders, for example, as direct reports, employees, drones, entrepreneurs, and so on. You write a sentence, too.

2. Ask people to notice whether this old frame limits them from seeing themselves as businesspeople. Discuss the issue in a reflective way.

3. Now ask people to write another sentence that represents a new frame of reference and then to act on it for the next week.

4. At the end of the week, have another coaching conversation with the same people. Ask for any insights, issues and dilemmas, and small things that could be changed to make a difference.

Simple but Powerful Things to Do to Turn Every Job Holder into a Businessperson

- Hold a collaborative gathering. Ask two questions: What jobs or functions do we do better than anyone else? What firms (or other areas of our business) would be interested in outsourcing that from us?

- Have a coaching conversation with every job holder about becoming involved in the business rather than being simply an employee. Brainstorm ways to "business" their job, knowledge, skills, and so forth.

- Have back-office people, such as information technology staff, work with customers on-site. The farther people are from the home office, the more they tend to act like businesspeople.

- Give service people a small discretionary budget between $100 and $1,000 to deal with any customer issue on the spot.

- Have all the MBAs shut off their computers and make sales calls or handle customer complaints at least 15 percent of the time.

- Show people the financial statement in your business so they become aware of the bottom line. Ask them to choose four or five things they can do to have an impact on that bottom line.

CHAPTER TWO

Mind-set first, technique second.

CREATING THE OPENING FOR COACHING

A New Cultural Clearing

In the past ten years, companies have gone through two distinct phases: (1) **survival** *(job cutting, cost cutting) and (2)* **transition** *(or improvement). In the next ten years, companies will go through a third phase called* **breakthrough.** *As Sears Chairman Arthur Hernandez has pointed out, "You can't shrink your way to greatness."*[1] *One of the critical factors driving this shift from improvement to breakthrough is velocity. It is no longer about time to market. It is about time to market in the face of dramatically increasing complexity.*

Intel produces its leading edge microprocessor chips every ninety days. Yet consider this: In 1980, when Intel introduced the 8089 microchip, it contained 29,000 transistors. When they introduced the Pentium chip in 1995, it had 7.5 million transistors. It is estimated that by the year 2010 the Pentium chip will contain over a billion transistors.[2]

The kind of leadership that was required to do "job cutting and cost cutting" or to make "improvements" was close enough to the management model that evolved after World War II to be operational. Today, as we enter the "breakthrough zone," leadership that is based on management by yearly objectives, delegation to different departments, and step-by-step change no longer fits reality.

We need leaders who can make the impossible possible. We need coaches and teachers who can set high goals and bring unlikely collaborators together, orchestrate the kind of dialogue needed to come up with creative and innovative ideas, and then create the kind of rallying momentum that drives a project to completion.

COACHING—A "BUZZWORD" OR A NEW CULTURAL CLEARING?

Today, coaching is certainly a hot buzzword in a world in which breakthroughs, winning the war for talent, and developing a world-class workforce are essential to success. In spite of the need, the culture in most organizations does not allow for or encourage coaching. The fact is that many leaders are much more interested in their next acquisition of technology than they are in making investments in human capital.

TABLE 2.1 *The three phases of business*

Survival	Transition	Breakthrough
• Restructuring	• Improvement	• Strategy of preeminence
• Managing head count, bricks, and mortar	• Leading—TQM programs, tools, techniques	• Coaching for breakthroughs that redefine marketplace
• Goal: stay alive	• Incremental goals	• Stretch goals—reach for
• Divest, job cuts	• Improve process	• Creative collaboration
• Fragmentation—low-cost producer	• Teams under same roof—do same thing better	• Web-based work style—create what never existed before

As one Fortune 100 executive told me, "We have just promoted one hundred people to vice president level, and not one of them has ever received any coaching. What's more, the people who report to them have never received any coaching either. If we don't address this now, as the competitive environment heats up, it will result in a huge gap in the leadership supply in the short- to midterm future." How did this happen?

Coaching first came into use in companies in the 1960s during a stable and predictable business economy. It was not seen as a way to create a future for the business or to battle with competitors. Rather, coaching was used in a remedial way during the annual review to address performance issues, and counseling was used to address people's personal problems. In the 1970s and 1980s, *executive coaches* (consultants) were brought in to deal with the hard cases. As one human resource manager of American International Group reported to me, "We have been doing coaching for years, but usually as a last gasp effort before we fire someone."

Four big myths need to be recognized and dispersed in order to introduce coaching into organizations. These myths constitute significant barriers to doing coaching in our jobs. If you can overcome them and develop a new mind-set, I predict that you will begin to put to use what you already know about coaching, based on learning experiences in business and other areas.

Four Myths That Represent Obstacles to Coaching

1. Coaching is someone else's job (human resources and consultants).

2. Coaching is for individuals and occurs behind locked doors.

3. Coaching is not about performance but about development.

4. Coaching is about identifying and filling gaps.

GE, Coca-Cola, Intel are led by men and women who personally and methodically coach leaders at all levels.

Noel Tichy[3]

MYTH 1   COACHING IS SOMEONE ELSE'S JOB

If you ask most business leaders how much coaching and teaching they are doing, they will say: "I know I should do more of it but I don't have the time," or "They don't report to me; I can't coach them," or "I have delegated this issue to human resources and training," or "We have an outside executive coach coming in." In every case they are saying, "It's someone else's job."

This often makes me wonder just what these managers think their job is. The curious thing about this is that if you ask people from the most admired high-performing companies in the world, you will hear an entirely different answer: "Coaching and teaching are my most important priority."

Noel M. Tichy, head of the University of Michigan's Global Leadership Program, an executive-development consortium of thirty-six companies, asks, "What separates the most admired, and 'winning' corporations from the 'also-rans?' Start with financial performance. The companies that have consistently grown the most and created the most shareholder value in the last decade are those like General Electric, Coca-Cola, and Intel. Yet at the same time it is fascinating that these firms are led by men and women who personally, enthusiastically, and methodically coach leaders at all levels of the organization."[4]

Jack Welch of GE spends a full month a year in "Session C" with business managers in every division to coselect talent for upcoming stretch assignments. He also has spent at least 15 percent of his time for the last ten years coaching and teaching sessions at GE's Crotonville Leadership Center.[5] Andy Grove of Intel teaches a business boot camp for all new engineering hires, which takes months every year. He says, "I have always felt a CEO should coach and teach, and I have always had the urge to do it."[6]

Roger Enrico of PepsiCo started a leadership and business-building course shortly before becoming chairman. He spent more than 120 days in eighteen months teaching.[7] Hubert Saint-Onge, head of strategic capability at the Mutual Group in Canada, worked hard to develop an informal coaching culture in which people coach and receive coaching in a boundaryless way.[8]

These leaders and others view coaching as something that lies at the heart of leadership, not as something that lies at its periphery. This will become essential in the next decade as the bar of excellence is raised higher and higher.

LESSONS FROM GREAT COACHES—BOB MASON OF POLAND SPRING

Bob Mason is the head honcho of Poland Spring's Boston distribution center, a $60-million division with 175 employees. Mason looks at coaching as his number one job. He is living testimony to the fact that even the busiest managers can find time to coach.

A former football player for the Washington Redskins, he says that learning to think of yourself as a leader and coach, not a manager, is half the battle. "I consciously schedule all my routine management tasks— monitoring the numbers of the business, routine meetings, customer calls—to fill a maximum of 25 percent of my time. This frees me up to spend 75 percent coaching people to bring their passion, brainpower, and commitment to the business."

When he first came to the company, he asked himself, "What should I do in the first thirty days?" Step 1 was to create a personal relationship with the "route men." He promised to spend one day on the route with each driver. As a former route driver, he offered to get behind the wheel and let people discuss whatever was on their minds. "I would arrive at the plant early, load the truck before they got there so they didn't have to do it, and be sitting in the driver's seat with the truck engine running and truck warmed, holding a cup of hot tea or coffee for them."

When drivers got in the truck, he would tell them, "Today isn't about delivering water. It is about you and me building a relationship. It is about you and me talking. I am interested in what I can learn from you about what is going well around here, as well as any real improvements we need to make." Boy did he get an earful. There were lots of ideas for making significant improvements, as well as some real problem areas that needed to be addressed. Mason's sessions became known as the "lab in the cab."

Mason believes strongly that thinking of yourself as a manager creates a mind-set in which you tend to tell people what to do and assume you know what the problem is rather than getting people to think for themselves or encouraging them to be involved. At his first meetings with his group, Mason, who wanted to create a collaborative atmosphere, found that he was the only one talking. When he asked why, someone reminded him of the supervisors who used to sit in the partitioned offices, doing everything in secret and telling people they could express themselves at meetings only behind locked doors. The offices had become a symbol of this culture.

Mason stood up and blasted his way through one plasterboard wall. Soon others did the same. During the next meeting in the team room that was created out of this destruction, there was lots of participation.

According to Mason, "I spend most of my time in coaching conversations with individuals and groups or interacting with them so as to help them accomplish what they don't think they can accomplish." He finds that getting people involved in caring about high goals for the company and bottom-line results is partly a matter of moving to open book management. "Once people see the goals and where they are now, you can show people all the things they do day-to-day that impact the P&L."

In addition to the "lab in the cab" and the collaborative team sessions in which people engage in dialogue on just about any business issue, Mason creates other forums for feedback. For example, every morning at 8:00, workers can come to a place in shipping where the trucks pull in called the "yellow line" to talk to Mason. He coaches them to refine their ideas, evaluate their thinking about problems, or adjust their attitudes. He strives to create a conversational atmosphere when doing formal performance appraisals, often taking people to the bleachers in the local football field.

Results? Since he came to the company, business volume has tripled and profits have doubled.[9]

REFLECTION ASSIGNMENT

Developing a Coaching Mind-Set I

1. Who have you coached lately?

2. Do you see coaching at the heart of what you do or as a subset of what you do?

3. What would it mean for you to coach others personally and methodically?

Coaching needs to impact individual and team performance in an integrated way.

MYTH 2   COACHING IS FOR INDIVIDUALS AND OCCURS BEHIND LOCKED DOORS

In sports or the arts, individuals are likely to receive coaching, but usually in the context of the group, the coach's primary focus. Furthermore, coaching is likely to occur publicly on the practice field or in the rehearsal hall. The coach intervenes in direct relationship to the performance cycle, whether it is between games (or plays) or during rehearsals.

When business leaders think about coaching in their businesses, it is in an entirely different way. Coaching is usually thought of as pertaining to individuals, not to overall team success. It takes place behind a locked door, often with forced politeness and awkward phrases. Furthermore, coaching usually occurs only during the annual (or semi-annual) review, even though the performance cycle has speeded up dramatically to weeks, days, or even minutes. In many cases, coaches are reluctant to move beyond the remote "management by objectives" process and intervene at all. But winning in today's highly competitive, high-velocity marketplace requires leaders who see coaching as their job, and they must develop a teachable point of view distinctly different from the prevailing one. They must see that (1) coaching is essential to achieving the company's most important goals, aspirations, and capabilities, not just as a remedial measure; (2) coaching is needed on the enterprise level and team level, not just for individuals; and (3) coaching must occur in boundaryless ways in relationships with customers, suppliers, alliance partnerships, and outsourcing arrangements. Table 2.2 illustrates this teachable point of view.

Following is an example of a leader with a teachable point of view coaching other leaders on an individual basis, building enterprisewide capability and performance across boundaries, as well as team coaching.

LESSONS FROM GREAT COACHES—PHEBE FARROW PORT, ESTÉE LAUDER

Port is the charismatic and pragmatic vice president of retail sales development for Estée Lauder Worldwide. She is Estée Lauder's chief field sales coach and mentor. One of her recent campaigns has been to transform her store managers from "inspectors" to "celebrators." As she walks into Macy's one day, an

TABLE 2.2 *The three levels of coaching—A teachable point of view*

Enterprise-Wide	Organizational	Individual
• Reaching goals by building strategic capability	• Reaching goals by building team capability	• Reaching goals by bundling individual capability
• Defining circle of competence, gaps	• Defining team competence, gaps	• Defining individual's roles, competence, gaps
• Creating alliances, learning that expands competence	• Bringing the right team together, team learning	• Personalized plan, igniting learning
• Forums for strategic dialogue to take place	• Focused dialogue around collective work products	• Conversations and thinking partner
• Forwarding action and coachable moments	• Forwarding action and coachable moments	• Forwarding action and coachable moments

announcement comes over the public address system. "Sue Jones in cosmetics exceeded her sales volume for the last three months by 25 percent and directly contributed to the store's profitability. Thank you, Sue."

Port swells with pride. She says, "It's a matter of catching people doing something right." This approach, inspired in part by Chairman Leonard Lauder, has resulted in the Estée Lauder brands (Clinique, Prescriptives, Tommy Hilfiger, Donna Karan, MAC, Bobbi Brown, Origins) capturing a full 30 to 50 percent of the cosmetics floor in most department store chains like Macy's and specialty stores like Bloomingdale's. "A lot of our success is directly related to the partnership with the retail sales partners."

Says Port, "The only way I can produce results is through 'lateral leadership,' coaching, and mentoring across traditional boundaries." She explains, "After all, Macy's and Federated Stores' managers and people don't report to me. You can't just dictate to them. You have to persuade and motivate, and negotiate." She holds collaborative gatherings that bring together Lauder sales and marketing people, CEOs of stores like Macy's, as well as store managers and cosmetic area managers. "Did you know that cosmetics make up 8 percent of your retail store sales?" she typically asks. "Did you know that the number one selling retail item in your store is no longer Levi's 501 Jeans but the Estée Lauder fragrance Pleasures?"

Former Chairman David Farrell of May Company was so affected that he asked Port to bring in some mirrors. He made his staff look in them and asked, "Do you have a cosmetics mentality?"

How did Port learn to be a leader? By following Leonard Lauder's example as a coach and mentor. "Since the early days, I observed him practicing what he preached, meeting floor people, encouraging unfiltered communication, coaching and mentoring employees, and being very results oriented. One of his philosophies that permeates the company is that 90 percent of people promoted are from within. The only way you can get a promotion is to become an effective coach and teacher. You have to coach people who work for you to bring them to the next level so they support you as you are ready to move to the next level. Mr. Lauder's famous quote is: 'You are only as good as your people want you to be.'"

According to Port, Lauder spent a limited amount of time with executives on store visits, preferring to meet with floor people. Says Port, "One day, I saw him reach across a counter and say, 'Sorry to interrupt. My name is Leonard Lauder. I hear you are one of the beauty advisors. Thank you for everything you are doing for Estée Lauder.'" As they walked away, Port said, "Mr. Lauder, you're so good at this." He replied, "I'm not so special. I put myself on a quota of three thank yous a day years ago. I suggest you do the same." Says Port, "I have to tell you, everywhere the man goes, he writes personal notes to people he meets."

Lauder does everything he can to create and preserve brand equity while encouraging employees to take risks. Port tells the story of a time she suggested what she thought was a creative new idea. He said, "No, absolutely not," but then said, "Now you know what no means, don't you? It means it wasn't consistent with our strategy, the timing wasn't right, it costs too much. Go back and rethink this."

"I never felt that I was cast aside in any way or penalized for making the suggestion. I approached him again about a year later. I presented my ideas again with a business plan and redefined end results. Mr. Lauder said, 'Now it makes sense. Let's do it.'"[10]

REFLECTION ASSIGNMENT

Developing a Coaching Mind-Set II

1. When you think of coaching, do you generally think of individuals or groups?

2. How has your thinking about coaching changed since reading this section?

3. What can you do to build more mechanisms for coaching into your daily work?

The bottom line in corporate America revolves around performance. A coach must make sure that every ounce of talent, skill, and teamwork surfaces day after day. If you don't, rest assured that there will be many competent competitors out there eager to take your place.

MYTH 3   COACHING IS NOT ABOUT PERFORMANCE BUT ABOUT DEVELOPMENT

In most companies, you will discover that there is little connection between coaching and performance issues. Conversations about coaching are usually about developing people for the future, with little connection to current performance. Development is not seen as a real-time activity that happens in the process of stretch assignments or in getting the job done, but as a separate and abstract activity. The same applies to learning.

Also, you will find a belief that there is one right way to develop people, for example, by sending people to business school programs. Or companies offer courses on leadership in their corporate universities or send everyone through a 360-degree feedback evaluation to see what their developmental needs are. These may be useful in the interim and ultimately necessary in terms of providing people with a basic stock of skills and capabilities in strategic planning, change management, Lotus Notes, and so forth. However, there is little evidence to suggest that significant human development or learning occurs.

There is much evidence that development occurs in the process when a coach selects people or groups, places them in stretch assignments where there are real performance goals, and then provides mentoring along the way. My experience has been that development occurs in the context of performance, through "accelerated experiential development" that brings people in touch with "diverse and adverse" circumstances. As Peter Senge has pointed out in the *Fifth Discipline,* only 20 percent of business learning occurs in the classroom; 80 percent occurs in the workplace.[11]

Coaching people to reach a stretch goal gives you the most accurate indicators of their developmental needs—much more effectively than 360-degree feedback. The most reliable way to know whether people have developed and whether coaching is effective is if they are able to produce results that were previously difficult or impossible.

This raises a lot of questions: Why doesn't it occur to managers to see coaching or mentoring as something that can be used to build both leaders and the business? Why doesn't it occur to managers that coaching, especially by recognized leaders, is the most effective way to have an impact on today's business performance, as well as on future development? Why are performance and development usually considered separate activities in the first place? Why are they handled by separate people in separate functions? The answer: The traditional corporation separated everything into bits and pieces—R&D, marketing, production and sales, performance and development.

The manager's job was to "manage" performance. The human resource manager's job was building new skills and capabilities, often with little connection between the two. In many companies, the human resources have been seen as an annoyance. In leading companies today, they are creating a close partnership with line managers to accelerate performance and development in an integrated way.

A good example of this is at Royal Dutch Shell, where Steve Miller's grassroots leadership has helped both to develop leaders and to improve Shell's market share. Miller has formed a partnership of line managers, human resources, and consultants. Figure 2.1 illustrates how performance and development must be linked to create consistent breakthroughs, the coaching challenge.

FIGURE 2.1 *The coaching challenge—linking performance and development*

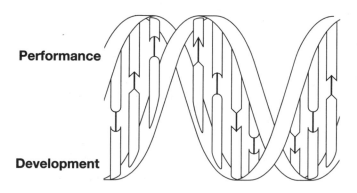

Performance

Development

We introduced coaching to build high-performance work teams, but there were no team goals created after eighteen months. It was all about individual development.

Manager in Fortune 500 company

LESSONS FROM GREAT COACHES—ROGER ENRICO, LEADERSHIP DEVELOPMENT AT PEPSICO

John Calloway, CEO of PepsiCo, discovered to his consternation in 1993 that division presidents at Pepsi-Co consistently held back more than half the budget slated for leadership development in order to fatten year-end profits. He asked Paul Russell, PepsiCo's director of executive development, to create "the world's leading executive development program."

Stepping up to the challenge, Russell perused leadership programs in other Fortune 500 companies, talked to Harvard leadership professor John Kotter, and met with many consultants. One day a colleague asked him whether he knew that Roger Enrico (then the head of PepsiCo's worldwide foods division) was thinking of doing something like that also. Says Russell, "I had an executive development structure in search of a guru. When Roger got involved, it went to a whole other plane." However, Enrico made it clear from the outset that he had something else in mind rather than the grand design Russell had been working on.

He told Russell that PepsiCo people didn't want a typical leadership course based on academic models and other firms' experiences taught by professors or consultants. They wanted to hear about the experiences of Enrico and other Pepsi leaders and be in a position to tap into their insights on real business challenges they were facing.

On the corporate jet home, Russell interviewed Enrico about his leadership experiences and observations. Enrico was intent on designing a leadership program that would have an impact on the performance of the business. The result was a fifty-page document that became the foundation for a PepsiCo program that focused on creating both personal and business breakthroughs.

The program begins with a five-day, off-site seminar led by Enrico. Enrico uses his five key leadership tenets, interviews with PepsiCo division leaders, and Socratic dialogue that challenges the students' fundamental thinking and attitudes. For the next ninety days the participants apply what they learn while doing their regular jobs and keeping in close touch with Enrico. The program finishes with a three-day workshop in which everyone shares the insights and lessons of the prior three months. It is not a mass rollout program. Only about nine people attend each seminar, which allows plenty of one-to-one time with Enrico.

People selected for Enrico's course must have a business-building idea important enough to become one of the top three priorities of their division. Enrico believes that it is hard to develop leadership unless it is business connected. He provokes participants into seeing themselves as leaders versus cogs in the wheel. "Nobody in this room can look at the company's problems and blame the turkeys at the top. You're now one of them."

Enrico believes that leaders should "think big and avoid being incremental." This is the only way to drive the competitive advantage for the future. "Furthermore," says Enrico, "as soon as everyone is on the bandwagon with one growth idea, a leader should be working on the next one." He does a lot of one-to-one coaching.

• Peter Waller, Kentucky Fried Chicken's (KFC) senior vice president of marketing in Australia, decided to take Enrico's seminar. He had the idea of linking four meal combinations into one Mega Meal to offer to families at a discount. Enrico gave Waller feedback that showed him he could transform his idea into a broader KFC strategy to win back lost market share based on bundling meal combinations. Enrico told the group, "It's the people who can see the connections between unrelated products and transform them into a value proposition who make great business leaders." Then he helped Waller create a slogan: "Take back the family." The slogan caught on around the world and resulted in the creation of KFC Mega Meals, sparking double-digit sales.

• When Bill McLaughlin became president of Gamesa, the ailing Mexican cookie company PepsiCo bought in 1990, recipes for the same brand of cookie differed by manufacturing site, workers doing the identical job were receiving different pay, and competitors were eating them alive. There was no teamwork at the top. Says McLaughlin, "I felt like saying, 'Forget it.'" Enrico assisted McLaughlin with a vision statement and team dialogue about a communication plan and pushed him to return to Mexico with a much more aggressive attitude. The company trained its employees in quality, implemented productivity bonuses, and invested in new distribution systems. Today, Gamesa can claim double-digit volume growth.

• Bill Nictakis, field marketing vice president at Frito-Lay, went to Enrico's program looking for a strategy for moving from salty snacks into broader snack categories. It was a hard idea to sell, given Frito-Lay's

$16 million write-off of Grandma's Cookies in 1985. Enrico helped Nictakis realize that he had to really pay attention to what people's objections were and take them seriously. The company spent $200,000 doing market research that helped overcome objections and, according to Nictakis, "Certainly helped refine our thinking." The result: Frito-Lay recently announced a joint venture with Sara Lee to develop, manufacture, and distribute a new pastry line.[12]

REFLECTION ASSIGNMENT

Developing a Coaching Mind-Set III

1. What are you doing to develop the next generation of leaders in your company?

2. Are you personally involved in coaching and teaching, or have you delegated this to human resources and consultants?

3. How do you integrate performance and development, for example, by setting stretch assignments and providing ongoing coaching and mentoring?

Masterful coaching is about expanding people's capacity to create the future they truly desire.

MYTH 4   **COACHING IS ABOUT IDENTIFYING AND FILLING GAPS**

LESSONS FROM GREAT COACHES—GLOBAL LEADERSHIP DEVELOPMENT

I am sitting in my office having a phone conversation about leadership development with Juliet Neufeld, vice president of corporate capability development for Zurich Financial Group. Neufeld is an inspired, dynamic, high-energy person who sees herself as one of Zurich's prime knowledge architects. Her role is designing a learning organization that affects performance and capability in a true partnership with line managers. She has a knack for combining different design elements in a blueprint so that the whole is greater than the sum of the parts.

She has had many conversations with me over several months about how to structure the companywide leadership program that the chairman has promised to send fifteen thousand managers in the company through in order to realize his vision of being a global powerhouse in financial services. He and other managers wanted a leading-edge program that would include creating a culture of coaching as a key leadership capability.

Neufeld says that she has been thinking about a leadership development program that is based on "creating futures, not just filling gaps." She explains that most leadership and learning efforts do not start with either personal or organizational vision but with identifying and filling gaps in people's personal attributes and competencies, that is, the usual round of Myers-Briggs, 360-degree feedback, and the like.

This usually leads to what Neufeld calls the PUSH approach to education—a prearranged set of training modules that everyone has to take. Says Neufeld, "There's an incredible difference between signing up for a course or engaging in a learning process because it will make it possible for you to realize your dreams and aspirations and having your attendance mandated by someone else."

We discuss the fact that despite decades of research, millions of dollars spent, and thousands of programs offered, there is not a shred of evidence that the PUSH approach to learning works. Why? For one thing, the focus is not on expanding people's capacity to produce the results they truly desire but on learning plans that someone or something external to yourself has designated. It is often not based on giving people the opportunity to discover and express their talents and gifts but on telling them what's wrong with them.

Coaching and training programs offered by business schools or corporate universities based on this approach place a premium on how entertaining the trainer is, how gourmet the food is, and how good the accommodations are, because participants aren't all that interested in attending. Says Neufeld, "Faculty that challenge the students and push them to learn receive much lower marks than those who simply put up fancy PowerPoint displays and tell jokes. The paint-by-numbers prescriptions that are offered often don't fit people's jobs or the situations and events that are unfolding in action. (Figure 2.2 illustrates the PUSH approach to development.)

Neufeld and I then shift the conversation back to designing a new approach to leadership development based on "creating futures versus filling gaps." According to Neufeld, "When people have a dream or aspiration that

FIGURE 2.2 *The PUSH approach to leadership development*

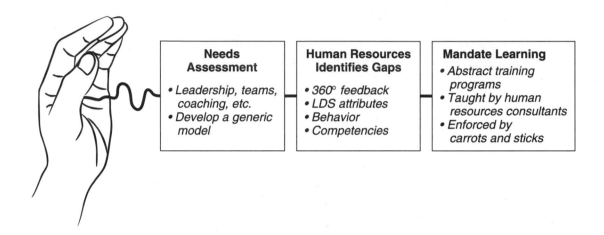

Needs Assessment	**Human Resources Identifies Gaps**	**Mandate Learning**
• *Leadership, teams, coaching, etc.* • *Develop a generic model*	• *360° feedback* • *LDS attributes* • *Behavior* • *Competencies*	• *Abstract training programs* • *Taught by human resources consultants* • *Enforced by carrots and sticks*

is burning a hole inside them, they start to show up as learners versus knowers." I add that when people are working on something they aspire to, they declare the attitude or skills gaps and pursue learning resources on their own accord. This is what is called the PULL approach to learning. As William Butler Yeats said, "Learning is not the filling of a pail, but rather the igniting of a fire." (Figure 2.3 illustrates the PULL approach to development.)

We then brainstorm a PULL approach to organizational learning to incorporate into Zurich Financial's Global Management Development (GMD) program, for an upcoming CollabLab session in Europe with the whole management development team. We sketch out a two-track system—one for everyone and

FIGURE 2.3 *The PULL approach to leadership development*

People Declare the Future	**People Declare Their Own Gaps**	**Coach Ignites Learning**
• *Based on personal, collective aspirations* • *Goals/projects* • *Performance measures*	• *Are responsible for their own learning* • *Coach is resource* • *Human resource tools are resource*	• *Recognized leaders teach key attitudes/ skills* • *Performance and development integrated* • *Daily coaching conversations*

one for high flyers—supported in part by something Neufeld is designing called Zurich's Virtual University in conjunction with her technology partner. If people have a goal and yearn to accomplish it, they want access to learning resources right now, immediately. Business leaders have been talking about just-in-time versus just-in-case learning for a long time, but until the Internet, the concept of the virtual university and distance learning wasn't really possible.

Neufeld's system makes possible enrollment, assessment, a wide variety of learning resources, and e-coaching on a real-time basis. Says Neufeld, "People can press a button, bring up their present role, generate an instant competency modeling map, figure out their gaps according to Web-based 360-degree feedback, and find the learning resources they need." She adds with glee, "Then simply by pressing another button, they can define a role they want in the future and have an instant competency map, gap analysis, and learning resources."

Says Neufeld, "A virtual university has some strong coaching and mentoring features. Enriched with lots of good content, a virtual university allows coaches to focus their conversations on shifting underlying thinking and attitudes, not regurgitating the same tips and techniques. Let's say the person you are coaching wants to learn how to run a project. They go to their computer desktop and switch on the virtual university that shows them such things as who is the company's resident expert on running projects here or anyplace in the world. There are some nifty tools that allow you to prepare for both one-to-one coaching sessions and team meetings by asking just a few questions. Then with just one keystroke you receive some guideline." I tried it. Not bad![13]

LEADERSHIP AND LEARNING—PROTOCOLS FOR THE PULL APPROACH

The following shows the PULL approach based on a two-track system. Track A is for everyone and is most powerful when it is set up on a computer or Web-based system. Track B is for developing up-and-coming leaders.

Track A

- Publicly post all upcoming jobs and assignments on your company's intranet so that people can apply and be chosen on the basis of merit. This will create a climate of possibility and opportunity.

- Begin to build what Neufeld calls a "performance based competency assessment" using standard job classification codes and other resources. Figure out the respective roles for all major jobs in your firm and the competencies that match them.

- Help leaders and their people make the "competency connection." A computer program should be available so that people can plug in any role, see a map of the competencies that are needed, figure out their own gaps, and develop a learning plan and resources. Design the virtual university so that people are required to pick a mentor and do 360-degree feedback on their current roles. This way, they can have answers in seconds.

- Make learning resources available on a self-serve basis. The virtual university concept allows people access to just the right tools, courseware, books, and experts at just the right time.

- Use a virtual approach for transactionally based learning that involves acquiring basic ideas, tips, and techniques. Use a face-to-face approach for courses that require fundamental shifts in thinking or attitude.

- Design learning resources that make sure people have the basic skills and competencies every manager needs today: strategic thinking, change management, computer skills, and the ability to lead project teams. Also include any skills specific to your industry or company.

A sample of a way to show jobs and desired competency is shown in Figure 2.4.

Track B

- Have recognized leaders select talented candidates for a one-year, high-flyer "boot camp." Develop people with a proven track record of success and potential.

- Link personal and organizational vision by asking: What are your goals and aspirations? Your passions, talents, gifts? How can they be used to add value?

- Assign or have each person designate his or her own stretch assignment or breakthrough project. Make performance objectives clear.

FIGURE 2.4 Sample job and competency ratings

Mentor	Job and Competency	Current	Required	Weight	Gap	Reason	Learning Resource	Journal
	Sales Manager							
Hemmings	✓ Budgeting	1	3	Somewhat important	(−4)		Virtual university	📓
Johnson	✓ Business functions	2	3	Somewhat important	(−2)		Publications	📓
Hemmings	✓ Coaching	2	3	Important	(−3)		Course, coach	📓
Hemmings	✓ Leadership	3	3	Critical				📓
Johnson	✓ Negotiating	2	4	Very important	(−8)		Virtual university	📓
Hemmings	✓ Sales forecasting	2	3	Very important	(−4)		Virtual university	📓
Hemmings	✓ Staff/Career dev	2	3	Very important	(−4)		Course	📓

- Again, make the "competency connection" by defining what role people will need to play in the stretch assignment or project. Map the attributes and competencies they will need. Create a learning plan. Use a virtual approach, as in Track A.

- Provide coaches and mentors who have the skills to help people develop in the necessary areas throughout the stretch project.

- Stay in regular communication throughout the project, allowing actions to evolve out of coaching conversations and what emerges in the process.

REFLECTION ASSIGNMENT

Developing a Coaching Mind-Set IV

1. Do you see coaching as your job or someone else's? Describe what you are doing.

2. Do you look at coaching primarily in terms of expanding people's capacity to create the future or in terms of identifying and filling gaps through assessment? Explain your answer.

3. Are you personally involved in designing and implementing an approach to integrating business performance and people development? Describe what you are doing.

4. Do you see coaching as something done in the annual review as a remedial activity or as a day-in, day-out proposition. Explain using examples.

GROUP COACHING ACTIVITY

Creating a New Cultural Clearing for Coaching in Your Company

One way to bring coaching into your company is to hold a collaborative gathering with a wide variety of people during which you initiate a conversation about coaching. The collaborative gathering could be with twenty or more

people from the top group or with up to one hundred or more managers throughout the company.

1. *Send out invitations to a collaborative gathering.* The invitation should state that you are inviting people to participate in a collaborative gathering to introduce coaches and a culture of coaching to your company. Say that coaching is about a new relationship between manager and employees that is based on a shift from being a *commander* to being a *collaborator.* Say in the invitation that coaching is about altering the way people see things so as to open up new possibilities for thinking and action that allow them to reach their goals. Ask people for their participation in this new conversation. (This collaborative gathering can take place in a two-hour session or could be lengthened or shortened depending on the size of the group.)

2. *Have a guest speaker set a context of coaching* using some of the following distinctions to help define what coaching is:

   - Stretch versus comfort zone

   - Fostering collaboration versus delegating to separate departments

   - Expanding people's capacity versus supervising

   - Objective observations versus arbitrary assessments

   - Intervening versus letting things drift

   - Learning versus knowing

   (15 to 30 minutes)

3. *Generate a new conversation about coaching.* Break into appropriately sized groups and ask people to share their beliefs and attitudes about coaching. To set this up, ask each person to write one sentence on a piece of paper that represents their *old* conversation about coaching. After that, give people an opportunity to shift their frame of reference and create a *new* conversation about coaching. Ask them to write this on a piece of paper as well. For example:

   The old conversation. Coaching is psychological. Coaching is about telling people the right thing to do. Coaching is about the answers. Coaching is for the annual review. I don't need coaching. It's not okay to ask for help.

The new conversation. Coaching is about expanding people's capacity to create the desired future. It is not telling people what to do, but asking them to examine the thinking behind what they're doing so it is consistent with their goals. Coaching is about giving people the gift of your presence, asking questions, listening.

(15 to 30 minutes)

4. *Ask people to have a conversation about how to bring coaching into your culture.* Start by having each person write a list of five next steps. An example might be the following:

    •   Hold other collaborative gatherings in other parts of the company.

    •   Find out who the best coaches in the company are and invite them.

    •   Inquire into past efforts to bring coaching into your company.

    •   Have people find coaches who will help them achieve their goals.

    •   Set up a coaching course.

    (15 to 30 minutes)

5. *Create a coaching breakthrough project* (optional). This is a way both to develop coaching skills and to achieve specific breakthroughs, by design. (See Chapter Nine, pages 205–206, on the breakthrough technique.)

CHAPTER THREE

In today's corporate world, you either perform to the maximum and elicit the same from the individuals on your team, or you don't get to play.

YOUR PERSONAL COACHING CONTRACT

Coaching in the New Economy

NEW COACHES BRING A SPIRIT OF POSSIBILITY

I can remember the day when Lou Gerstner was named CEO of IBM, when Seiji Ozawa was named head conductor of the Boston Symphony, and when Mike Ditka was named head coach of the New Orleans Saints. There is always a spirit of possibility in the air whenever a new coach with a solid reputation takes over a team, whether in business, sports, or the performing arts.

There is a belief that here is a leader who can, at last, make it possible for a talented group (individuals) to achieve its real potential and perhaps perform at extraordinary levels. There is usually a corresponding belief that the coach will apply some magic process that will move an organization from mediocrity to excellence. Often enough, it proves to be true.

There is a real sense of possibility, opportunity, and challenge that anyone coming into a new role feels, along with an implicit (or explicit) contract, usually based on very clear expectations, for example, to win a championship, to raise a theater or ballet company to new heights, or to turn a corporation around 180 degrees. In business, the coach fulfilling a contract is usually measured by whether or not he or she can deliver on economic performance, measured by an inspired and re-vitalized team, innovative new products in the pipeline, operational excellence, jumps in sales fig-ures, and higher customer satisfaction.

People coaching in business, sports, or the performing arts generally have a one- to three-year period to prove their worth. If they are not able to do so, we can be sure that others will be com-ing along to replace them. Fortune 500 CEOs have in recent years shown themselves to be par-ticularly vulnerable.

Every two to three years of the last decade, fully one third of the Fortune 500 CEOs have been replaced because they could not deliver. The same 30 percent replacement figure applies to the armies of rank-and-file managers in any corporation today. This is the reality. You either perform to the maximum and elicit the same from the individuals on your team, or you don't get to play.

NEW COACHES HAVE THE ADVANTAGE OF PERSPECTIVE

Why is it that a newly hired general manager, coach, or conductor can come in and do miracu-lous things with the same talent and customers as his or her predecessor? One reason is that suc-cessful coaches tend to expect success, regardless of the circumstances. It simply does not occur to them that they could fail. Second, winning coaches seem to have a vision and values that they translate into a teachable point of view, as well as a "system" or an approach that is based on the mastery of a few fundamentals. For example, marketing guru Jay Abraham says there are three fundamental ways to grow a business. These ways are so disarmingly simple and powerful that they are often overlooked: "Increase the number of customers, increase the number of transac-tions, or increase dollar volume per transaction."[1] Focus on the fundamentals consistently and miracles will happen.

One of the other advantages that new leaders, managers, or coaches have going into a new or-ganization is perspective. They have a studied sense of detachment that allows them to look at the business or group and see things as they really are, in part because they do not have pride of authorship. They are able to look at what is really possible, as well as at the current situation. They are able to acknowledge what is working and what is not working because they have nothing to protect. This together with their past experience allows them to gain insight into what's missing—insight that can make a difference.

It is very easy for most managers to lose their perspective once they become involved in an organization. They may start with a vision and values, a teachable point of view, and a focus on the fundamentals, but soon the existing culture has a way of taking over and they become entangled in people, circumstances, and events. René Jaeggi, CEO of Adidas, told me at the end of a strategic seminar that he had sponsored and participated in with thirty vice presidents, "Ich ühle mich gut" (I feel good). Two weeks later, when I saw him in his office, he said, "I've been sucked back into the monster"—the prevailing management culture.[2]

THE PERSPECTIVE OF THE NEW COACH

You may not be the newly hired CEO, general manager, team leader, conductor, or coach, but why not take that perspective anyway? Imagine for a moment that you are your own successor. You have been asked to come in and transform the group and the individuals in it into a successful team. Before accepting the job, however, you want to size things up.

The first thing that you would want to consider is whether the team really has the possibility of succeeding. Often people make the mistake of jumping into a job or situation in which they could never succeed, no matter what they did. They may work incredibly hard, but it is like building a castle on sand. Some questions to ask might include: (1) Are there smart, sophisticated, highly talented people who have a hunger or yearning to be part of something greater than themselves? Or are people resigned, cynical, or sarcastic? (2) Does the company have a leading edge technology, as well as one or two "hot" products in the pipeline? Or are they living off the outdated stuff in the warehouse? (3) Are they making sales? Running a tight ship? And so on.

Then look at what's missing that could make a difference: (1) leadership with the edge or the ability to make tough decisions, (2) a business vision of possibility, (3) a new and powerful strategy plus the ability to execute it, (4) operational excellence, (5) a successful approach to innovation, (6) exceptional marketing and sales—and so on. (If you are not a general manager, come up with your own list of questions.)

Now, let's assume that your answers are satisfactory and you are ready to commit yourself. Create a personal coaching contract that says just what your commitment will be.

YOUR PERSONAL COACHING CONTRACT

The following are a few guidelines for creating your own coaching contract. For each guideline coaching tips are provided that will help you get started. You may add other items so that you coaching contract is specific to your situation.

- Commit to a Personal Coaching Mission

- Commit to Selecting the Best Talent

- Commit to Articulating Shared Goals and to Providing Feedback

- Address Performance or Capability Gaps Immediately

- Commit to Recognizing anmd Rewarding People

Commit to a Personal Coaching Mission. Focus on an extraordinary and tangible result. Coaches are needed not to produce ordinary results but to produce results that are out of the ordinary. Sir Colin Marshall, chairman of British Airways, achieved his goal by spending 30 to 40 percent of his time coaching.[3]

Whether you are a CEO, department head, or project leader, ask yourself, "What would an extraordinary and tangible result be for my area? What is the single biggest challenge we are facing?" You might need to develop the next generation of leaders, turn your organization around 180 degrees, come up with a breakthrough product or service, increase sales 40 percent, or build more value for customers. Once you decide what you want, commit to spending 25 to 30 percent of your time coaching to it within a specific time frame.

In 1985, Sir Colin Marshall, chairman of British Airways, declared that the airline would become the "world's favorite airline." This goal was reached in three years.[4]

PRACTICE ASSIGNMENT

My Coaching Mission Statement

1. Write a mission statement that focuses on accomplishing your single most important business challenge.

2. Include how you intend to transform individuals and the group so that they are capable of meeting this challenge.

3. Mention key leadership and team practices that you will imbue your group with.

Commit to Selecting the Best Talent. Find the best talent available and match it to the task. Think in terms of the kind of people you will need to bring on board to achieve your goal. Masterful coaches are connoisseurs of talent who recognize people's passions and gifts that others do not see. They also keep in their minds a whirling Rolodex of the best people in their fields. For example, Robert J. Oppenheimer, head of the Manhattan Project, was not the best physicist in the world, but he knew where to find them and how to enroll them.

The best coaches are also highly skillful at matching talent to tasks. They use "appreciative" inquiry to do this, utilizing people's strengths and making their weaknesses irrelevant. They recognize that in a Web-based, free-agent marketplace, it is possible to gather the most talented people available to work on a project without necessarily increasing fixed costs. (See Chapter Seven, on investing in relationships.)

Coaching Tips for a "Talent" Interview

- Keep a whirling Rolodex, whether on paper or electronically, of all the talented people in your field and those that are adjacent to it—scientists, artists, engineers, anthropologists, MBAs, and so forth.

- Select talented candidates to interview for your next project, keeping in mind that innovation comes from differences—from juxtaposing multiple talents and gifts.

- Ask questions that reveal whether people are bright, enthusiastic, and have expertise you need.

- Ask questions to find out whether people have a passion for impact.

- Pay little attention to grades and schools but a lot of attention to letters that teachers or employers have written about candidates.

Commit to Articulating Shared Goals and Providing Feedback. Shared goals and feedback inspire collaboration. Your coaching contract should include ways to articulate goals and challenges that inspire individual commitment and team collaboration. As one middle manager at 3M told me, "The idea of producing a breakthrough product for an enthusiastic customer group gets people excited about collaborating. Cutting costs by 10 percent just doesn't make it." People commit themselves to goals that are big enough and intriguing enough to subordinate their egos to and collaborate around when they realize they cannot achieve them on their own.

Your coaching contract must also provide for regular coaching feedback. Research shows that when people have clear performance goals (not just behavioral ones) and are provided with regular feedback on their results, they improve as much as 125 percent. (See Chapter Ten, on giving feedback.)

Coaching Tips for Building Team Commitment and Team Collaboration

- Articulate an inspiring goal or challenge that answers the question: What do we want to create together?

- Ask each person to write a business case for action: Why should we do this?

- Ask each person to write why they are passionate about the goal—or why they are not.

- Continue the dialogue until the team comes together, objectives are agreed on, conflicts have been ironed out, and people are ready to jump into action.

- Challenge individuals to take on tough assignments that further their professional development.

- Discuss the importance of feedback at every juncture.

Address Performance or Capability Gaps Immediately. Commit to addressing gaps on a just-in-time basis. In the traditional organization, business leaders managed by objectives. As one General Motors plant supervisor told me, "We managed by objectives, passed out goals, and then essentially said, 'Come back at the end of the year when you have the results,' not realizing we were abdicating responsibility for coaching." This may have been all right in a low-performance or medium-performance environment, or yesterday, but not in the high-performance environment that exists today.

It is essential that you as a coach put in your contract that you will address performance and development gaps at the earliest possible moment. This may involve moving beyond the individual or group and extending the team's circle of competence through outsourcing or joint ventures.

Coaching Tips for Addressing Performance and Development Gaps

- Identify any gaps in performance or development with respect to mission and goals. Create mind-maps or use other visual tools to describe them.

- Discuss any obstacles that might exist with respect to eliminating the gaps, for example, mental models, skilled incompetence, or the need to develop new skills and capabilities.

- Brainstorm with the intent of coming up with lots of solutions to eliminate those gaps, then choose the best solutions.

- Create an action plan.

Commit to Recognizing and Rewarding People. Masterful coaches recognize that in a knowledge economy it is important to give everyone credit both for their intellectual output (a special report) and for their tangible work products. They look for innovative ways to reward people. A Motorola manager on the Iridium satellite phone project reports that she rewards star performers for a job well done with special prizes. For example, she may pull a broad bandwidth of brainpower from a team that includes Ph.D.s, MBAs, salespeople, and customer service workers to brainstorm for an hour at lunch about the star performer's most intriguing business problem.

It has been shown that rewards and recognition often increase productivity and performance. Microsoft, General Electric, and PepsiCo not only pay people for performance but also offer special bonuses—an adventure vacation, a second home in the mountains, or college tuition.

Coaching Tips for Giving Rewards and Recognition

- Make it a habit to recognize and validate people's talents and gifts.

- Acknowledge people generously for who they are, not just for what they do: "The way you handled this tough assignment shows your commitment to excellence."

- Look for inventive ways to reward people.

- Remember that positive perceptions of pay influence positive performance.

TEN RULES FOR BUSINESS COACHING IN THE NEW ECONOMY

In my first book I said that masterful coaching was a journey. The person who puts on a coach's hat will be faced with many different dilemmas, puzzles, and questions: "Does being a leader automatically make me the coach?" or "Do I have to wait until people give me permission to coach them?" or "How do you find the time to coach?" This book cannot answer every question, but the ten rules listed in Exhibit 3.1 will help you to map the territory of coaching in the context of doing business in the knowledge economy. By referring back to these ten rules (or guiding principles) and reading them again and again, you will gain the insights necessary to discover your own answers. The rules are explained in more detail in the text that follows.

RULE 1   KEEP YOUR COACHING CONVERSATIONAL

One of the keys to making coaching work in any business is to let go at the top. Let go of the need to make the decision, the need to have the answers, and the need to tell others what to do. Hierarchal attitudes and behavior tend to get in the way of effective coaching.

There are two reasons for this: (1) People tend to react strongly to authority figures who strut their tail feathers, and (2) people react strongly to coaching feedback, especially if they think it is arbitrary. The combination will always make people defensive. The question is, How do you keep hierarchal attitudes and arbitrary assessments out of the way of effective coaching? The an-

EXHIBIT 3.1 *Ten rules for business consulting in the new economy*

1. Keep your coaching conversational.

2. Use face-to-face, phone, and e-mail communication.

3. Focus on mind-set first, techniques second.

4. Shift knowledge workers to higher level thinking tasks and work products.

5. Create virtual mastermind groups and coach people on how to think and interact.

6. Employ a breakthrough strategy, not just improvement techniques.

7. Create robust feedback loops.

8. Expect something new from everyone.

9. Coach customers to solve problems for themselves.

10. Make sure that all processes are capable of just-in-time delivery.

swer is, Minimize them. One of the best ways is for managers to keep their coaching conversational and two-way.[5]

I guarantee you will feel much more at ease coaching others if you talk to people in a conversational and collegial way rather than in a superior or condescending way. People will be much more at ease in receiving your coaching. Notice the difference between saying, "Based on our shared goals and in the spirit of honoring our coaching relationship, here's what I see you might change to produce desired results. How do you see it?" and "I'm the boss. Change this or else."

Social settings help to keep coaching conversational, for example, a coffee shop, a walk around the lake, or a two-hour flight to Cincinnati. Being in relationship with someone actually creates more space to be authentic and to make promises or requests for behavioral change that will lead to desired results. Conversational coaching is also important with groups. You are there to foster quality dialogue that will lead to insights not attainable on an individual basis, not just to give all the answers.

RULE 2   USE FACE-TO-FACE, PHONE, AND E-MAIL COMMUNICATION

One of the keys to coaching is being able to sustain a relationship (communication) between when the goals are set and the results are delivered. One of the biggest obstacles managers have is keeping up the coaching conversation over time—especially scheduling face-to-face meetings with busy people spread out across different time zones.

The solution to this problem isn't to have your secretary call her secretary, to wait till next year for the big meeting in Frankfurt, or to abandon coaching in frustration. It is to let people know in advance you intend to sustain your coaching relationship using multiple media. According to Michael Dell, "Management in business today is different combinations of face-to-face, ear-to-ear, and keyboard-to-keyboard."[6] Each has its place. Virtual communication doesn't replace people; it just makes them more efficient.

Says one major account manager at AT&T who uses e-mail coaching, "Hey! If it is possible for people to meet, fall in love, and get married over the Internet, why isn't it possible to use it for coaching?" I have found that a combination of face-to-face meetings or a series of phone conversations, followed by e-coaching, is often very effective. There is also something about the electronic medium that makes it easier for people to disclose their dreams, aspirations, and vulnerabilities, as well as to provide frank coaching.

By reading between the lines in an e-mail message someone sends you, you can pick up on squishy commitments, unexamined beliefs and assumptions, and promises that have been dropped. E-coaching also gives you the time to frame your responses so you can lead the coachee to respond creatively rather than react emotionally.

RULE 3   FOCUS ON MIND-SET FIRST, TECHNIQUES SECOND

Masterful coaches intuitively know that reaching breakthrough goals and bringing about real change usually starts with a shift in mind-set. They distinguish themselves from the midlevel or novice coach precisely because they know that *thinking drives behavior.* They know that when people change the way they think, they change the way they act. The merely "competent" or "beginner" coach tends to rely on tips and techniques. These may work for a little while, but people usually revert to form under stress and pressure because their underlying mental models have not changed.

According to Jay Abraham, referred to in the *Wall Street Journal* as the highest paid marketing consultant in America, "When I interact with people, my intent is to impact them in a short period of time. I do everything I can to give people a whole new dynamic mind-set, rather than merely focus on methods or techniques."[7] If you give people the right mind-set, they will generally figure out the techniques on their own. For example, I often tell entrepreneurs to be master architects who work *on* their business, not employees who work *in* their business. This small shift in thinking produces profound changes in behavior. (See Chapter Sixteen for an interview with Jay Abraham.)

Shifting a mind-set starts with having a teachable point of view about what it will take to be successful. For example, in the industrial economy, productivity (efficiency) was the key. In the quest for efficiency, people did not have time for relationships. Today, the rules have changed 180 degrees. Success now comes from investing in relationships that lead to new opportunities. If you are coaching people who are too busy being efficient to create relationships with colleagues and customers, your teachable point of view might be, "Pursue opportunities before efficiencies." (See Chapter Seven, on creating a mission-critical teachable point of view.)

1:1 COACHING ACTIVITY
Getting to Underlying Thinking

Next time you see someone experience recurring breakdowns, coach the person on the underlying thinking (mental models) that are driving his or her behavior and the recurring breakdowns. Use the questions in Figure 3.1 to guide you:

FIGURE 3.1 *The iceberg diagram*

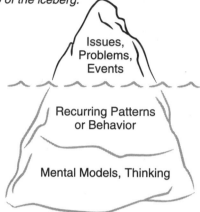

The issue, problem, event is just the tip of the iceberg.

1. What's the issue, problem, event?

2. What's the recurring pattern or behavior?

3. What is the underlying mental model, thinking?

4. How does it need to change?

Issues, Problems, Events

Recurring Patterns or Behavior

Mental Models, Thinking

The following are some examples of mental models that might get people in trouble.

- I am my position.

- Don't rock the boat.

- I need to be in control.

- The enemy is out there.

- I "have" to versus I "choose" to.

- The way we do things here is . . .

- Our usual method is . . .

RULE 4 SHIFT KNOWLEDGE WORKERS TO HIGHER LEVEL THINKING TASKS AND WORK PRODUCTS

Structure coaching relationships based on a compelling business goal or problem that will stretch people's minds and skills, rather than on problem attitudes or behaviors. If people have enough at stake in reaching the goal or solving the problem, the attitude or behaviors that are in the way will tend to clear up.

It is an absolute waste to treat talented knowledge workers as if they were cogs in the wheel by either allowing them to stay in jobs that do not require them to really think or allowing them to spend their days carrying out routine, repetitive tasks. These jobs would be better done by machines. One of the key responsibilities of a masterful coach, especially as we move deeper into the knowledge era, is to shift knowledge workers to higher level thinking tasks.

This attitude was summed up very well by a manager I spoke with who was in charge of a manufacturing area at General Electric. He said, "I see it as my job to create and design projects that engage the brainpower of the average worker." Redesigning the nature of jobs and processes themselves in order to make more use of knowledge capital is a project in itself.

At Dell Computer, for example, most order-entry tasks are carried out by the customer over the Internet. Dell's customer service people spend most of their time on higher level thinking tasks, such as consulting with customers on their technology needs or brainstorming in teams to come up with customer solutions.

1:1 COACHING ACTIVITY

Shifting Knowledge Workers to Higher Level Thinking

Start by looking at what five to ten people in your group do every day. Ask them what is trivial that they could stop doing. Then ask how much time is spent doing routine repetitive tasks that are too important to put aside. Can these be automated? Then ask, "What could you work on that would make a difference?"

RULE 5   CREATE VIRTUAL MASTERMIND GROUPS AND COACH PEOPLE ON HOW TO THINK AND INTERACT

One of the most effective ways of reaching a breakthrough or solving a complex problem is to create a "mastermind" group of unlikely collaborators. The idea of a mastermind group is to juxtapose multiple perspectives, talents, and gifts in order to increase the possibility of a creative and innovative solution. It also breaks down the guild mentality that tends to defend and constrain.

One of the greatest benefits of living in a virtual age is the possibility of creating virtual mastermind groups of the most talented people you can find, rather than being constrained by "bricks and mortar." Imagine the power of bringing together an extraordinary combination of people, methods, and resources from all over the world to engineer a business breakthrough around your biggest challenge.

The most important business skill of the twenty-first century will be the ability to communicate on-line in such groups. A coach creating a virtual team must (1) clarify the mission that will inspire people to collaborate; (2) create an extraordinary combination of people; (3) connect everyone by using some groupware; (4) transform chat rooms into "knowledge rooms" by creating shared goals, team norms, and sustainable dialogue about the best way to produce a collective work product; and (5) coach with the intent of transforming how people think and interact. (See Chapter Thirteen, on virtual teams.)

I suggest adopting Roger Schwarz's guidelines from his book *The Skilled Facilitator* for other face-to-face and electronically distributed teams.[8] (See Chapter Seven, page 180, for these guidelines.)

RULE 6   EMPLOY A BREAKTHROUGH STRATEGY, NOT JUST IMPROVEMENT TECHNIQUES

Breakthroughs are about making the impossible possible. Having said that, breakthroughs don't require that you be the CEO with a big budget or have a Ph.D. from MIT or an MBA from Harvard. Breakthroughs involve seeing what you and others are doing to produce results in a given domain—innovative, new, high-performance light bulbs; selling computers over the Internet; delivering hot pizza—and then doing something different.

The Breakthrough Strategy

- Define extraordinary results.

- Practice systematic abandonment.

- Do something different.

GROUP COACHING ACTIVITY
The Breakthrough Strategy

The next time you are coaching your team to produce a breakthrough, put aside your Total Quality Management tools and use this three-step breakthrough strategy. Keep in mind that the more you juxtapose multiple perspectives, talents, and gifts in the process, the more likely it is you will produce a breakthrough solution.

1. *Define extraordinary results.* Sit down with your team; set some reasonable goals and objectives that are the kind that "keep the farm running." Then set a breakthrough goal that represents an extraordinary result in an area in which you need one—attracting and retaining the best people, speeding up product development, increasing sales, increasing profit. For example, Clorox wanted to find ways to turn bleach, a smelly product that, if spilled, could ruin your clothes, into a growth business.

    The extraordinary result we want to produce is

2. *Practice systematic abandonment.* Once you define an extraordinary result, the next step in producing a breakthrough is to abandon things that have worked up to now but that have built-in limitations in terms of business performance. In the case of Clorox, a breakthrough team discovered that the first thing they needed to do was challenge the concept of selling liquid bleach in big bottles.

    What we need to systematically abandon to produce the breakthrough is

3. *Do something different.* Once you let go of what you need to abandon, brainstorm what you need to do differently to produce the extraordinary result. Be sure to include ideas from people who are on the fringes of your group or industry, as this is often where the most innovative ideas come from. In Clorox's case, they began selling bleach crystals that didn't smell in small boxes that weren't heavy. Sales skyrocketed.

    What we can do differently to produce the extraordinary result is

RULE 7   CREATE ROBUST FEEDBACK LOOPS

Traditionally, coaching feedback was thought to occur between a leader and a team member, often during the annual review. By contrast, masterful coaches, intent on building a highly competitive, high-performance organization, have a much broader concept of feedback that starts with being a keen observer of everything that happens on their turf: the speed and enthusiasm with which people walk and talk, what's still sitting in the warehouse, quality issues, key sales data, and so forth.

Masterful coaches consciously and intentionally design robust feedback loops in all areas of their businesses where performance matters. For example, one of the best forms of coaching feedback you can receive is from your customers—the experts on everything about your products and services that works and doesn't work. Today, with the help of toll-free numbers and e-mail, collecting customer feedback is easier than ever. In a high-velocity economy, where competitors are trying to do everything better, faster, and cheaper, timely and accurate feedback is essential. Coca-Cola collects data from smart vending machines via cellular phones and infrared signals. A computer-based restocking program analyzes the data and then produces delivery slips for the drivers.

Then again, it won't make any difference how many feedback loops you create if you don't listen to the news—good or bad. To promote a climate of feedback, Jacques Nassar, CEO of Ford Motor Company, sends e-mail to employees that shares news, the good and the bad, with everyone. He also reads hundreds of employee comments each month and makes sure that follow-up occurs.[9]

GROUP COACHING ACTIVITY

Brainstorm Feedback Loops

With your group, look at the areas in which you need feedback. Set up a session to brainstorm creative feedback loops. Choose the ones you will use. Assign accountability for the design and implementation of each one.

RULE 8   EXPECT SOMETHING NEW FROM EVERYONE

A company in India named Tata builds the majority of cars produced in that country. According to one manager, "People here recognized that we couldn't get a promotion every two years. So the question we asked ourselves was how to reinvent what we do every two years, as well as the way we work, so that we are motivated and stimulated?" This led to a companywide coaching and mentoring program: "Expect something new from everyone."[10]

This is an apt motto. Today, as advanced manufacturing techniques perfect the art of making duplicates, value will be increasingly placed on innovation. If innovation is desired, the coach must create space for crazies, kooks, and mavericks. It also means a coach must learn how to care for and feed new ideas rather than let a sigh, frown, or yawn suffocate them. If an idea succeeds, talk about it. If it does not, learn from the mistakes and try something else.

What's new with innovation? We have gained the insight that it comes from differences. The more you juxtapose talented people, perspectives, and resources around a business challenge, the more likely it is that you will light creative sparks. John Seely Brown, chief scientist at Xerox's Palo Alto research and development center, brings together scientists, artists, MBAs, anthropologists, and software engineers to brainstorm solutions to customer problems. This approach helped Xerox to launch the PC revolution in the 1980s.[11]

As we move from a work world of "places" to "spaces," in which people from all over the world can meet virtually to discuss a customer issue, dream up an innovative solution, or grind out a prototype, the possibilities expand exponentially. Digital technology makes it easier to assemble a team. Ten years ago, whether someone would work on a project depended on what country he or she worked in. Today, it depends on talent, educational background, or experience.

RULE 9   COACH CUSTOMERS TO SOLVE PROBLEMS FOR THEMSELVES

Companies have a responsibility to give the highest possible value to customers. One of the ways they can do this is to coach customers to help them learn to solve their own problems. For example, Fidelity Investments, Schwab, and other financial service firms encourage customers to make trades themselves over the Internet. This frees their registered investment representatives to spend more time counseling customers as to what constitutes a smart investment decision.

In the next decade, transactions in many fields will increasingly be moved to the Internet, including routine sharing of information and communication. Telephone and face-to-face communication will increasingly be used in a coaching and counseling capacity as employees help customers to make smart decisions.

Technology may be the ultimate way to connect a customer with a firm, but it has to start with trust. Here are some other guidelines for coaches:

Anticipate What the Customer Wants. The key is to establish an intimate relationship with customers whereby you understand their strategies, desires, needs, and preferences. This allows you to recall their needs intelligently, to anticipate their needs before they even articulate them, and to tailor products to their needs.

Educate the Customer. Educate customers in new trends or technologies that will influence their businesses. In fields like high-tech or financial services and medicine, it is hard for even the most sophisticated customers to keep up with what you can offer. Educating customers also includes showing them how your products and services can make them profitable. For example, Phebe Farrow Port of Estée Lauder shows the managers of department stores such as Macy's that it is cosmetics, not Levi's 501 Jeans, that are the biggest profit makers.[12]

Deal with Customer Complaints Immediately. Andy Grove acknowledges that Intel made a huge mistake when it ignored customers' responses to its announcement that there might be a flaw in its Pentium processor chip. Intel refused to replace chips unless there was a verified problem, assuming that only a few scientists would make such a claim. When customers rebelled, Intel's stock fell off the shelf.[13] By dealing with customer complaints immediately, you not only preserve the customer relationship and your company's brand equity, but you also learn how to improve your products and services from the people who know the most about them.

RULE 10   MAKE SURE THAT ALL PROCESSES ARE CAPABLE OF JUST-IN-TIME DELIVERY

I have always felt that work should be a gift to the human spirit and that an organization should be a place in which people joyfully work to celebrate their personal qualities of excellence by providing value to a customer, rather than being something people merely do to make a living. Thus, when I first heard of reengineering as a way to make people in groups more productive, I found the idea repugnant! "Another engineering solution to a human problem." Simply put, the idea behind reengineering is that if you break a job down into too many pieces and involve too many people, no one will be able to see how the process works and the work will break down.

When I read Hammer's book on reengineering, I did gain a few insights: (1) delivering value to customers in a timely and reliable way works better if people have a view of the whole process, and (2) simplifying your core processes is a good way to reduce handoffs, eliminate waste, and make sure that products can be delivered to customers on a just-in-time basis. Then, while coaching some reengineering projects, I discovered that although a helicopter view of the whole process is important at the beginning, it is best to spearhead projects with quick successes.

Then there was the human side of the equation. A few years back I did a coaching program at NUMMI, a joint venture of Toyota and General Motors in California. I was shocked when I met some people on the assembly line whose entire job consisted of attaching car doors with three bolts and a power drill.

Then I read about GM's Saturn plant that had developed a brand new way of building cars based on empowering workers in tight, autonomous teams. Each team has a specific function, such as building engines, chassis, or doors, and each team member is trained to do approximately thirty different jobs so that no one gets bored. Workers can retrieve data from a Web-based system and analyze any problems and fix them. Saturn's success shows that if you give workers more sophisticated jobs and tools to work with, they will produce better products and services.

YOUR FIRST THIRTY DAYS AS A MASTERFUL COACH

Now that you have made your coaching contract and understand the rules for coaching in the new knowledge-based, digital economy, what are you going to do next? Start by taking the stance that you are a new coach taking over your team (even if you are not). What would you do in the next thirty days (1) to build high performance; (2) to increase strategic, team, and individual capability; and (3) to do so in an environment of change and complexity and high competition?

DAY 1   DISCOVER WHAT IS REALLY EXPECTED OF YOU

Ask questions. Then slow the conversations down so that people have time to be explicit in their answers. Listen to what people are saying, as well as to what's behind their words.

DAYS 2 TO 5   RELATE TO, INTERVIEW, AND OBSERVE THE PLAYERS

Find out where they are now. This is an excellent way to begin to build a personal relationship with people and engage them in the task. When you ask people, "What do you think?" they get involved. Gather facts and data. Ask, "What's working and what's not working?" You will learn a lot about the group's goals, problems, capabilities, morale, and so forth, even if you have been with the team for some time. (See Chapter Two, on investing in relationships.)

DAYS 6 TO 9   PONDER AND ORGANIZE YOUR FINDINGS

Take time to mull over what you have learned from these interviews. What does it mean? How do you see the team's resources, assets, talent, teamwork, or motivation? What are the major breakdowns that need to be addressed?

DAY 10   WRITE A PERSONAL COACHING MISSION STATEMENT

Create a simple statement of the major challenge you face and what you intend to accomplish with the team and the individuals on it. Focus on key results you want to achieve. The statement should be transformational. Once you write it, write five or six bulleted points that describe your teachable point of view for successfully achieving the mission.

DAYS 11 TO 12 HOLD TEAM MEETINGS

Have a dialogue about your mission statement, teachable point of view, and where we are now. Make a short presentation and answer questions. Give your definition of coaching—what it is and is not. Then provide your findings from interviews—what's working and what's not working.

DAY 13 CREATE A SHARED GOAL

Ask people to focus on a goal that represents an extraordinary result and that will inspire both personal commitment and team collaboration—greater sales, much faster cycle time, dramatically improved quality and service, and so on.

DAY 14 ASSESS CAPABILITY GAPS

Hold a one- to two-hour session to assess the group's capability gaps in regard to the goal and how to fill them. Determine your strategic capability today (core competence as a company). Decide how to expand it to meet the goal. What is your organizational capability today in terms of providing with absolute reliability what customers expect? Where does it need to be? How can you achieve this? What is the level of leadership required to meet the challenge? How will you develop the leaders you need?

DAY 15 CREATE TEAM GROUND RULES

You need ground rules for how the group will think and interact. For example, ask people to (1) make decisions consistent with their vision and highest values, not their reactions to others, circumstances, or events; (2) pursue opportunities through an attitude of collaboration; (3) share all relevant information with others on the team; (4) build shared meaning by expressing their own ideas, then explore others' ideas; and (5) discuss the undiscussable.

| **DAY 16** | **DETERMINE THE FLOW OF COMMUNICATION** |

Insist that communication flow through e-mail and that groupware be installed. If people are not connected, connect them within two weeks. Everyone in your organization should be connected to e-mail. Insist that communication flow through e-mail to enhance the possibility of collaboration and eliminate wasted time at meetings. Also, gain access to a groupware package. Launch training that allows your group to do projects to improve business processes independently of time and distance. Learn to coach in this medium. (See Chapter Thirteen for an interview with Tom Sudman on creating virtual teams to collaborate on projects.)

| **DAYS 17 TO 20** | **DESIGN "BREAKTHROUGH" PROJECTS** |

Find projects that can be completed in eighty hours while you coach the team. Setting only long-term goals makes it difficult to intervene in a way that has a meaningful impact on individual or team performance. Coaching has the greatest impact when people are hotly engaged in pursuing short-term performance goals under time pressure. Based on your mission and goals, create one or more breakthrough projects to be achieved in eighty hours that will spearhead a breakthrough on a larger level, such as new product innovation, customer care, or operational excellence. Each success becomes an opening to a widening circle of successes. (See Chapter Nine, page 205, for more on designing and implementing breakthrough projects.)

| **DAYS 21 TO 22** | **ASK TEAMS TO SHARE THEIR WORK PLANS IN WRITING** |

Help each breakthrough project team to share a written work plan. Act as a thinking partner to enhance it. Each breakthrough project should be focused on a performance opportunity in the business. Team members should be selected based on relevant talents and gifts, not status or rank. The breakthrough goal should be challenging but attainable and should elicit the attitude, "This is what we have all been waiting for!" Act as a thinking partner in creating (or reframing) written work plans that focus on doable actions. Be available to discuss issues as they come up.

DAYS 22 AND ONWARD

LET ACTIONS EMERGE

Actions will come from daily coaching conversations with people in the group. It is very important to be available to discuss emergent issues with individuals or groups. This also provides an opportunity to provide a teachable point of view or to offer feedback, individually and to the group. A good questioning protocol is to ask, What are the accomplishments and insights? Issues and dilemmas? Next steps?

DAYS 22 TO 29

PROVIDE FEEDBACK

Provide feedback and learning to individuals or the group on a just-in-time basis. Every leader should have at least four conversations a year with every person on his or her staff to look at performance and to create a professional development plan. Aside from these formal sessions, feedback and learning should be on a just-in-time basis. Is the team making strategic assumptions that could lead to breakdowns? Explore them. Is a team member about to step on a political land mine? Intervene in a way that is challenging and supportive. Does the team need a course on how to write a business plan? Provide it. (See Chapter Ten, on giving feedback.)

DAYS 22 TO 29

SEIZE COACHABLE MOMENTS

Pay attention to coachable moments when they occur and seize them. These occur in every minute of every hour of every day. Masterful coaches seize coachable moments (or critical incidents) to deliver their teachable points of view on a wide variety of issues: (1) personal ethics and legal responsibility, (2) entrepreneurial attitudes, or (3) teamwork and collaboration. Many managers do not recognize coachable moments and lose the opportunity to have an impact.

DAY 30   ASSESS PROGRESS

Check on what has happened, progress toward goals, and what has changed. Make adjustments on the basis of what has changed since starting out. This is also a good time to recognize and reward people formally, not only for what they have accomplished but also for how they have grown and developed in the process. Launch new eighty-hour breakthrough projects based on previous successes.

CHAPTER FOUR

You can't tranform others until you are willing to transform yourself.

GETTING IN SHAPE FOR COACHING

Finding Practical Ways to Get Ready

The purpose of this chapter is to get you ready for your new career as a masterful coach. It doesn't matter what your passion is—business, golf, tennis, or the cello—there is always a period at the beginning (and at the start of each season) when you have to get in shape. It is said that Jack Nicklaus, after winning eleven golf majors, went to his teacher from his college days and said, "Teach me how to play golf." Jack Grout then took Nicklaus through all of the fundamentals, often talking about his own mentors.[1]

The key leadership issue in today's economy is to make knowledge workers more productive.

There is an aspect of getting in shape in the performing arts as well. Benjamin Zander, conductor of the Boston Philharmonic Orchestra, leaves a piece of paper on his music stand prior to each rehearsal so he can ask the players to indicate how he is doing with respect to bringing out the best in them.[2]

Let's say you are the kind of business leader who has ruled from on high and has spent the last ten years either in Total Quality Management or reengineering (job cutting and cost cutting). Let's say as well that you have recently been struck by lightning and have discovered (again) that "the knowledge in people is our most important asset." You have realized that rightsizing meant, in many cases, taking your company's knowledge assets and throwing them into the nearest river.

There has to be a better way. Peter Drucker has said that the key leadership issue in today's economy is to make knowledge workers more productive. That means letting go at the top and committing yourself to being a masterful coach, teacher, and facilitator—remembering that knowledge is social. The same applies if you always believed in coaching but never had time to devote much attention to it or to develop the necessary skills and capabilities. You now want to develop the perspective, reflexes, and muscles that you have never used before.

One of the issues that comes up around coaching is confidence. Some businesspeople question whether they have the necessary seniority, style, skills, technical ability, and so on. In most cases, people have more coaching assets than they are aware of. They usually err not on the side of grabbing the brass ring and going for it but on the side of being too tentative. They act like new fathers or mothers who are afraid to do anything wrong—putting aside their intuition and insights and looking for a list of rules. There are no rules. Any rule you create may be appropriate one day and inappropriate the next. A good way to gain confidence is to become aware of the coaching assets you already have.

YOUR PERSONAL COACHING ASSETS

Masterful coaches have the following five assets. Exhibit 4.1 lists them and they are discussed in the following paragraphs. After you read through the material, you will have a chance to do your own personal coaching asset inventory.

EXHIBIT 4.1 *Five assets of masterful coaches*

1. A burning desire to lead, coach, and teach

2. A powerful results orientation

3. Emotional intelligence

4. Ability to be a good generalist and a good specialist

5. Generosity of spirit

ASSET 1   A BURNING DESIRE TO LEAD, COACH, AND TEACH

One of the first things people want to know is the qualifications for a masterful coach. Knowing what they are allows you to take stock of your personal coaching assets. Yet the question inevitably leads to making a list and overlooking the obvious. The most important coaching asset is to have a burning desire to coach people in a way that makes a difference. If you have that burning desire, it can make up for a lack of experience, methods, and techniques to some extent. If you don't have the burning desire, then all the techniques in the world won't help you. *Do you have a burning desire to lead, coach, and teach others?*

ASSET 2   A POWERFUL RESULTS ORIENTATION

Coaching is concerned with accomplishment, not psychology. One seeks a coach to "produce results" that are difficult or impossible to produce today. One seeks a psychologist to "feel better." Results can happen only if the coach has a strong results orientation. Coaches must be able to set the highest goals and standards and be relentless in holding themselves and others accountable to them.

Goals are only a first step. You can't coach people on goals; you can only coach them on the one to three things to do that are necessary to reach those goals. Drive the same simple messages home with consistency. "Don't just focus on the numbers," says Tom Kaiser, president of Zurich American Insurance Group. "Focus on customers, employee satisfaction, and cash. The numbers will be there."[3] Remember in speaking with team members that people either have the reasons or they have the results. *How do you measure up?*

ASSET 3   EMOTIONAL INTELLIGENCE

Every time I start to write about holding people accountable for results, I worry that some readers will forget that coaching always takes place in a relationship with a human being who has his or her own point of view, goals, and feelings. To coach a human being, you can't just think with your head; you have to think with your feelings. It is called "emotional intelligence."[4]

In years past I held many leadership programs with French Canadians. Few had academic degrees, but many had the kind of basic human wisdom that comes with an open mind and an open heart. They were often superb team leaders and builders who had mastered the most subtle but complex nuances of human nature. Today's MBAs, engineers, and finance managers are often just the opposite; they have degrees that allow them to deal with technical issues, but they have not developed enough emotional intelligence to deal with the human ones. *Where do you stand in terms of emotional intelligence?*

ASSET 4   ABILITY TO BE A GOOD GENERALIST AND
A GOOD SPECIALIST

As a generalist, do you have some provocative new ideas about leadership or the business? Do you have a balanced view of things? Can you bring a group together across boundaries? If you were my coach, I would also want to know whether you had the special expertise I needed. Coaching on special skills always needs to be grounded in a community of practice. People don't go to a sports or music coach; they go to a tennis coach, cello coach, and so on. *As a coach, if you don't have all the special skills I need, are you willing to play the role of learning resource?*

ASSET 5 GENEROSITY OF SPIRIT

As I said earlier, coaching is a way of being, not just a technique that allows you to help other people achieve success. The coaching asset that I ascribe to that way of being is "generosity of spirit" toward others. This generosity of spirit compels you to say, "What's the problem? Would you like a thinking partner for that?"

Generosity of spirit allows you to give people the gift of your presence in any conversation. It motivates you to give authentic feedback that helps someone grow and learn, as well as to give praise that affirms the person. People with generosity of spirit give others credit. It is amazing how many people in organizations are misers when it comes to praise, operating as if dishing out more than just a little will render them empty. *Do you act from a generosity of spirit?*

PRACTICE ASSIGNMENT
Your Coaching Assets Assessment

Rate yourself between 1 and 5 on the survey shown in Exhibit 4.2 (1 being weak and 5 being very strong). You probably are strong in some of these areas and weaker in others. Then mull on the following points to capture the learning. The idea is to validate and build on your strengths as you work to overcome your areas of weakness.

CAPTURING THE LEARNING

My strengths are in the following areas:

- The specialist skills in which I have an above-average level of competence are:

- The generalist skills in which I have an above-average level of competence (for example, being a thinking partner or a project manager) are:

EXHIBIT 4.2 *Coaching assets assessment*

	1	2	3	4	5
1. You have a burning desire to lead, coach, and teach, as well as a positive attitude toward learning.	☐	☐	☐	☐	☐
2. You are effective at building professional relationships and have a reputation for people skills.	☐	☐	☐	☐	☐
3. You possess basic human wisdom or emotional intelligence, and other people have said so.	☐	☐	☐	☐	☐
4. You are able to deliver a simple, powerful, consistent message to your team that shapes, limits, and defines thinking and behavior.	☐	☐	☐	☐	☐
5. You have a powerful results orientation that you re-create in others.	☐	☐	☐	☐	☐
6. You have an ability to teach others your ideas, to share your knowledge, and to ignite learning in others.	☐	☐	☐	☐	☐
7. You have the ability as a business leader to see the strategic big picture and to have a balanced view of complex situations.	☐	☐	☐	☐	☐
8. You show generosity of spirit by giving people the gift of your presence. You are generous with your ability to give authentic feedback that praises and corrects.	☐	☐	☐	☐	☐
9. You have specialist or subject-matter expertise that relates to your business—for example in R&D, marketing, or production.	☐	☐	☐	☐	☐

My areas of weakness are:

- A few of the things I intend to work on, either to build on strengths or develop weaknesses, in order to become a masterful coach are:

ON BECOMING A GURU—MY OWN EXAMPLE

On my business card it says GURU, *personal, organization, and world issues.* Why guru? Not for self-aggrandizement. I prefer the term for both its traditional and its transformational aspects. I enjoy transformational change. I have never been that interested in transactional change. I have also never liked the terms *consultant* and *trainer,* because these terms seem so run-of-the-mill. Sometimes I don't even use the word *coach,* referring to myself as a conversation partner instead.

I started out doing transformational coaching at the fairly young age of thirty. My strongest qualification was my passion for the work. I didn't just want to make a living—I wanted to make a difference. I had some entrepreneurial business experience running periodicals. This gave me some strong leadership skills. However, my specialist skills were somewhat limited. Some people would have said that although I was very perceptive, I lacked emotional intelligence. It took me a while to realize that it was about contributing to people, not cleverness.

I made a conscientious attempt to develop wisdom in the way I spoke to people. I went to the library and checked out many, many books, especially on quotations, wrote them down on three-by-five cards, and then practiced reading them to the trees in my backyard. In fact, I used to walk around the woods for hours reciting quotes from Henry Ford, Gandhi, Thomas Watson, Swami Mukdananda, Theodore Roosevelt, Martin Luther King, historian Lewis Mumford, architect Paolo Soleri, and others. I would sprinkle these quotes into my workshops and at some point began mixing them up so I couldn't tell what I had said, what some guru or another had said, or what had been said by some business titan.

As a journalist at the time, I was able to use my position to interview more than one hundred people who were masters from different fields—especially business, philosophy, science, and the arts. I read their books, signed up for their courses, or signed on for short-term work assignments. These people and others provided excellent role models. I noticed that they could engage people in conversations during which new possibilities would appear out of nowhere or people would be faced with reality, enter into despair, and then rise again to new heights.

I knew I wanted to coach and teach people in this way, but I was haunted by insecurities. The idea of standing in front of a room and talking, which is what I wanted to do, terrified me. I also wasn't sure I was ready to coach people in various kinds of leadership positions.

See yourself differently, act differently, starting right now!

As part of my personal development program, I studied oriental physiognomy and learned how to analyze people's character, personality, thoughts, and moods by their facial expressions and body types. I learned that I could look at people and tell about their past, present, and future. I learned to tune into what they were thinking, how they were feeling. I don't know how I do this, but I do. I am at least 85 percent accurate (make that 87 percent). Along with studying people's faces, I became an inveterate people watcher. I observed people in business, at home, in the subway, in restaurants, in the supermarket. It is amazing what you can learn about people just by watching what they eat.

One day, in conversation with a friend, Dave Korkosz, about both his personal and professional life, I was able to help him gain insight into some things he was doing that were creating unintended results. He called a few days later to tell me that not only had our conversation had a powerful impact on his business results but it had also been what he called "life altering." From this point on, it was a matter of looking (waiting) for the opportunities to set off on my career as a guru.

TEN STRATEGIES FOR GETTING IN SHAPE FOR COACHING

Following are ten strategies you can use to get in shape for coaching. There may be some others that you develop or discover that will get you on the right track, but at least these will help you start. They are listed in Exhibit 4.3.

STRATEGY 1   DECLARE YOUR INTENTION TO BE A MASTERFUL COACH

Many people spend their whole lives getting ready for the rest of their lives. Then they discover, often too late, that the opportunities have slipped away from them and, like seeds in a packet, have gone past their expiration date. You can start being a masterful coach today. First of all, declare your intention to be a masterful coach and start to see yourself that way instead of as someone still get-

EXHIBIT 4.3 *Ten strategies for getting in shape for coaching*

1. Declare your intention to be a masterful coach.

2. Study with a master, dedicated teacher, or coach.

3. Create a personal coaching project with one to three people.

4. Sign up for a personal transformation course.

5. Become an obsessive people watcher.

6. Practice the left-hand column exercise weekly.

7. Keep a journal; do regular practice and reflection assignments.

8. Go to spring training or orchestra rehearsals.

9. Develop emotional intelligence; acknowledge emotions.

10. Learn something completely new outside of work.

ting ready. Act that way in everything you do, starting right now. The power that declaring a public commitment to being a masterful coach (or to anything) can have is amazing.

In my own case, I decided to put a date on the calendar to do my first personal (professional) transformation seminar. That was my public declaration that I was going to become a masterful coach. However, while enrolling attendees I actually began to see myself as a masterful coach, based on the kinds of interactions I was having and the feedback I was receiving. I had about three months to prepare to do something that would demonstrate enough mastery that I would be able to continue with the work that was my passion.

Thomas Watson of IBM once said that you can become an excellent leader in a minute. When people asked how, he declared, "By refusing to do anything less than excellent work from this minute on."[5] That is the kind of approach I took as a "guru in training." I committed to causing the success of each person with whom I interacted (in a way that didn't prevent the person from causing his or her own success). I also disciplined myself so that every word that came out of my mouth could create value for people. Then I disciplined myself to listen so that I would give each person the gift of my presence, listening with a high quality of attention, as if he or she was the only person in my universe. In most cases, this worked.

The same kind of declaration of commitment can work for every manager who wants to become a masterful coach. Once you have made the declaration, start to see yourself in a manner that is consistent with that declaration. Keep in mind that "the best way to do is to be." Ask yourself, Who do I need to "be" when I go about hiring new recruits? How about a "connoisseur of talent" versus a "hiring manager" or "slot filler"? Who do I need to "be" when I call the first team meeting? How about a value-shaping leader? How would a masterful coach handle this botched customer order with the people in shipping?

Note: Starting to act as if you are a masterful coach does not imply that you don't need to develop yourself as one. Quite the contrary, you will be sure to meet many obstacles. Remember: (1) keep your spirits up in the face of adversity, (2) look for openings to do coaching, (3) learn something new about coaching every day, and (4) solicit honest feedback.

PRACTICE ASSIGNMENT

Being a Masterful Coach

Declare to someone your intention to become a masterful coach. Have a conversation with that person. Think about the various coaching situations in which you are involved. How do you have to be different in those situations?

To become a great leader, put aside your job title, expertise, and ego, and surrender to letting someone else coach you for awhile.

One of the best ways to learn how to coach is to seek out great coaches and have some powerful experiences of being coached yourself. If you look at the masterful coaches and teachers in the spiritual tradition, sports, the arts, or business, most have been molded by a very intensive experience with one or more coaches or mentors. These experiences not only gave them the inspiration, role models, and life experiences necessary to become great coaches and teachers, but also made them much better players. One of the great lessons that even the best players learn is what it means to put aside their own job titles, expertise, and egos and let someone else coach them for awhile.

Managerial leaders could learn an enormous amount about coaching by finding a masterful coach in their own or a related field. If you think you don't need coaching, it is probably because either you are not stretching yourself or you may be too arrogant and have an attitude of knowing versus learning. Chris Argyris has pointed out in an article called "Good Communication That Blocks Learning" that successful people often arrange their lives so that they do not have to learn the lessons from failure.[6] If this is true of you, declare a stretch goal that pushes you beyond what you already know how to do, and then ask someone to coach you.

If there is not a masterful coach in your company with whom you can work in complete openness and candor, consider bringing someone in from the outside. In either case, look for someone to whom you can expose not only your dreams and aspirations but also your ignorance and incompetence.

PRACTICE ASSIGNMENT

Finding a Coach or Mentor

Find someone you respect who is accomplished in an area in which you would like to develop. Decide what you would like the person to coach you on. Go and have a conversation with that person.

A project with a clear focus is often the glue that holds a coaching relationship together.

STRATEGY 3   CREATE A COACHING PROJECT WITH ONE TO THREE PEOPLE

It has been said that everything that goes wrong in the typical corporate training program can be stated in four words: *It's just like school.* School is based on the idea that knowledge is about acquiring information, not building new skills through practice. For the most part, business has been going down the same dead end. In truth, as most of us have discovered, people learn best when they practice, fail, and try again under the guidance of a mentor who can share relevant knowledge and experience.

That being the case, I strongly recommend that you find one to three people who want to achieve a specific stretch goal and create a coaching relationship in which together you design a "coaching project" that will help them to realize that goal. Tell them that you want real feedback about how you are doing as a coach. Look for people who might be open to such an experiment—those who could benefit from your knowledge and wisdom and who are insightful enough to give you their perspectives when you ask, "How am I doing?"

I used the term *project* by design here. Projects that are about accomplishing something are the glue that holds a coaching relationship together. Coaching relationships based on things like changing attitudes and behavior tend to suffer from the laws of entropy. I have found that although managers are willing to be somewhat introspective about their thinking and attitudes when they get in the way of producing desired results, they resent any such conversation otherwise.

A coaching project could take many different forms: (1) a successful presentation to the board, (2) a new marketing campaign or product development effort, (3) making a big sale, or (4) winning back a lost customer. If you need to focus on behavioral or attitudinal changes, create mini-coaching projects, such as supporting someone in sharing with the boss what's really on his mind, or listening better at the next team meeting.

If you get in over your head, find a mentor to talk over what's happening. Depending on the nature of the project, you might want to find two or three conversation partners. Just as there is an art to getting the most out of a coach, there is an art to getting the most out of a coachee. Ask the coachees to coach you on making them greater. Do the same thing when coaching a team. Ask, "What can I do to bring out the best in you?"

PRACTICE ASSIGNMENT

Creating a Coaching Project

Think about who can be approached about creating a coaching relationship and coaching project. Have a conversation with the person to set it up. Who might serve as a thinking partner for you on the coaching project? Go and have a conversation with that person as well.

STRATEGY 4   SIGN UP FOR A PERSONAL TRANSFORMATION COURSE

Ralph Waldo Emerson said that who you are speaks so loudly, it drowns out what you are saying. One of the most reliable steps a person who aspires to becoming a masterful coach can take is to go through some kind of experience of personal transformation. It has been said that personal transformation is a key to organizational transformation. Let me give you an example from my own experience.

A number of years ago, I started a company called Relationships, an educational corporation that gave transformational seminars on a variety of subjects. Over the years, people often asked me how I prepared myself to do this kind of work. Basically it involved (as I mentioned earlier)

Personal transformation is essential for organizational transformation.

putting a date on the calendar for the first leadership seminar, building a team, and enrolling a big crowd. The seminars were business oriented but delved into areas of personal transformation as well. We would spend an hour setting a context by making some distinctions about leadership or other topics. The next fifty hours or so would involve engaging participants in a dialogue, with the idea of producing breakthroughs in results and for people.

The idea was simple. Each participant would go to the front of the room. I would go to the back of the room with my facilitation partner and we would engage in a conversation that lasted anywhere from three minutes to three hours about whatever the person's breakthrough was. This was a one-to-one interaction. For most of the seminar, the ground rule was for the participants in their seats not to interrupt the dialogue. This created a space for me to work and, at the same time, prevented people from reacting and interfering.

I would talk to people about their visions or issues from a place of relentless compassion, making new distinctions, exposing people's blind spots, and interjecting what the Buddhists call *crazy humor*. In most cases, the person's issue would touch at least 30 percent of the other people in the room. The result was that people learned the leadership lessons they needed to learn while observing others learn. By the time the last few people would take their turns, it was amazing how much they had transformed as a result of just listening to the dialogue, self-reflecting, and gaining insights. They would often express themselves with a new clarity and power about their business issue, and with wisdom, compassion, and humor regarding others. It was awe inspiring.

People would write to say that there had been some mysterious breakthrough in their high-level coaching and teaching skills, which they said they had absorbed from me, as if by osmosis, and from long hours of self-reflection. It was interesting because we never said very much in these programs about how to be a coach or how to teach.

PRACTICE ASSIGNMENT
Transformational Learning

Sign up for a course that is transformational.

> *The face never lies. Everything you say reveals you.*

STRATEGY 5   BECOME AN OBSESSIVE PEOPLE WATCHER

There is a great line from Sherlock Holmes, "You have eyes, but you do not see." Holmes could observe people and see things that were invisible to others. These observations gave him insight into his cases and allowed him to crack them.

One of the most important ways to get in shape for masterful coaching is to become a different kind of observer, one who notices things about people, situations, and events that are transparent to others. For example, a masterful coach doesn't just look at someone's face, as if it were a statue, but notices the subtle expressions of mood and temperament. A masterful coach doesn't just listen to someone's words, but notices the discrepancy between verbal and nonverbal communication. A masterful coach doesn't just hear someone's opinions, but listens for the assumptions behind them.

It is inconceivable that you can do all of that observing without being a passionate people watcher. I once went with my daughter Vanessa to the Metropolitan Museum of Art in New York to see an art exhibit by Van Gogh and other painters. There were hordes of people. I walked through the galleries looking around, undisturbed until I felt a tap on my shoulder. "Dad, you're staring at people." I was caught red-handed. Instead of looking at the paintings, I was looking at the people studying the paintings, which in truth I found more interesting.

It is important to separate observations from assessments. Most people tend to observe scantily, then rush to judgment, based on their prejudices toward certain kinds of people or behavior. Why does that guy have a tie on? He must be a stuffed shirt. In general, it is a good rule of thumb to observe longer, and when you do make an assessment, to make sure you can validate it.

One of the ways I have trained people to coach is to go with them to a public place and observe people. I once sat observing people with Susan Fletcher, a coachee from the La Relève program in Canada, in a cafe in a government building. As part of learning how to be a good leader and coach, Fletcher wanted to improve her ability to "size people up." At first we observed people going about their normal business. Then we started watching people's facial expressions more closely for signs of temperament, observing their physiognomy for signs of character and personality, looking at their dress and guessing their occupations, guessing whether they were likely to be a leader or not, rating their level of animal energy, and so on. In some cases, we would overhear their conversations and guess from their opinions what their mental models might be. We would sometimes introduce ourselves to people as "people watchers" and ask questions to validate our findings. (If you do this in an open and friendly way, my experience is that people will generally be open and friendly.)[7]

If you want to get in shape for coaching, join the amalgamated people watcher's union. (It is fun.) Start with your next phone call. Who is on the other end of the line? What does he or she want? What do the person's way of articulating things and tone of voice suggest to you? What does the person want to achieve? What can you do to make the person successful?

What about that new person you are recruiting? Don't just observe obvious things like academic and career background. What is the person's level of passion and enthusiasm? How badly does he or she want to have an impact? How about your next board or sales meeting? The boss is looking at his watch. Why? There are many opportunities to watch people—at night as you go about your life or on weekends.

PRACTICE ASSIGNMENT
Becoming a People Watcher

Create five to ten opportunities this week to observe people. Go out with a partner and observe people, then compare notes.

The coaching communications are usually those that we think but don't say.

STRATEGY 6   PRACTICE THE LEFT-HAND COLUMN EXERCISE WEEKLY

We have already said a lot about authenticity. It is one of the major personal and cultural issues related to introducing coaching into business, teams, or one-to-one relationships. The issue is not that people don't have the sincere intention to speak with openness and candor. It is that they don't know how to be honest and open and, at the same time, not create a blowup in their relationships. The anxiety that most of us feel in being authentic results in us making undiscussable potentially embarrassing or threatening information needed for growth and learning. This behavior is called *avoiding*.

I have found that most people, especially senior managers, are classic avoiders when it comes to giving straight feedback. I worry about people who cannot fire one person on the team because they "care," but who can turn around and fire thousands of people without feeling either deep caring or remorse. It is absolutely impossible to be an effective coach if you fall into the avoider category, so you must give it the most emphasis when getting in shape for coaching.

A great tool to use and to practice with is called the Left-Hand Column Exercise, developed by Chris Argyris.[8] Here's how it works. Think of a relationship you have with someone (or a group) that is driving you up the wall. Then take out a piece of paper and draw a line down the center from top to bottom. On the right-hand side, write down a conversation that you had that was not as successful as you would have liked. (Do it to the best of your ability.) In the left-hand column, write down all the things you thought but did not say, those things you made undiscussable in order to protect yourself or the other person. See Figure 4.1 for an example of this technique.

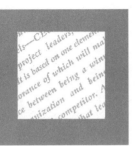

PRACTICE ASSIGNMENT
The Left-Hand Column Exercise

1. Use a left-hand column exercise before or after your next meeting with someone.

2. Observe coaching communications buried in your left-hand column that could have made a difference.

FIGURE 4.1 *The Left-Hand Column Exercise*

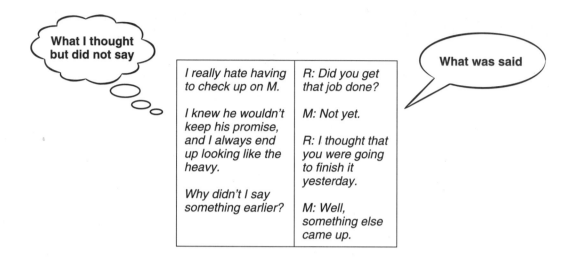

3. Practice saying the person's name and delivering the message in such a way that it is empowering, not invalidating.

4. Say, "When you do [this], it makes me feel [this way]." If you don't tell the person how you feel, you may not get the message through.

5. Ask whether the other person has any undelivered communications for you. After all, coaching is really a two-way communication.

6. For particularly difficult conversations, role-play with a colleague. Then reverse roles to see the other person's perspective. It will be an eye opener, but an effective way to prepare.

The idea in using the left–hand column exercise is not to say everything you think but to say those things that can make a difference in the situation. Everyone is in situations in which he or she would profit from saying some of what is in the left-hand column—or saying it earlier rather than later.

For example, someone once worked on business development for me. I saw that this person was willing to send out marketing letters but resisted picking up the phone and talking to a CEO or other decision maker. I found myself being unduly patient with this person but secretly resenting him for his lack of effort. One day this employee got through to a CEO on the phone but became so nervous that he hung up. I finally pulled him aside and talked to him about the things in my left-hand column. I stated my willingness to coach him, but he told me what we both were thinking but not saying—that he wasn't right for the job. Today he is off doing something else that fits him. This change could have been made six months earlier, to everyone's benefit.

STRATEGY 7   KEEP A JOURNAL; DO REGULAR PRACTICE AND REFLECTION ASSIGNMENTS

Over the years I have noticed that most managers are extraordinarily reactive. Instead of reflecting on the deeper patterns behind people's behavior, circumstances, and events, they tend to react in the moment. As a result, they lean toward easy answers and quick fixes rather than toward finding fundamental causes and solutions. Their behavior may change for a short time, but then they often revert to form. I would put 90 percent of what happens in most company training programs into this category.

Masterful coaching deals with transformation, not merely a change in form. It requires the ability to recognize and alter underlying patterns that shape, limit, and define thinking and behavior, rather than the ability to deal with the symptoms. You must develop a reflective stance rather than a reactive one. It doesn't happen overnight, especially if your pattern is to be reactive. In training "master level" coaches in our one-year coaching program, we help people develop this ability by having them keep daily journals of what they are learning, and through monthly practice and reflection assignments.

Keeping a journal involves taking five to ten minutes a day to record your observations about your strengths and areas needing improvement as a coach as you think and interact with others in your organization. A sample entry might say, "It was great being the coach at the last team meeting. I focused on working with the group to build some shared goals and some shared understanding"; or "I noticed at my performance review with Joe that I was thinking about a lot of things that could have had an impact that I was withholding for reasons I don't really understand. I seem to avoid conflict like the plague"; or "I spent an hour coaching the customer team on being not only service-oriented but also sales-oriented. Had difficulty getting people to shift their mental models. I will talk to Jim from Regional Sales about this."

Practice assignments involve doing something. Reflection assignments usually involve thinking about something. Each month participants do one or the other and then summarize in writing what they learned. The coach usually responds with a phone call, a letter, or an e-mail. The following is a smattering of some practice and reflection assignments.

REFLECTION ASSIGNMENT
Observe Yourself, Your Group

Observe yourself over the next month in the course of doing your job. Specifically observe your external behavior. Then observe yourself internally to find what is producing that behavior—your thoughts and feelings. Also observe your group's external behavior and its internal culture—how it feels to be in that group, how group members think, cultural assumptions, and so on. Record your observations.

PRACTICE ASSIGNMENT
Sit at the Foot of a Master

Go with a masterful coach to a team meeting, individual coaching session, or even a customer gathering. Pay attention to how the coach thinks and interacts with people and to the conversation process, not so much to the specific content. Write down two or three nuggets that you learn from this.

PRACTICE ASSIGNMENT
Offer to Be a Guru

Offer to act as a consultant in a discussion between two colleagues in which there are competing agendas and priorities. Your role will be to listen for twenty to thirty minutes and then give feedback to each of the participants. Offer to be a facilitator at the next big team meeting in order to sharpen your coaching skills. Write down what you learn and where you felt stuck or ineffective.

REFLECTION ASSIGNMENT

Curl Up with a Good Book

Read one of the following books over the next month: *Shogun,* **by James Clavell;** *The New Strategic Rules,* **by Kevin Kelley (editor of** *Wired***);** *Care of the Soul,* **by Thomas Moore; or** *Emotional Intelligence* **by Daniel Goleman. Summarize on one page any insights you have from this.**

STRATEGY 8   ## GO TO SPRING TRAINING OR ORCHESTRA REHEARSALS

Every year when spring training rolls around, Boston Red Sox fans dream of winning the World Series. The Sox, and dozens of other teams, head for Naples, Florida; Scottsdale, Arizona; or wherever. The same thing happens in basketball, tennis, and golf. A great way to get in shape for coaching is to visit one of these camps and observe how the coaches interact with the players. There are positive motivators like Rick Pitino of the Celtics, screamers like Bill Parcells, and arm-around-the-shoulder types like Harvey Pennick, the legendary golf coach. Whatever their style, you will be able to learn lots about what coaches do to bring out the best in their players.

If you prefer the arts, take a Friday afternoon off and buy a cheap ticket to the symphony orchestra rehearsal in your area. For example, there is no doubt that Benjamin Zander is a top-flight conductor. But he sees himself more as a teacher than as a maestro. His preconcert talks include virtuoso performers, politicians, students, and businesspeople. At one of these talks, someone asked, "Is an orchestra conductor a good model for leadership?" He replied, "It's the worst! There is a saying: 'Every dictator aspires to be a conductor.' I practiced that model of conducting for years. It wasn't until I was about forty-five that I realized something amazing: The conductor doesn't make a sound. The conductor's power depends on his ability to make other people powerful. That insight changed everything for me. I started paying attention to how I was enabling my musicians to be the best performers they could be. My orchestra noticed the change immediately. They asked, 'What happened to you?'"[9]

Another form of spring training is to gather some of the best coaches in your organization for a one-day collaborative gathering about coaching. Ask people to tell you (the group) what they do. Ask them to include a learn-by-doing practice session for things like writing marketing copy with eye-grabbing headlines, making a sales presentation, reengineering a process, designing a circuit, and so forth.

PRACTICE ASSIGNMENT

Learning from Great Coaches

- Visit a practice session for the arts or sports, or create other opportunities for watching masterful coaches.

- Set up some group practice and learning sessions for your team in areas in which they need to improve.

Companies today want people's passion, but they don't want to know their emotional pain. If you kill the pain, you also kill the passion.

STRATEGY 9   **DEVELOP EMOTIONAL INTELLIGENCE; ACKNOWLEDGE EMOTIONS**

Years ago, when I started my career as a coach, people told me the only way to achieve break-throughs was through soul renewal. In recent years, especially since the advent of "paradigms," the cognitive approach has been raised as a new sacred cow: think and ye shall find (or rather, think differently). I subscribe to this approach, but it's not a complete picture. I have seen hundreds of people attempt to change their beliefs and assumptions about someone or something, but remain trapped on a bodily (visceral) or emotional level. For a breakthrough to occur, these holds need to be released.

What does all of this mean in terms of getting in shape for coaching? Stop being a stuffed shirt, a "professional," or a robot. Get out of your head. Be a real human being. Tell it like it is. You can't coach people to acknowledge their emotions if you have no experience acknowledging your own. In business, you need an edge to make tough decisions, but you also need compassion and feeling. Acknowledging emotions doesn't make you look soft or weak. In fact, it will make you look stronger in other people's eyes.

The next time you feel entangled in a goal or problem and the cognitive approach has only taken you so far, ask yourself what you are really feeling. You will discover that there are many situations that you cannot think your way out of. You can only feel your way out of them. I have noticed in working with thousands of people that the moment of true insight and the emotion often come at the same time.

I've discovered that if people take their fingers off the control button and open up, several interesting things happen. First of all, they begin to look a lot more radiant and exude a lot more energy, as if all the cells (molecules) in their body had been rearranged. They also usually arrive at a moment of true insight into their situation—often involving a revelation about their own foolishness. At the same time, they begin to demonstrate a lot more emotional intelligence in terms of themselves and in their interpersonal relationships. In other words, as people begin to get more in touch with their own feelings, they also begin to become more in touch with the feelings of others. It shows up as wisdom, compassion, and humor.

I often tell people, "Cool is dead. To be moved is to be alive. To be alive is to be moved." To help people to express emotion in business, I use a lot of humor. I find that if people can laugh they can, in the process, let go of a lot of other feelings. Second, I often ask people to tell me about how they are feeling as they speak. This creates the space for them to express as much emotion as they feel comfortable with.

One Caveat: Just because someone feels something does not make it accurate. For example, imagine this dialogue: "Joe isn't trustworthy." Q: "How do you know that?" A: "I don't know it, I just feel it." Though people's feelings are valid, they are not necessarily accurate and often need to be validated with logic or data before any rash action is taken. Intelligence is a matter of integrating body, mind, and spirit.

PRACTICE ASSIGNMENT

Developing Emotional Intelligence

What are some situations that might be troublesome to you? Acknowledge any emotions that you have about them that you have not expressed previously. Go and have a conversation with those you need to talk to in order to clear the air.

STRATEGY 10   LEARN SOMETHING COMPLETELY NEW OUTSIDE OF WORK

Executives (managers) often forget, when coaching others based on their accumulated knowledge, wisdom, and years of experience, what it feels like to be a learner or what is involved in the process of learning. As a result, we can lose touch with the fact that we are coaching a human being, as well as lose touch with what is involved in helping anyone learn something new. One of the best ways to get in shape for coaching is to learn something completely new—preferably outside of work.

Michel Renaud of Renaud Pemberton Consulting in Montreal, Canada, is a world-class executive coach. Renaud recounts a story that many business leaders will identify with: "A number of years back, I read George Leonard's book *Mastery.* In this book he talked about being masterful at something and how that was different from being good at something. I was good at a lot of things—sports, business, among other things—but I wasn't great at anything. I thought about mastering something new in my profession, but frankly my passion for this wasn't there. I decided to develop a passion outside of work instead. I chose salsa dancing. I wanted to be great at salsa, not be what Leonard calls a 'dabbler, obsessive, or hacker.'

"Taking on something that is a passion is exciting, but also demands that you learn, which can be embarrassing to one's ego. Salsa took me to the places where I thought I wasn't good enough, where I thought it was boring, and where I wanted to run away and quit. It seemed that I would never learn everything that I needed to learn to be a great salsa dancer. I never took on a commitment to master something as I did this, and I stuck with it. It has opened my whole life to the experience of growth and learning. Salsa also took me to new places I had never been before in my professional life.

"I asked myself, 'What if I worked at my work in the same way I work in salsa?' First of all, it affected my coaching because it allowed me to balance my life and feel much more available to people again. I have a great teacher, and the more I take classes (three nights a week), the more it begins to put me in touch with what it takes to be a masterful coach. My teacher stretched me but, at the same time, was very patient with me. As a result, I feel much more committed to the goals of the people I am coaching. I have a greater understanding of what they need to learn and the whole process they have to go through to learn it.

"As I myself am on the road to mastery in a very vivid way, I can apply it to others who are committed to mastering something in a very tangible manner, relating my experience to theirs. For example, I have a client in Pittsburgh, in the oil and gas industry, who was promoted from vice president to president. He is a brilliant strategic thinker and operations analyst, but he is weak in terms of team building. He keeps playing to his strong suit, rather than develop his weaker side. He keeps thinking that if he does the things he is good at he will succeed. But sooner or later the monster comes out of the closet. I told him a story wherein he could relate his experience to mine, and it had a transformational impact.

"I said, 'I am very good at following the music in salsa with my legs and feet, but my arm movement is weak. I saw right away that my tendency was to do more of the things I am good at doing and not expose the things that I am not good at. It was a big hurdle for me to focus on those areas where I was weak, rather than work on those areas where I am good. When I did this, people started asking me: Why are you making all those crazy movements with your hands? It doesn't look good. You were a better dancer before. I had made a lot of progress but had reached a plateau and couldn't seem to move to the next level. Then one day, suddenly, my hand movements evolved and it all came together.'

It's not just what you learn that is new. It's what learning does in terms of your own renewal.

"Somehow, I was able to convey all of this to the president in a way that the message really got through because I wasn't coming from my head or from concepts I found in a book, but from the difficulties of my own learning experience. I told him, 'You have two choices as a business leader. One, to continue to work off your strengths and, if you are lucky, you will succeed anyway. The other is to choose to develop your weaknesses, so you can be more complete as a businessperson. Either way is okay. If you choose to let me coach you on your weaknesses, then you may want to tell people what you are doing so that they understand that you are a learner. This will encourage them to be learners as well.'"[10]

PRACTICE ASSIGNMENT

Mastering Something New

What is something new that you can learn to master that is outside of your normal activities? How can you go about learning it?

SUMMARY: GETTING INTO SHAPE FOR COACHING

You probably have loads of coaching assets that you might be unaware of. It is important to become aware of what these are. The five masterful coaching assets that I consider vital are these:

1. A burning desire to lead, coach, and teach

2. A powerful results orientation

3. Emotional intelligence

4. Ability to be a good generalist and a good specialist

5. Generosity of spirit

There are also certain things that you can do to get into shape for coaching. I recommend the following:

1. Declare your intention to be a masterful coach.

2. Study with a master, dedicated teacher, or coach.

3. Create a personal coaching project with one to three people.

4. Sign up for a personal transformation course.

5. Become an obsessive people watcher.

6. Practice the left-hand column exercise weekly.

7. Keep a journal; do regular practice and reflection assignments.

8. Go to spring training or orchestra rehearsals.

9. Develop emotional intelligence; acknowledge emotions.

10. Learn something completely new outside of work.

CHAPTER FIVE

It's not in the 360-degree feedback or appraisal forms; it's in the quality of conversations.

THE SIX-CAP COACHING SYSTEM

Coaching Conversations

Coaching conversations are special conversations in our culture. Coaching conversations are those during which we speak and listen with the commitment to reveal possibilities yet undreamed of for people, as well as to transform those possibilities into reality. They are different from conversations of mere opinion, conversations of sharing information, or conversations in which everything we say is an expression of the resignation we feel: "It can't be done," "Why bother?" and so on.

Paul Lafebvre of the Canadian Centre for Management Development told me that a coach is a "merchant of possibilities" who wakes people up to their dreams. When I was a young man, a woman named Mary Tess Crotty told me I was ready to do coaching programs that would transform people's (organization's) lives, igniting my aspirations as well as my fears. The directors of the Mars project said, "We believe we can put a scientific payload on Mars," the equivalent to a hole-in-one in golf. The coach of the 1980 Olympic hockey team told his group of college players they could win the gold medal, making them believe this was possible, even against the Russian team that could have beaten any group of NHL pros.

A coach is a merchant of possibilities—distinct from counselors or therapists, who usually ask people to describe their problems and who see their job as prescribing some kind of treatment. A coaching conversation is one in which we coach people into realizing their possibilities, first by believing in them and second by interacting with them in a way that expands their skills and capabilities. This usually involves the coach observing the person or group, making assessments, and providing what's missing that will make a difference—a new idea, fresh approach, or an innovative solution. See Exhibit 5.1 for a "recipe" for coaching conversations.

A coach needs to manage not only the conversation with the coachee but also the conversation that the coachee is having with himself or herself. There are usually two conversations going on in the coachee's head. The first is all about possibility: "I can become a CEO or the leader I want to be." "I know I can nail this big presentation to the board. After all, I've done it before." "I can get this 'killer app' to market before the competition." "I am sure I can not only make the sale but also deliver on service in a way that wows the customer."

EXHIBIT 5.1 *A recipe for coaching conversations*

1. Open by clarifying the purpose of the conversation.

   Talk about goals, problems, development steps.

2. Find out how others perceive their world.

   Listen to their story. How do they assess their possibilities, choices, situation?

3. Remove obstacles to success.

   Coach by asking versus telling. What are the barriers (such as attitude, mental models, behavior, lack of skills)? How can they be removed?

4. Provide what's missing that can make a difference.

   Brainstorm leverage solutions; offer your suggestions; create an action plan.

The other side of this conversation is a psychological conversation in which people take their attention off what they are creating and put it on themselves: "I am not sure I am smart enough to be CEO, or whether I have leadership potential." "Remember the time I bombed on that speech to the Rotary Club?" "I don't know whether the customer likes me."

A masterful coach interacts with people so they keep their internal conversations focused on what they are creating rather than on themselves. This means having conversations for possibility and action that keep people focused on their vision, not dwelling on psychological conversations that create too much focus on their self-doubts. It is important to acknowledge small wins and gains to help people believe in themselves. It is also important to deliver feedback so that people see it as empowering rather than invalidating. Having said that, I am now going to be deliberately provocative to show that social convention often gets in the way of effective coaching.

The backbone of any coaching conversation involves finding out who people are, not just in terms of their jobs but who they are in terms of what they passionately care about.

A COACH HAS A CERTAIN WAY OF SPEAKING AND LISTENING

A lot of people today expect a coach to talk to them like a combination of Peter Jennings, Mister Rogers, and Mother Goose. The prevailing belief is that a coach should always talk in a nice, modulated, "reasonable" tone, tiptoeing around people's every sensitivity. As Lou Holtz of Notre Dame has said, "It has become politically incorrect to push people to excel." In reality, this is a lot of foolishness.[1]

If you look at the most successful coaches in business, sports, and the arts, they may aspire to come off as something other than a crusty old bastard, as many thought about Harold Geneen, former chairman of ITT, or as an enfant terrible like Steve Jobs was on the first Apple team. In reality, given the pressures of producing results in a world of change, complexity, and competition, while working with people who sometimes "just don't get it," it is not always possible to be nice, reasonable, and modulated.

As Jack Welch has pointed out, it is hard to be a successful CEO today without sometimes appearing to be on the lunatic fringe. There needs to be some tolerance for the coach to do his or her job, to speak with both toughness and compassion, just as there needs to be room for the coachee to take risks, make mistakes, and learn from them. Forget Peter Jennings. Forget Mister Rogers. Forget Mother Goose.

Treating others with dignity and respect means being willing to have inspiring and empowering conversations in which we declare possibilities. It also means having the difficult conversations with people in which we enter the lunatic fringe, making unreasonable demands or requests or giving feedback that calls people to account. It sometimes takes a bittersweet quality (both tough and compassionate) to get through to people. We also need to remember that the person (group) we are coaching is a human being with his or her own point of view, thoughts, and feelings.

There is a wonderful story that illustrates this. It happened at the last game of the 1985 NCAA basketball championship. John Thompson was coaching for Georgetown University and Dean Smith was coaching for North Carolina. The two star players that year were Michael Worthy, who later became a Los Angeles Laker, and Patrick Ewing, who later became a player for the New York Knicks. Needless to say, playing the "Final Four" was a stretch for all concerned and both coaches had pushed their teams way beyond the point they had thought possible. They were tied up with one minute left on the clock when a freshman, Michael Jordan, scored a basket that put North Carolina two points ahead. Steve Jones of Georgetown got the ball with more than enough time to score. Jones inexplicably threw the ball to James Worthy on the other team. It was a mistake that will stay with Jones for the rest of his life. Thompson realized this in a second and, instead of yelling at Jones, walked up to him and gave him a big bear hug, whispering support and reassurances in his ear.[2]

Coaching conversations involve finding out people's vision or destination, where they are starting from, and the direction they need to move in order to get there.

COMMITTED SPEAKING AND LISTENING

What distinguishes a coaching conversation? For one thing, it involves committed speaking, which starts with a sincere and honest intention to help others make a difference. It also involves interacting with people in a way that is both more challenging than most managers are used to and more supportive. It is important to build trust and to let people know where you are coming from so they will be open to your interpretation rather than debate you or go into reaction. It is also important to bring people to choice.

Let me emphasize that committed speaking means speaking with a commitment or intention to make a difference. This involves not only expanding people's sense of what is really possible but also bringing them face-to-face with their current reality. I want people to say, "Wow, that just opened my eyes," not "Oh, that's interesting." You sometimes need to adopt a warrior's spirit and communicate with a requisite level of honesty and openness, making people aware of their blind spots or patterns of self-deception.

When I was eighteen, Mike Feinstein, my boss on the delivery truck for the Newton Center Market, pulled me aside and said, "Robert, you don't know how to work." Ouch!!! "That's B.S.," I said, protecting myself. He then picked up a banana box, put it on his shoulder, and walked down the street imitating my slouched, slow, lilting gait. I may have reacted in the moment and resented him for it, but I've never been the same since.

To be an effective coach, as part of your tool kit you have to be able to communicate with an edge—one that is sharp enough to extricate people from the reality in which they are lodged. This requires not only having the courage to communicate penetrating insights, but also putting emotional energy behind it so that people will get it. Most people in business do not have an edge (or have a very crude one). They may say they want to have an impact, but their theory-in-use (what they actually do) is to act so as not to offend anyone. The point is not to offend people but to touch them with new possibilities and extricate them from the reality in which they are stuck.

It is difficult to be effective at committed speaking unless you are also a committed listener. It's a matter of listening from a commitment to making a difference in people's lives as well as in their organizations. As people talk about their goals and problems, most other people just listen to the story and the words. The kind of advice these people give is at about the same level as you might find in the publications in the supermarket aisles.

A masterful coach listens in a much deeper way, not just to what people are saying but also to the whole network of underlying perceptions, beliefs, and assumptions. In most situations, the issue that people face is an inability to surface, question, and revise mental models that prevent them from acting on good advice.

Committed Speaking Guidelines

- Communicate with a sincere and honest intention to make a difference in others' lives.

- Share your sincere and honest intentions so that others know where you are coming from.

- Communicate with honesty and authenticity those things that are needed for growth and learning, even though it may make others uncomfortable at first.

- Communicate with enough edge to make people aware of their blind spots and to penetrate illusions.

- Be a human being, not a robot; deliver your communication with emotional energy so people "get it."

- Balance toughness and compassion.

Committed Listening Guidelines

- Communicate from a commitment to listen, whether you agree or disagree.

- Ask yourself, "Why am I about to give advice before attempting to understand this person?"

- Listen to bring out people's ideas, insights, or half-baked thoughts that contain hidden nuggets.

- Listen for the underlying context that shapes people's perceptions, who they are, how they see their possibilities, and their behavior.

- If you are committed to breakthroughs for people and breakthroughs in results, be more rigorous:

  - Listen for discrepancies between verbal and nonverbal communications.

  - Listen for "rut" stories that will get people stuck or "river" stories that will move people along.

  - Listen for interpretations people make about their world that will get them into trouble.

  - Listen for beliefs or assumptions that are creating blind spots and counterproductive behavior.

  - Listen for the good, too.

MASTERFUL COACHES OFTEN SAY THE ONE THING THAT CAN MAKE A DIFFERENCE

One of the main differences between an advanced beginner and a competent coach has to do with the difference between *listening to* and *listening for.* The advanced beginner listens to the words in people's stories, the masterful coach listens for the structure of interpretation that lies underneath them. Are they telling a rut story or a river story? Are people interpreting things in a way that will make them feel like a victim or make them feel empowered? See Exhibit 5.2 for a visual representation of the difference.

EXHIBIT 5.2 *Listening "to" versus listening "for"*

Listen to	Listen for
The words	• Stories—river versus rut
	• Facts versus interpretations
	• Verbal explanations versus emotional subtitles
	• Rigorous thinking versus jumping to conclusions
	• Unexamined beliefs, assumptions

Another difference between the advanced beginner and the competent coach is the deliberate intention to intervene when it seems appropriate. A limitation of both the advanced beginner or reasonably competent coach may show up in a reluctance to ask questions that really challenge people's perspectives. They also may simply give up too early and defer to people's thinking, out of an assumption that pushing would be disrespectful. Along the same lines, there is the tendency of the merely competent coach to believe that giving one's own point of view, even if it can help, is a cardinal sin, and that coaching is always about asking questions and listening.

A masterful coach is one who can say that one thing that can make a difference. This brings us to the next level of coaching, which has to do with having the coaching conversation that is appropriate to the needs of the coachee and the situation at hand.

THE SIX-CAP COACHING SYSTEM

Part Two of this book introduces a five-step masterful coaching model as a way to assist businesspeople in structuring coaching relationships over time—starting with developing a teachable point of view, investing in relationships, setting aspirations, and so on. Coaching people through these steps happens in conversations.

There are six distinct kinds of conversations that a coach needs to be able to use. Each type of conversation requires putting on a different "coaching cap." I'm using the coaching cap as a metaphor to assist you in distinguishing the different conversations, as well as to help you to broaden and deepen your coaching practice.

It has been observed that people tend to identify with one conversational style that has worked for them in the past—always being candid, always being diplomatic, and so on. Coaching *agility* suggests that you be able to switch styles as easily as you could switch caps. Just thinking of the six styles as caps can help you to see new possibilities and openings for action during your coaching conversations. The six caps are as follows:

- Declaring Possibilities Cap
- The Assessment Cap
- Teaching and Advising Cap
- Drawing Others Out Cap
- Reframing Cap
- Forwarding Action Cap

The guidelines for each coaching cap are given on the following page.

THE SIX-CAP COACHING SYSTEM IS A TWO-WAY STREET

You can use the Six-Cap Coaching System as your own frame of reference, the coachee can learn how to use it, or both.

Learn to separate the different kinds of coaching conversations from one another. Keep them separate and do not try to have too many different kinds at once. For example, if you start a conversation about declaring possibilities (Cap 1), you probably would not want to move to forwarding action (Cap 6). The result is often nearsighted goals and misfired actions. You also would probably not want to be making assessments (Cap 2) and advising (Cap 3) at the same time. The result would be hurried assessments or shoot-from-the-hip advice.

In effect, whenever you are trying to have more than one conversation, you are like a juggler with too many balls. You are likely to hear, "I'm confused; what are we talking about?" The key is to have one conversation at a time.

Move beyond one preferred kind of coaching conversation so you have more coaching agility. Become aware of your own tendency to have one or two preferred conversations. You may be very good at setting goals and planning but fail to recognize the need to have a conversation about them where you surface, question, and challenge assumptions behind the goals. If you do not draw others out (Cap 4) and help them to reframe goals (Cap 5), the plans they make may not be powerful enough. Regardless of your preferred conversational mode, you can become aware of which cap you have on and switch caps as needed to broaden your range of options.

Listen for conversational cues to decide which cap you should be wearing. The first rule is that there are no rules, as each person or interaction is different. The second rule is to not make a belief system out of any one approach. Teaching or advising others is fine, but not when what is needed is to draw people out. Listening to people's views is excellent, but not when they are making assumptions that need to be challenged.

Trying to have more than one kind of conversation at a time can be very confusing for the coachee. Pick up on conversational cues that it's time to put on a new cap or change caps. See Exhibit 5.3 for some of these conversational cues.

EXHIBIT 5.3 *Conversational cues about when to change caps*

1. The Declaring Possibilities Cap

   Put it on: When people have labeled them-selves "losers" or say they have "no choice."

   Take it off: When people can't buy into the "what" because they don't see the "how"; put on the Assessment Cap.

2. The Assessment Cap

   Put it on: When the coachees clearly need to talk about a concrete plan to get from where they are to where they want to be.

   Take it off: When people start talking about "whether or not we are going to act on this"; put on the Forwarding Action Cap.

3. The Teaching and Advising Cap

   Put it on: When people solicit your wisdom or request advice after you have spent time let-ting them talk things out themselves.

   Take it off: When you hear a lot of "yes buts" or when people start debating with you or are not open to your interpretation; try the Draw-ing Others Out Cap

4. The Drawing Others Out Cap

   Put it on: When people express that they feel misunderstood; when they have the seeds of a brilliant idea but are expressing it in a vague, inarticulate way; or when they don't buy into your advice.

   Take it off: When people are interpreting things in a disempowering way, have jumped to conclusions, or are making assumptions or inferences not validated by witnessable data or examples; try the Assessment Cap.

5. The Reframing Cap

   Put it on: When you pick up red flags such as a crooked mind-set (interpretation), poor atti-tudes, crazy thinking, or limiting beliefs and assumptions.

   Take it off: When people seem to have the appropriate mind-set and are ready to get on with it, or when they ask for a how-to technique; try putting on the Forwarding Action Cap.

6. The Forwarding Action Cap

   Put it on: When people have had enough strategizing and theorizing and need to do something, when they don't see any openings for taking successful action, or when they need a technique to execute effectively; also when people are depressed and discouraged.

   Take it off: When doing the same thing harder doesn't produce different results; this could lead to putting on the Declaring Possibilities Cap or the Reframing Cap.

Deliberately announce which cap you are putting on. In a coaching conversation, you might say, "We have been declaring some possibilities that seem achievable in reality, but you seem to be expressing a lot of questions about how we will achieve it. Shall we take the Possibilities Cap off and put on the Assessment Cap?" Or the coachee might say, "I have been listening to your advice and I really appreciate it. At the same time, I have had some ideas bubbling up in me. Can you (we) put on the Drawing Others Out Cap for a while?"

Perhaps you pick up on the fact that the person is basing ideas and proposals on some far-fetched assumptions about customers and colleagues. You might say, "Look, I need to put on the Reframing Cap here and challenge your assumptions." Or you might say, "I am now going to be deliberately provocative, in order to get you to think differently." By announcing your intention, you help the person understand, without taking it personally, why you are asking probing questions or challenging assumptions.

Don't think of the process as linear. Although there are six coaching caps, they are not necessarily six steps in a logical order. They are more like navigation points. It is up to each coach and coachee to use the caps in relationship to what is happening in real time.

DRILLING DOWN FOR MORE INSIGHTS

The following section describes each cap and includes some recipes for its use based on trigger statements or questions. You can use these recipes in a wide variety of practical situations with profound results.

CAP 1   DECLARING POSSIBILITIES

Masterful coaches trade in possibilities that haven't been dreamed of or imagined, rather than in goals. It is not that we shouldn't set goals, it is that most of us set them *without* having a conversation about what's really possible. The result is that the goals we set are often within a limited horizon of possibility. Masterful coaches expand people's horizons of possibility through something called *declarations*.

Declarations involve looking into ourselves and declaring what is possible based on our commitment versus looking into our circumstances and describing what's possible based on convention.

Declarations have the power to bring something into existence that no one would have predicted or dared to imagine. They have the power to generate a conversation that goes way beyond the originator.

What are you willing to declare as possible? A declaration is different from a *vision,* which is usually much broader. When a declaration is stated well, it is imaginable visually and usually very simple and focused, for example, "put a man on the moon" or "best team leader in the organization." Declarations tend to force people to look at the possibility of a new future and to undertake the necessary steps to bring it to pass *today.*

Is it really true that you have no choice but to settle for less? Often in coaching you are asked to counsel people as to a course of action. In most cases, the possibilities people see are severely limited. For example, I once coached the marketing group of a New York fashion house. Its sales and distribution were shrinking due to the president's intimidating manner and its product styling. I suggested that the team give feedback about product styles to the president and to the design group he managed. They said, "The last person who did that was fired." Acknowledging that it meant settling for less, they said, "We have no choice." I responded, "Is it really true you have no choice? How about suspending that belief?" I then made a declaration that there were other possibilities besides the ones they saw. The team came up with a short list of things, including building more trust with the president. One year later, the problem was solved and sales were soaring.

Let's experiment. People in groups are often hesitant to voice new ideas for fear of challenging authority or orthodoxies. This can have a stifling effect, so to counteract this I often say, "Let's have a conversation about possibilities. Let's scan the horizon, based on the notion that someone somewhere has a better idea, come up with some intriguing possibilities, and put them forward without necessarily having to commit to them." This is a way to nurture some "creative space" or a climate in which people will generate inventive and effective ideas. If the team comes up with something that makes sense, I suggest, "Let's leap the abyss and do an experiment."

 Possibilities are made through powerful commitments.

GROUP COACHING ACTIVITY
Declaring Possibilities

The next time you feel your team is resigned to its fate, ask the members to stand up and make three declarations. Do it publicly with as many people as possible.

1. I declare that what is possible is what I (we) say is possible.[3]

2. I declare that what looks impossible (difficult) is possible; specifically. . . .

3. I declare my commitment to this possibility coming to pass even in the absence of evidence or proof.

CAP 2	MAKING ASSESSMENTS

One of the first things you will probably do in entering a coaching relationship is to find out what people's goals and aspirations are. The next thing you will most likely do is put on the Making Assessments Cap to find out where people stand with respect to their goals. Whereas declaring possibilities often requires passion, making assessments requires cool, factual analysis. It usually involves an *evaluation* of the person's (group's) strengths and weaknesses, as well as a determination of what's missing that, if provided, will make a difference. Making powerful assessments is the basis of planning, of providing feedback, of discerning what gaps need to be filled, and of deciding what the coach (coachee) needs to work on: What happened? What's missing? What's next?

Let's look at the possibilities and form a realistic assessment of "what's so" right now and what's missing. For example, once Sir Colin Marshall had made his declaration of the possibility to make British Airways the world's favorite airline, as mentioned in Chapter Three, he began asking airline leaders at all levels to assess what was needed to make it happen. The answers included putting the airline's operations under the marketing department in order to create an awareness that instead of moving people as if they were suitcases, they needed to move them as if they were valued clients. The answers also included making sure that the lights were on in the boarding ramps and that the food was warm and easy to unwrap. All these suggestions, and many more, were actually implemented. Today British Airways not only ranks as one of the best in the world, it is also one of the most profitable.[4]

Assess people's talent. Ask about their passion, best work, what they're doing that's cool. I have asked hundreds of executives what was the most important part of their jobs, the part that made everything else easier. Invariably the answer is "hiring great people." How do you find out who is great? According to John Seely Brown, chief scientist at Xerox's Palo Alto research center, "I don't necessarily pay a lot of attention to people's academic credentials. What I do pay a lot of attention to in hiring is people's passion for impact and boldness, the desire to make a difference." Says Brown, "I also pay a great deal of attention to what kind of letters of recommendation people have, assuming I know the people writing the letters. I want people with great intuition who can get things done."[5]

Assess learning edges and growth spots. A coach must assess not only people's passions, talents, and gifts, but also their level of motivation, their learning edges, and their growth spots. According to Bob Meekin, director of organization effectiveness at Becton Dickinson, there are three questions to ask: (1) Do people have the desire to reach the goals? (If not, what could be blocking them?) (2) What core capabilities do people need to develop that are normally expected in their role? (For example, consultants may have a good technical ability but be ineffective at building powerful relationships.) And (3) What new capabilities need to be developed?[6]

Let the other person speak first in order to calibrate what you need to say, then give your assessment. It is sometimes important to be able to make assessments with an edge that is sharp enough to penetrate illusions.

Observe longer than you normally would before making assessments.

1:1 COACHING ACTIVITY

Making Assessments

Look at the possibilities you have dreamed of for people or that they have dreamed of for themselves. Observe what people do to make the possibilities a reality.

1. Say the person's name.

2. Ask, "What are your (our) goals and intentions?"

3. "What are the talents and gifts that you bring to the enterprise?"

4. "What's missing that, if provided, would make a difference?"

CAP 3   TEACHING AND ADVISING

One of the thing that distinguishes a coach from a therapist is that a coach usually has a teachable point of view to communicate with passion—be it about innovation, quality, service, or whatever. In addition, a coach often offers or is solicited for advice.

Michael Schrage, author of *No More Teams,* speaking about chief information officers, asked, "Why not a Chief Wisdom Officer?"[7] The question we should ask when we put the Teaching and Advising Cap on is, What constitutes good teaching or advice? Here are some simple principles to follow: (1) give advice that is caring and candid, (2) give advice that is practical, (3) give advice that is wise, and (4) give advice when people are open to hearing it.

"Are you open to some advice?" A masterful coach listens a long time before offering advice, unless time is short. One of the things I have noticed in coaching seminars is how often people make hasty assessments, offering advice before really attempting to understand someone. The advice they give is usually unwanted, irritating, and way off the mark. This has led me to tell people, somewhat tongue-in-cheek, *The best advice is the advice you never give.* To avoid giving unwanted advice, I look for openings and then ask, "Would you like my advice?" Sounds simple, but it's not

always done. This gives people the power to say no. If people feel they have the power to say no to your advice, they will also feel they have the power to say yes. If people say no, don't take it personally; you may be speaking to them at the wrong time.

"This is going to be caring, but candid." Leaders with the most sincere and honest intentions are often unaware of the things that they do to sabotage themselves. The role of the coach is to make people aware of what they are unaware of. John Gardner, executive, teacher, and leadership guru, writes, "Leaders need advisers who will guide them lovingly and candidly through the mine fields of arrogance, overweening pride, fixed ideas, vindictiveness, unreasoning anger, stubbornness, and egotism."[8]

Sounds good, but just how do you broach one of these subjects on any given day? It is useful to announce your intentions so that people know where you are coming from. For example, René Jaeggi, former CEO of Adidas, told me that his judo master in Japan used to walk up to him on a weekly basis and announce, "I love you, so I have to hurt you." He would then proceed to give him some tough feedback.

Let's look at what's practical. Ralph Waldo Emerson once remarked that before asking for advice, he usually did a lot of thinking on his own, only to wind up bewildered as to the best course of action: "All I need is for someone to tell me what to do." Sound familiar? A few years back my brother Jimmy, who is a furniture sales rep in New England, found a rep from another area encroaching on his territory. He stewed about it but kept his mouth shut, fearing the other rep's political connections. He called his mentor, who told him: "Do exactly as I say, Jim. You're too nice. Get some street smarts. Call that other rep and tell him, 'Stay out of my territory. If I catch you in my territory again, you're going to get a phone call.'" He did exactly as he was told and never had a problem again.

What is the wisest thing to do? There are two kinds of advice, the kind that involves strategizing and scheming and the kind that is based on wisdom. Chogyam Trungpa has written that there is a basic human wisdom that can help the world's problems, based on age-old principles: (1) focus on what you really want, (2) walk a mile in the other person's moccasins, (3) use strength wisely before it becomes weakness, and (4) try new approaches.[9] See Exhibit 5.4 for what can happen from developing any trait too much.

When crafting advice, I generally ask three questions: (1) What is the *practical* thing to do—the best means to the end? (2) What is the *wise* thing to do? Step back from the heat of the moment

EXHIBIT 5.4 *Too much of a good thing*

This *good* thing . . . . breeds this *monster*

Confidence . . . . Sense of infallibility

Quickness. . . . . Overhastiness

Sharp wit. . . . . Abrasiveness

Alertness. . . . . Narrow focus

Dedication. . . . . Workaholism

Control . . . . Inflexibility

Courage . . . . Foolhardiness

Perseverance . . . . Resistance to changes

Charm. . . . . Manipulation

Thriftiness. . . . . False economy

Commitment . . . . Blind faith

and look at the deeper and broader view. (3) Putting aside shoulds, coulds, and woulds, what does the person want to do? Put your advice out as an option to consider, not as gospel. If people are not open to your interpretation or start debating with you, let them sleep on it or recognize that it may be time for you to change caps.

1:1 COACHING ACTIVITY

Teaching and Advising

Ask people to tell you about situations in which they were stuck or ineffective during the last week so you are not dealing in hypothetical situations. Listen carefully as they tell their stories. If you listen long enough, people

will reveal themselves and you will get an insight into fundamental causes for the problems they are having—whether their thinking, behavior, wrong actions, or whatever. Then ask, "Are you open for some advice?" Only continue if they are. Give them the advice and see whether it makes any sense to them. Remember to

1. Teach the student, not the subject.

2. Give advice that is pure, practical, and wise.

3. If people resist, remember that tomorrow is another day.

4. If they debate, try drawing them out.

CAP 4   DRAWING OTHERS OUT

In many cases, when you offer advice, people would be better served if you took that cap off and put on the Drawing Others Out Cap and listened. The Latin root of the word *educate, educare,* doesn't mean to put in, but rather to *draw out.* Drawing out actually has two dimensions. The first is listening with empathy, the second is listening for people's brilliance. This involves adopting a stance that people can do their own thinking and discover their own answers. Figure 5.1 illustrates this.

Tell me more. All people want at least one person in the world to understand them. A masterful coach is someone who can suspend the impulse to give advice and instead listen with compassion and understanding and without judgment. This creates the opening for coaching. By contrast, coaches who wag their self-righteous fingers or who lecture only put people off. To move beyond this, hold your tongue or say, "Tell me more." This allows people to unburden themselves and allows you to walk a mile in their moccasins.

The idea is to listen empathetically without agreeing or disagreeing. If someone says, "The boss is a jerk," the coach doesn't say, "I agree," or for that matter, "I disagree." Give people the space to sort through their thoughts and feelings. They often come to a realization of their own foolishness.

FIGURE 5.1 *The process of drawing others out*

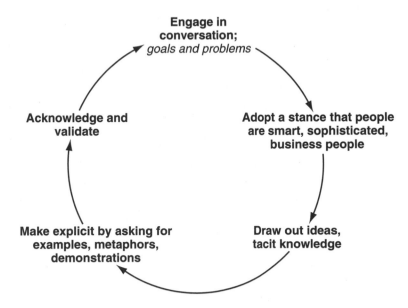

"You know what, he's not really a jerk. We just got off to a bad start in that last conversation." Asking them to tell you more also helps people express ideas they have never articulated before.

What do you think? Someone once described what it was like to have dinner with Prime Ministers Benjamin Disraeli and William Gladstone. After leaving Gladstone's company you would walk away thinking, "He's brilliant." After leaving Disraeli's company you would walk away thinking, "I'm brilliant." Disraeli, although a superb statesman and orator, was an expert at drawing others out. He was known for engaging people in conversations by asking, "What do you think?" You will discover that it is impossible for people to answer that question without becoming involved. The key lies not just in the asking, but in listening for people's brilliance.

That's a great idea! Another sign of mastery is to be able to draw out ideas people know only on a vague, intuitive level. One of the best ways to grease the wheels is to acknowledge and validate new, good ideas (or even fragments of ideas) as they start to flow. Instead of responding in long-winded monologues, respond with short declarative statements like, "That's interesting," "That's a great idea," or "Absolutely brilliant!" Of course your acknowledgment needs to be sincere and honest, and be prepared to answer the question, "What makes you say this is such a good idea?"

Give me an example or metaphor. A few years back a group of people from Honda decided to build the next generation of cars. They asked the design team to build a new concept car based on the notion, "Let's gamble." This led the team to come up with a metaphor, "Theory of Automobile Evolution." The metaphor helped to draw out their thinking on how cars would evolve in the crowded streets of Tokyo. The answer was, "man maximum, car minimum," and led to the development of the popular Honda City Car, which was short and tall, so it could easily fit into small parking spaces.[10]

The next time people are struggling with expressing a creative idea, ask them to describe it in terms of a metaphor: "What's it like or not like?" By connecting thoughts from different realms, like "automobile" and "evolution," metaphors can help jump-start the creative thinking process. Asking for examples is also an excellent way to assist people in articulating ideas they are struggling to express on a conceptual plane.

Would you like a suggestion? A lot of people today think that a coach should never put in his or her own ideas. To me that is as absurd as the coach who doesn't know when to shut up and listen. The idea is to learn how to contribute your ideas in an empowering way. A good technique, after you have heard someone out, is to ask: "Would you like a suggestion or do you just want to ponder it for awhile?" This gives people a choice, although in most cases, they will ask for a suggestion. To disagree with people in a constructive way without squashing their ideas, say, "It's my belief that. . . ." When you share ideas as "beliefs," not as absolute truths, people will be much more open to hearing you.

1:1 COACHING ACTIVITY

Drawing Others Out

The next time someone comes to you with a problem, rather than following the urge to give advice, discipline yourself to continue asking questions to understand not only the problem but also what it means to the person. Keep asking questions and listening with the intention of helping that person find his or her own answers (discover his or her own brilliance).

CAP 5   REFRAMING

Masterful coaching, at its core, is neither about offering advice nor about hearing others out. It is about interacting with others in such a way that their frame of reference is altered. There are just three things you need to do in this kind of conversation: (1) as people speak about their goals or problems, learn to pick up on red flags—a "why bother" attitude, a "silo mentality," or beliefs and assumptions about the business that don't seem to fit reality; (2) demonstrate to people how their way of thinking about things will get them into trouble; and (3) provide people with new frames of reference that allow them to see things differently and act differently. See Figure 5.2 for how this process works.

Let's make a distinction here. The job of a leader today is not to make all the decisions. It is to make distinctions, performing small, inventive acts with language that alters people's frames of reference and allows them to move beyond conventional possibilities and choices.

FIGURE 5.2 *The cycle of reframing*

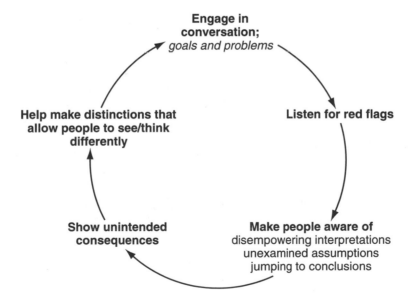

I often talk about the difference between *pursuing your passion* and *pursuing your pension*. Most people are so involved in pursuing their pensions that they don't know they are trapped in that pursuit or that pursuing their passion is even possible. Just mention the word *passion* and suddenly a new possibility comes into play. Making distinctions is based on two questions: What assumptions is the person making unknowingly? What distinctions can I make that will allow the person to create something new?

That's one possible interpretation; what's another? People often make interpretations about themselves, their business, or the world, and then act as if their interpretation is a fact. For example, Daimler Benz once asserted in the *London Times* that the world market for cars would be limited to ten thousand. The limiting factor? It was thought that it would never be possible to train more than that many chauffeurs. IBM founder Tom Watson predicted in the 1950s that the world market for computers would be about one thousand. The limiting factor? Storage space. Whenever I suspect that people are not separating facts from interpretation and are getting themselves into trouble, I say, "That's just one possible interpretation. What would be another interpretation—one that would be more insightful, empowering, or accurate?"

Aren't you making an assumption? Do you have examples or data? Often in coaching, you are in a position to encourage people to do the "right thing," such as speak up at the big meeting. People resist based on totally unexamined assumptions. For example, "The CEO is going to be there and if I say what I am thinking and feeling, I will definitely be fired." In most cases I've found that there is little or nothing to corroborate such an assumption.

Ask questions with the intent of penetrating people's illusions: "Do you have an example of people being fired for speaking their minds or is it just an assumption?" Invariably people say, "No, but it could happen." Once people agree that it is an assumption, work with them to find ways to test it. For example, I tell people to try a mini-learning project, like being much more authentic at the next meeting. This often leads to people reframing their views of the world.

Bridge conversations. The coach's role in reframing is to engage people in conversations in which they act as a bridge between an old interpretation and a new one. Here are some examples:

- From being an employee to being a businessperson

- From pursuing your pension to pursuing your passion

- From focusing on what's predictable to focusing on what's possible

- From do-it-yourself to doing it with a group

- From face-to-face meetings to virtual meetings and teams

- From being a victim to being empowered

- From complaining about something to making requests

REFLECTION ASSIGNMENT

Reframing

Think of the people you are coaching or of your group as a whole. Where are there breakdowns or potential breakdowns? What thinking is behind the breakdowns or might cause a breakdown in the future? How can you reframe people's thinking?

CAP 6   FORWARDING ACTION

Any CEO will tell you that everything is happening ten times faster than it did a decade ago, in large part due to technology. You can't sit in your corner office pondering strategy or policy or be a guru who just focuses on altering people's managerial frames of reference. You have to define stretch goals, make decisions, and then jump into action. At the same time, you have to be able to energize and forward the action through others. *Action language* is much more likely to make something happen. Change your thinking from wishes and dreams to *declarations,* from predictions to *promises,* from complaints to *requests,* and from judgments about others or the organization to *offers.* See Figure 5.3 for some more examples of action language versus passive language.

Declarations again. To put it simply, masterful coaches encourage people to make as many commitments as possible, starting with their own declaration of commitment to a vision or goal. A

FIGURE 5.3 *Examples of action language*

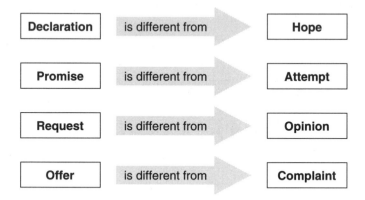

Action Language

All action is initiated or stalled by the language we use. Coach people on using action language to make things happen.

Declaration	is different from	Hope
Promise	is different from	Attempt
Request	is different from	Opinion
Offer	is different from	Complaint

coach is much more likely to generate action when he or she publicly declares a commitment and begins moving the organization in that direction. A declaration from an organization's leader not only opens new possibilities but also generates excitement and focuses people on what needs to be done.

What's your promise? Action is much more likely to ensue if people make promises with explicit conditions of satisfaction—such as who, what, or by when—than if they make predictions, such as "This will happen if. . . ." I've observed that people know this on an unconscious level and go out of their way to weasel out of committing themselves. Some of my favorite weasel strategies include "We'll see," or "That's a definite maybe," or "It all depends." A coach not only elicits powerful promises from people but also listens for people's sincere commitment.

Do you have a request? One of the other ways to encourage action is to ask people to make powerful requests of team members, customers, or vendors. A powerful request is one that asks someone to do something that in the normal course of events would be considered unreasonable. The key to being able to do this is to recognize that just as you have the power to ask, people have the power to decide whether to comply. "You say the new product can be ready in ten weeks.

Is it possible to ship it in six?" or "We need another $25,000 to complete this new systems integration project but have run out of budget. Can we borrow it from yours?"

The next time you are in a restaurant, instead of complaining to your dinner partner about your overly done steak or cold pasta, how about asking the waitperson to ask the cook to dish you up another? Making such requests feels empowering, and—unlike complaints—can actually make something happen.

I would like to remind you of your commitment to. . . . Masterful coaches create a climate of breakthrough not only by making powerful promises and requests, but also by holding others accountable. By holding people accountable for their commitments, coaches "force" them to bring out the best in themselves.

There are no better practitioners of this than some of today's leading CEOs. They simply can't countenance or even understand procrastination. The usual obstacles don't seem to exist for them, and they don't expect such barriers to slow down their staffs either. When you agree to do something, you do it. And intervening acts of God, customers, and competition are no excuse for not being done on time.

We do people a disservice when we don't expect them to honor their word.

A conversation for action involves the coach (1) stepping back and seeing new possibilities and actions when people are stuck, (2) providing a fresh perspective that gives people new insight into dilemmas, (3) giving people a tip or a technique that gives a new action rule, or (4) returning people to themselves, to their promises, and to action when they just want to give up.

GROUP COACHING ACTIVITY
Forwarding Action Through Action Language

Next time you are in a group and there is a lot of complaining going on about other people, other departments, the "bosses", or whatever, say, "No more complaints, only requests, promises, or offers." Then coach the group on

keeping this ground rule. You will find that the quality of the conversation will change completely and actions will be forwarded.

Before we leave this chapter, I should say that there are other coaching caps that you may want to consider wearing, for example, a Planning Cap. If you want to use another cap that is appropriate for you or the people you are coaching, it's your choice.

SUMMARY

To sum up, there are three kinds of coaching conversations: (1) conversations during which we create partnerships with others, (2) conversations for possibility in which we declare what we will bring to pass, and (3) conversations for action that focus on how to actually make things happen.

The more your goals are in the breakthrough zone, the more likely there are going to be breakdowns, which can result in sadness, anger, and upset. When that happens, it is human nature to stop and get into conversations where we argue for our own limitations: "I can't do it," "This is impossible," or "Why bother?"

A masterful coach's role is to support people in holding what happens in a way that is consistent with who they really are, what their visions are, and what they are magnificently capable of. This might mean interrupting people's psychological conversations by affirming them, or urging people to look at something in a different way, or it may involve helping people to focus their attention on what needs to be done. Simply put, coaching is about returning people to themselves, to their promises, and to action, regardless of what happens.

PART II

THE METHOD™— A FIVE-STEP COACHING MODEL

Now that we have established a coaching mind-set in Part I—with the intent of creating a new cultural clearing—Part II will deal with providing a simple, powerful coaching method. Though many leaders and others today are coaching "intuitively"—and this is commendable—it is my belief that being an "intuitive coach" is insufficient to foster a culture of coaching, to produce breakthroughs, or to solve complex problems. The intent here is to provide a simple, powerful, universally applicable method that leaders at all levels can use to achieve extraordinary and tangible results.

The intent is not to take the intuitive skill and artistry out of coaching, but rather to provide some kind of structure or road map. The aim is to make coaching a distinct discipline and practice.

As a case in point, today many professionals say they do coach, but they follow no particular method or model as they would in medicine, law, education, and so forth. Companies may want to bring in outside coaches to supplement the coaching of their own leaders, but if they do they are likely to find themselves in a grab-bag situation as to the "what" and "how" of coaching. For one practitioner, coaching might be "career counseling" or might involve "intensive debriefing of 360-degree feedback." For another, it might be psychological counseling.

THE BEST METHOD FOR THE WIDEST AUDIENCE.

In the coming chapters, I would like to provide what is missing that might make a difference. It is something I call *Masterful Coaching—The Method*™.[1] The intent is to offer a powerful, concise, step-by-step model that people in business leadership roles can use that has a wide variety of practical applications. The intent is to create not the best model but rather the best model for the widest audience.

The book's target audience is people in leadership roles within organizations, and the model clearly reflects this. The model is based on the premise that you are in a position to coach a talented group of people who need to achieve significant results with colleagues amid change or complexity. The people you are coaching may consist entirely of direct reports, or they might be unlikely collaborators from other areas of the business, including partners that you have brought together for a special project. If you are not a leader in charge of a group with line responsibility—a human resource professional or an outside consultant—you will find that the model can easily be extrapolated with a little imagination.

Although the model starts with the leader clarifying his or her personal coaching mission (or mandate), the road map for how to go about this process is highly collaborative. For example, a masterful coach does not accomplish goals by telling people what to do but by linking goals to people's inner aspirations and by acting as a thinking partner.

I have consciously and intentionally reframed the question of whether coaching is for individuals or groups from an "either-or" to a "both-and" proposition. The fact is that any individual you coach will always be "coupled" to a group, and vice versa. The individual's thinking and attitudes shape the group and in turn the individual is shaped by the group. As a coach, I shift my attention back and forth between the two, depending on which focus I think will make a bigger difference at the moment. The model can be used for coaching either individuals or groups, depending on what you feel you need to focus on in the moment to produce the best possible results.

The Method™ is not a blueprint. It serves to map the territory so that you can go from A to Z in any coaching relationship. A map is a good metaphor, because any serious coaching relationship is a journey out of which emerges both diverse and adverse experiences that you did not anticipate at the beginning. At the same time, The Method™ definitely works. As many people have told me, it is the missing piece in the puzzle.

Let's walk quickly through the five-step model so you can see that it is nothing mysterious, and that it is something that you can immediately act on. Each of the next five chapters will deal more in depth with each step.

Step 1. *Develop a personal coaching mission and teachable point of view.* This involves thinking about what your personal coaching mission (your mandate) is—business growth, product innovation, faster cycle time, and so forth. It may also include things like developing top talent or getting people to work as a real team with a passion for winning. To assist in this process, Chapter Six offers a template called a Performance Excellence Scorecard. Once you define what your Personal Coaching Mission is, you will need to develop a teachable point of view about how to achieve it. Your teachable point of view is something you will need to communicate powerfully through ideas, stories, metaphors, and so on. One of the signs of a masterful coach is not only the desire to teach but also to seek coaching and teaching from others.

Step 2. *Invest in relationships.* The only way you will be able to achieve your coaching mission and get your teachable point of view across is to invest in relationships. First, consciously decide with whom you want to invest in a relationship, for example, a coach for yourself, talented direct reports, creating a great group, colleagues in other areas, or alliance partners. Invest in relationships by giving people the gift of your presence and by finding out about their goals and aspirations. Masterful coaches are able to enroll people in a mission by finding ways to link their goals and aspirations to what needs to be accomplished.

For example, they might say, "Your committed participation in this project could be an opportunity for accelerated experiential development." Once people are enrolled, the next step is to look for openings to initiate coaching conversations. The key to coaching conversations is to keep coaching conversational: "Would you like a thinking partner on that?"

Step 3. *Plan stretch goals collaboratively.* It is important in today's knowledge economy for leaders to move beyond telling others what to do and to engage people in collaborative inquiry about what needs to be achieved. If the mission is to grow the business, the idea is not to show off your infinite wisdom but to get out on the table every idea that people have in their heads about growing the business. Start with clarifying the overall mission for the group and what your general performance expectations are of the individuals or unit.

There are three questions the coach asks in this step: (1) Where are we now with respect to the mission or performance expectations? (In other words, people need to face reality.) (2) What would be a stretch goal that would foster performance and development? and (3) What's missing that, if provided, would make a difference? What is missing is not always obvious. This becomes the basis of a plan.

Step 4. *Forward the action.* The role of the coach, once planning is done, is to generate action. Often people may feel overwhelmed by the goals and plan. The most simple and logical thing a coach can do to generate action is to take larger tasks and break them into smaller projects. The conversation should be about coming up with performance opportunities right now that can be translated into short-term, breakthrough goals and doable actions. The idea is to empower individuals or groups around these projects, to help them to make as many commitments as possible, and then to encourage them to jump into action. It is vital that the coach learn to determine not just those high-leverage actions that the coachee *should, could,* or *ought* to take, but also those actions that the coachee is most likely to take.

Step 5. *Provide feedback and learning.* The role of the coach at this point is largely to observe people as they make a committed attempt to perform and to intervene in the event of unintended results. Engaging people in a dialogue using the triple loop learning model can be very effective. "Here's your goal. Here's the unintended result. How do you have to *be* different, how do you have to *think* differently, how do you have to *act* differently to obtain the results you want?" (See Chapter One, page 22 for an explanation of the triple loop learning model.)

This becomes the basis of providing feedback that builds self-esteem, corrects, and stretches. The feedback is reflected in designing (revising) the performance and development plan. Masterful coaches recognize that people learn best not from the classroom but from experience, and they therefore customize experiences to the individual. For example, they may expose people to outside thought leaders, create stretch assignments, or send people to courses.

At this point, I would like to acknowledge the reader. The fact that you are reading a book about masterful coaching says something about who you are, in terms of your commitment to excellence and your desire to make a powerful contribution to others. My promise to you is that, by the time you finish reading these chapters on The Method™, you will be able to take everything you know about coaching and put it to use in a powerful and profound way. Like the many people I have shared it with already, you are going to be able to look in the mirror and say, "Now I can do it!" Here's an outline of the model for your reference as you read.

MASTERFUL COACHING—THE METHOD™, A FIVE-STEP MODEL

Step 1. Develop Your Coaching Mission and Teachable Point of View

- Define your personal coaching mission—your mandate.

- Develop a teachable point of view about how to succeed.

- Teach it through ideas, stories, metaphors, and demonstrations.

- Seek coaching for yourself; take a reflective stance.

Step 2. Invest in Relationships

- Decide which relationships to invest in.

- Engage others by discovering their passions, goals, and aspirations.

- Enroll people by holding out positive possibilities.

- Look for openings to initiate coaching conversations.

Step 3. Plan Stretch Goals Collaboratively

- Do not tell others what to do; be a thinking partner.

- Together assess *where we are now* with respect to the mission.

- Set *stretch goals* that foster performance and development.

- Identify *what's missing* that will make a difference.

Step 4. Forward the Action

- Break what's missing into a few small projects or doable steps.

- Focus on doable steps that others will act on.

- Encourage people to use action language.

- Ask What happened? What's missing? What's next?

Step 5. Provide Feedback and Learning

- Be a keen observer of intended and unintended results.

- Ponder how people need to be different, think differently, act differently.

- Frame feedback so that it builds esteem, corrects, and stretches.

- Customize challenging experiences that foster accelerated learning and development.

Principles are like compasses. They are always pointing the way.

STEP 1. DEVELOP YOUR COACHING MISSION AND A TEACHABLE POINT OF VIEW

Sharing Ideas and Stories of What It Will Take to Succeed

It is twelve o'clock at London's Heathrow Airport. The passengers of a Virgin Atlantic flight from New York have just emerged from the plane, disgruntled after a two-hour delay at Kennedy and a long flight. A Virgin Atlantic official is there to greet them at the jetway and to apologize personally for the delay, offering quadrupled frequent-flyer miles. No, the official is not Bill Marks, Virgin's station manager at Heathrow; it is Richard Branson, the founder of the airline.

When Branson started Virgin Atlantic, he had a mission to wrest away a big chunk of the airline business from big carriers like British Air and, especially, TWA, whose chairman he once heard explain why they were taking lettuce out of the sandwiches. To realize his mission, Branson had a teachable point of view: "Put yourself in the customer's shoes."

Branson not only makes personal appearances at the airport but also frequently flies from London to New York, helps the crew serve drinks, and plays his guitar for passengers. Before these flights, he meets with crew members and talks about putting themselves in the customer's shoes. Word gets around the whole company pretty fast.[1]

DEVELOP YOUR PERSONAL COACHING MISSION

Whether you are a CEO of an airline, a functional head in a manufacturing business, or a team leader in a call center, Step 1 of The Method™ starts with deciding what your Personal Coaching Mission—your mandate—is. It represents exactly what you desire or are expected to achieve, as well as what you need to do to attract talent and build a great group. It also represents whatever renewal mechanisms are required to move your organization from where it is to where you want to be.

For example, if you are a sports coach, your mission might be to win the championship. The renewal mechanisms that would support that mission might be to attract top talent, put together an effective offense and defense, and make sure that people work together as a team. If you are a conductor of a symphony orchestra conducting Beethoven's Fifth, your mission would be to deliver a world-class performance, and so forth.

As a business leader, your mission or mandate might be to grow the business, to develop a breakthrough product that alters customers' buying habits, to create a highly effective process organization that affects time to market, to open up new markets on the global stage, to dramatically increase sales, or to develop a best-in-class reputation for service. To further develop this mission, you need to clarify what initiatives you will take, the results you will expect, and the renewal mechanisms that will allow you to achieve it.

PRACTICE ASSIGNMENT

Developing Your Personal Coaching Mission

There are a number of key questions that you can ask yourself to develop your Personal Coaching Mission. Either write the answers down or talk them through with a conversation partner. After answering the questions, write a one-paragraph statement that describes your Personal Coaching Mission.

1. What is your role and responsibility in the organization?

2. What is your biggest leadership, coaching, or teaching challenge?

3. What is your greatest business-building opportunity?

4. What is your greatest business obstacle?

We have found in working with Motorola University that in addition to answering these questions, an effective tool for further developing a Personal Coaching Mission that includes these different dimensions is to have a coaching conversation that is based on using a Performance Excellence Scorecard. The scorecard defines your mission in all of its aspects. The notion of a balanced scorecard that includes both performance and development is important.

Following is a template of a scorecard that you or others in your organization could use. First, sit down and think about the questions on the scorecard. Then have a conversation about it with your manager. Once you have done that, publicly post your Personal Coaching Mission and your Performance Excellence Scorecard in your office and in other appropriate areas. This is a way of telling others what you feel responsible for and for what you expect to be held accountable. (If you do not prefer the scorecard concept, an alternative is simply to follow the steps for developing a coaching mission outlined in Chapter Two.)

PRACTICE ASSIGNMENT

Translating the Coaching Mission into a Performance Excellence Scorecard

Fill out the Performance Excellence Scorecard by reflecting on the following questions by yourself or with a thinking partner.

1. What are the company strategies and business objectives? *For example:* Grow the business.

2. What is your overriding coaching mission or mandate? *For example:* Grow your business unit; attract top talent; build teamwork; create a passion for winning.

3. What are the current-year initiatives? *For example:* Develop leaders who can open up new markets, build innovative products, speed up time to market, open up new markets.

4. Define business results. *For example:* Promote three leaders who can open new markets, introduce three new products, reduce time to market to four months, increase sales 24 percent, set financial goal of 14 percent profit before taxes.

   Note: **The preceding examples are based on a senior leader, but the same scorecard could be used by leaders at all levels.**

5. Define *renewal mechanisms* based on Malcolm Baldrige Award criteria. Say what you will do with one or more of the following:

   - Leadership development

   - Strategic planning

   - Customer and market focus

   - Core process renewal

   - Knowledge management/information systems

   - Human resources

6. Why are you passionate or interested in this? What do you have at stake in all this?

Performance Excellence Scorecard

- Company Strategies and Business Objective

- Your Overriding Coaching Mission—or Mandate

- Current Year Initiatives

- Define Business Results

- "Renewal Mechanisms" to Work on Based on Malcolm Baldrige Criteria. What you will do with one or more of the following:

  - Leadership development

  - Strategic planning

  - Customer and market focus

  - Core process renewal

  - Knowledge management/information systems

  - Human resources

DEVELOP A TEACHABLE POINT OF VIEW ABOUT HOW TO ACHIEVE THE MISSION

The next step, after clarifying your personal coaching mission, is to develop a teachable point of view about how to achieve it. A teachable point of view represents your particular perspective, philosophy, or approach on how to move your organization from where it is to where you want it to be. It can be developed by mining previous professional experiences for hidden lessons, by pondering a complex business situation until you arrive at a moment of true insight, or by studying other missions.

Often when a leader steps into a new role and is faced with what looks like an impossible business challenge, it is clear that meeting this challenge will require establishing a whole new dynamic mind-set in the company or group. Developing a teachable point of view and communicating it through ideas, stories, or metaphors is a powerful tool. (This is very consistent with what we have said about triple and double loop learning.)

Examples of Teachable Points of View

- *Mission:* Develop next generation of leaders.
- *Teachable Point of View:* Leaders are developed not in the classroom but through challenging experiences.

- *Mission:* Build individual or company productivity.
- *Teachable Point of View:* Instead of focusing on productivity, focus on relationships that will lead to opportunities.

- *Mission:* New product innovation.
- *Teachable Point of View:* Innovation does not happen by delegating but by collaborating. The more juxtapositions of different talents and gifts there are, the more innovation there will be.

- *Mission:* Create and keep customers.
- *Teachable Point of View:* Shift from one-size-fits-all to one-size-fits-one.

LESSONS FROM GREAT COACHES—COMMUNICATING YOUR TEACHABLE POINT OF VIEW

One of my favorite examples of this is Roberto Goizueta, the late chairman of Coca-Cola and a Cuban immigrant who rose from the technical side of the company in an era dominated by marketers. Goizueta's mission was to transform Coca-Cola from a mature business to a growth business. When he took over,

Coke was in battle with Pepsi, spending untold millions of dollars in advertising to gain tenths of a point in market share. Goizueta looked for a strategy, a way to create a dynamic mind-set in the company.

In the mid-1980s, Goizueta had a simple but powerful insight. He asked his executives, "What is the daily average consumption of beverages per capita by the world's four billion people?" The answer was sixty-four ounces, and less than two ounces was cola. He explained that they had to stop thinking in terms of "share of market" and think in terms of "share of stomach."

Coca-Cola people had invested too much energy in the idea that the enemy was Pepsi. Instead it was coffee, milk, tea, or water. Goizueta undertook a nonstop campaign to get his teachable point across to thousands of employees. He told stories about his grandfather's grocery store in Cuba before the revolution, urging people to think with the common sense of a shopkeeper. He explained the importance of drumming up business and told stories about Coca-Cola employees who went into hotels and office buildings looking for places where Coke wasn't being sold and having a machine installed. He painted these people as heroes, which had the immediate impact of inspiring the local troops to get out and do the same. Goizueta was enormously successful. Coke's market value was $13 billion in 1981 and has grown to over $272 billion in 1997.[2]

Developing your teachable point of view will take pondering the question: "What's your share of stomach?" The rest of this chapter is devoted to supporting you in developing a teachable point of view that will allow you to achieve your mission. A teachable point of view applies not only to your basic mandate but also to other aspects that may be interrelated. A teachable point of view that has the power to shift mind-set is not always obvious and often requires considerable pondering to define it.

There is an interesting sidelight to the story about Goizueta that illustrates this. In the mid-1990s, a group of top executives from CitiBank were in a strategy session about building their business. After being told the Goizueta story, they asked themselves: "What's our share of stomach?"

The following five coaching tips are explained in more detail in the rest of the chapter. The coaching caps to use in this are also listed.

Coaching Tips for Developing a Teachable Point of View

1. Reflect on your life experiences to come up with a few teachable insights.

2. Reflect on your coaching mission and develop a teachable point of view on how to succeed.

3. Formulate a teachable point of view for success in key areas of concern.

4. Communicate your teachable point of view through ideas, stories, metaphors, and examples.

5. Eagerly seek coaching yourself—take a reflective stance.

Coaching Caps to Use for Developing a Teachable Point of View

- Put on your Teaching and Advising Cap to create or shift context or culture. Preach; be an evangelist of your vision and values. "Good ideas drive out bad." (See page 119.)

- Put on your Drawing Out Cap to find out people's thoughts and attitudes and ask, What's missing? (See page 122.)

- Then put on your Teaching and Advising Cap or your Reframing Cap. (See pages 119 and 125.)

REFLECT ON YOUR LIFE EXPERIENCES TO COME UP WITH A FEW TEACHABLE INSIGHTS

A masterful coach is not a neutral therapist who listens and never says anything, but a values-shaping leader who affects people's vision and values. Coaches do this through communicating their passion, purpose, and perspective. They gain credibility by making decisions that are consistent with the high values they espouse, and they expect others to do the same. They deal with dilemmas that come up in business in a way that is consistent with their ethical codes and legal responsibility.

Masterful coaches approach everything they do in a purposeful way, based on who they are, what they stand for, and what they want to accomplish. Although they are usually down-to-earth people who know how to get along with others and can joke and laugh, they are rarely off purpose.

I once asked Joan Holmes, executive director of the Hunger Project, how she dealt with personal conflicts and petty upsets in her own life. She said, "Quickly."[3]

Masterful coaches also tend to have a particular perspective that is forged by their parents, teachers, coaches, and most importantly, their life experiences. Perhaps one of the greatest lessons comes from being placed in diverse and adverse circumstances. One important key is learning to profit from your life experiences by synthesizing them. For example, as I once heard Sumner Redstone, chairman of Viacom, say in an interview on television, "Success comes from failure." You learn much more from failure than you do from success.

Andrew Grove, chairman of Intel, wrote a book called *Only the Paranoid Survive.* Grove discusses growing up in Hungary when the anti-Communist revolution was crushed by Russian tanks. The experience taught him to be a worrier and to take nothing for granted, especially when things are going well. He was able to apply these insights to his career as a businessperson and to teach them to Intel managers. In business, paranoia may not be a disease but a road to creativity, productivity, and financial performance. Grove's paranoia led him, in part, to drive the Intel team to develop two generations of chips at once.[4]

Developing a teachable point of view often starts with thinking about the core beliefs and values that shape how you think and interact with others. Another powerful key involves taking a reflective stance regarding the adventure we call life, and profiting from your own life experiences. This can lead to creating your own treasure trove of insights.

REFLECTION ASSIGNMENT

Reflecting on Who You Are and Your Key Values

Write three or four short sentences in response to the following:

1. Big ideas (values) I passionately care about . . .

2. Core beliefs and values about success in my field . . .

3. The guiding principles I will operate from as a coach . . .

The following story may inspire you to gain insights into how you can profit from your life experiences.

LESSONS FROM GREAT COACHES—USING YOUR LIFE'S LESSONS

When Coach Phil Jackson took over the Chicago Bulls, he wanted to integrate his two passions—basketball and spiritual exploration. He learned the principles of selflessness and compassion growing up as the son of a Pentecostal minister. Later, by sitting on a cushion practicing Zen Buddhism with a master, he learned that awareness was everything. From the Lakota Sioux, who believe that the enemy is sacred, he learned not to let anger cloud his mind in competitive battle. He also learned from his own coach, Red Holzman, that the power of "we" is stronger than the power of "me."

According to Jackson, "It struck me that the Lakota way and posture could serve as a paradigm for the Bulls to become champions. A Lakota Sioux warrior didn't try to stand out from his fellow band members; he strove to act bravely and honorably, to help the group accomplish the mission. Also, to a Lakota warrior even the enemy is sacred." This teachable point of view became a centerpiece of Jackson's coaching. It led him to coach Michael Jordan about being a team player. It led him to talk to Dennis Rodman about controlling his anger while at the same time being compassionate.

The decor of the Bulls' team room is intended to establish a private place for heart-to-heart conversations with players, a hideaway where the team can watch game tapes and talk about their strengths and weaknesses. Jackson used the team room to communicate the idea of interconnectedness. In Jackson's view, the rudiments of teamwork are selflessness in action and interconnectedness, as illustrated by the Hopi proverb, "One finger can't lift a pebble."[5]

REFLECTION ASSIGNMENT

Translating Life Experiences into Teachable Insights

Create a time line from the time you were born until today. Write down five to ten of your most significant life events, the major insights gained from them, and the people and situations that you can apply these to.

_____

Key life experience

Insight gained

People and situations it applies to

_____

Key life experience

Insight gained

People and situations it applies to

_____

Key life experience

Insight gained

People and situations it applies to

_____

Key life experience

Insight gained

People and situations it applies to

He held out a vision, he laughed, he cried, he motivated us with human emotion.

REFLECT ON YOUR COACHING MISSION AND DEVELOP A TEACHABLE POINT OF VIEW ON HOW TO SUCCEED

Every great coach, whether in business, the performing arts, or sports, has a core mission and a teachable point of view about what it will take to succeed. This usually involves spending some time reflecting on the nature of one's goals and priorities as an individual and as an organization and then developing a point of view about how to achieve the goals effectively. Often a masterful coach will want to transform the prevailing paradigm and reframe people's thinking—contrary to the prevailing way of doing things.

A favorite example of mine is when Chris Galvin became CEO of Motorola. He noticed that the company was facing some serious issues due to a lack of collaboration with customers and colleagues. Nokia had displaced Motorola as the number one maker of mobile handsets. Iridium, Motorola's global satellite phone, took two years longer to bring to market than expected, and Motorola's different divisions would often go to outsiders for components rather than buy in-house. The result was that Motorola's stock fell off the shelf.

To build the company, Chris Galvin first developed a teachable point of view about collaboration. He started with a rare exercise of public soul-searching about the "warring tribes syndrome" in an article in the *Wall Street Journal,* where he publicly acknowledged that Motorola's engineers did not collaborate well. This was sure to get people's attention. Then he put on his coach-and-teacher's hat and spoke repeatedly to people in the company about changing the rules of engagement—*customers first, Motorola second, your business third.*

The result was that a new mind-set was established, customer and operational issues were addressed, and Motorola's stock doubled in the following year.[6]

REFLECTION ASSIGNMENT

Developing Your Mission–Critical Point of View

This reflection may take many hours or days. Give yourself the chance to mull it over before jumping to any conclusions.

1. What is your Personal Coaching Mission—talent acquisition, business growth, operational excellence?

2. What is your point of view or thinking about achieving it? What appears to be the limiting factor?

3. What would be a different point of view? How does your thinking need to change? Consider how the most successful businesses in your industry or others might approach this.

4. Develop a mission-critical teachable point of view in no more than a few sentences or a short paragraph. What's your "share of stomach"?

Think about **what** *you want to achieve, then develop a teachable point of view about* **how** *to achieve it.*

LESSONS FROM GREAT COACHES—FROM COMPETITION TO CREATION

I met Gary Peck, an executive vice president of Adidas, at the Tarrytown Conference Center in New York about five years ago. Peck, a South African who was chosen for the Olympic team in water polo, was in charge of design and development of Adidas textiles. He had previously worked for Nike. On that spring day in Tarrytown, I asked the Adidas team, "What's the vision?" Peck stood up, went to the thought board, and drew a picture of an ass and a foot beside it. He said, "That ass is Nike's and the vision is to kick it."

In a recent conversation I reminded Peck of this story. He said, "Let me clarify the different place I come from in coaching my team today. A year or so ago, our whole industry was in a real downturn. It forced me to realize that our competition was not Nike but that we needed to compete with ourselves to create what never existed before. I developed a teachable point of view that has to do with focusing on creating rather than the competition. I always ask, 'What's missing?' instead of focusing on 'What's wrong.' I believe that you are only limited by your imagination.

"About a year ago, at the Atlanta trade show, I noticed that the only thing that had changed about the show over the years was the booths. All people had done was to package things differently. When I went home, I noticed that my son Justin and his buddies didn't really give a damn about a lot of the sports that Adidas, Nike, and Reebok make shoes and textiles for—football, baseball, basketball. They are often more interested in alternative sports like roller-blading or snowboarding, where they can be independent of the kind of rules and regimentation you find on teams. It seemed to me that this was only the beginning.

"So I had a conversation with some of my team members about new sports, things like snowboarding, mountain biking, snow-biking, in-line skating—sports that didn't exist when we were growing up. We wondered, what if we were to put together a collaborative package of products that facilitated the needs of all of these new athletes? A lot of companies lie to themselves and their customers saying this particular shoe or shirt can be only used for basketball or tennis. We noticed there was a whole line of products that were general but functional, and that we could lasso all of these by opening a new product category.

"We drew up a business plan for this special business unit called Terrain—sports that can be played on any terrain. The point of view that evolved was 'one person, different sports.' However, it was very hard to get people to cooperate because everybody was used to keeping different products in separate categories, as well as reporting up in traditional ways. For example, the designers in textile and footwear are not only in different categories but also report to different organizations. Terrain and 'one person, different sports' became a way for me to challenge the orthodoxies of our business.

"I had to coach, teach, and preach the message over and over again until the organization came into alignment with it. It doesn't sound like much from the outside, but from the inside this meant a big shift in thinking and actions. I told people to take the customer's point of view rather than their own points of view about separate product categories and organizations. The customer wants to use the same shoes for many different sports. It eventually started to get through and led to a major realignment of our business. Today, the Terrain business is growing by leaps and bounds."[7]

FORMULATE A TEACHABLE POINT OF VIEW FOR SUCCESS IN EACH KEY AREA

Although your primary mission might be innovation, operational excellence, or building your business (about which you already have a teachable point of view), you may have other subgoals, designated tasks, and priorities that also require a teachable point of view.

Think about the other areas that you are concerned with as a business leader and then develop a teachable point of view around each of them. It could be a point of view about how to treat people so that they bring their whole selves to work, or a point of view about how to get people to shift from thinking in terms of functional stovepipes to thinking in terms of processes and teams.

It could also include ways to run a successful team meeting so that everyone's contributions are recognized and valued; how to answer the phone so as to say, "This is a world-class company"; or how to pack cases on a truck so they don't get scratched.

REFLECTION ASSIGNMENT

A Teachable Point of View About Each Business Concern

Develop a teachable point of view about every possible subarea. For example, What is your teachable point of view about strategy, people, processes, technology, or accomplishing key tasks? Then indicate the individuals or groups with whom you will share it and when.

1. My concern is ─────────────────────────────────

   My teachable point of view is ──────────────────────

   Others to share it with ────────────────────────────

   When I will do that ───────────────────────────────

2. My concern is ——————————————————————————

   My teachable point of view is ——————————————————

   Others to share it with ——————————————————————

   When I will do that ——————————————————————————

3. My concern is ——————————————————————————

   My teachable point of view is ——————————————————

   Others to share it with ——————————————————————

   When I will do that ——————————————————————————

4. My concern is ——————————————————————————

   My teachable point of view is ——————————————————

   Others to share it with ——————————————————————

   When I will do that ——————————————————————————

5. My concern is ——————————————————————————

   My teachable point of view is ——————————————————

   Others to share it with ——————————————————————

   When I will do that ——————————————————————————

LESSONS FROM GREAT COACHES—FROM VENDOR TO BUSINESS PARTNER AND COACH

I met Reg Stalley, director of marketing at Royal Tire of England, at a seminar I held on masterful coaching. I introduced myself as an oddball whose passion for making a difference didn't always make for a smooth fit for me into corporate culture. Stalley introduced himself and said, "I'm an oddball, too," cracking the room up.

Stalley was in the middle of driving a cultural change effort, a powerful new retail marketing partnership with Royal Tire's customers. He is known for doodling or staring off into space during meetings as the group churns up a complex problem, then suddenly saying, "Don't you think the real issue is . . . and if we just made a few small shifts in strategy and action we would crack it wide open." Bingo! There is a group "aha."

I asked Stalley about the cultural change he was undertaking and his teachable point of view: "We are shifting from a 'selling in' to a 'selling out' approach. Rather than just sell tires to the stores, we want to help the stores sell the tires off their shelves. [It] may not sound like much, but it is a huge culture change for us. All of our marketing programs are designed to help our salespeople 'sell in'—a point of view of being a vendor.

"Today, our salesforce has to shift from being a 'vendor' to being a 'business partner and coach,' and that's a hell of a difference." Stalley uses mantras, metaphors, and accumulation of argument to get his point of view across. "I tell people in advance that it won't come easy. Think about it—for the last twenty years, I have been coming in, shaking your hand, selling you the tires, thanking you for the sale, and walking out and leaving it to your own devices to get them off your shelf. Now I come in one morning and I say, 'Good news, I am now your business coach and your business partner.' I then tell people in a very personal way, 'I need to ask you to do something that is a stretch. I want to talk to you about the need for new ways of being and thinking, as well as taking different actions.'"

In addition, Stalley and Royal Tire wanted to make sure that the salesforce had the necessary training and tools. These included the following:

- Creating powerful forums to obtain the account managers' input

- Providing account managers with coaching and negotiation skills so that they focus on interests rather than positions in discussions with dealers

- Providing a new set of computer-based tools that allow the salesforce to analyze key components of the dealer's business, giving them feedback about what to buy and how to sell in a way that immediately allows them to make more money

The dealers' reaction is often "Wow!" Says Stalley, "The combination of our teachable point of view in shifting mind-set, the coaching and negotiation skills, and tools that directly impact the dealer's business give us the credibility we need to make this work."

People with a high level of personal mastery cannot afford to choose between passion and reason, head and heart, any more than any of us would choose between seeing with one eye or walking with one leg.

Peter Senge[8]

COMMUNICATE YOUR TEACHABLE POINT OF VIEW THROUGH IDEAS, STORIES, METAPHORS, AND EXAMPLES

Clarity is power. To get your message across, you need a clear, well-articulated message. Instead of getting stuck finding the right words, focus on expressing what you passionately believe in. If you do that, the words will be there. Always communicate with the intention that your words will have an impact. Frame your message so that it speaks to the person or group you are addressing. What do I need to say here that will move Joe? How can I express myself in a way that will break the grip of resignation on this group?

Catalytic Mechanisms for Getting Your Message Across

- Make distinctions that allow people to see things in new ways.

- Use accumulation of argument.

- Use stories, metaphors, and example.

- Add your own emotional energy.

Make Distinctions That Allow People to See Things in New Ways. Make distinctions with the view that good ideas drive out bad ideas—from authoritarian to collaborative management, from playing it safe to taking risks, and so on. In leadership seminars, I talk about two kinds of people: *chocolate* and *vanilla.* Vanilla people are security-oriented. Chocolate people are oriented toward making a difference. Vanilla people are oriented to being successful, often not recognizing that failure is always following them. Chocolate people are oriented toward making a contribution.

After making these distinctions, I ask people which they are. I hold this mirror right up to people until they start to see that they have been plain vanilla their whole lives and until they can imagine the possibility of being a leader. It's a simple distinction, but it produces breakthroughs.

Use Accumulation of Argument. The coach's role is to confirm the teachable point of view through an accumulation of argument. I once gave a talk to the corporate finance group at Quaker. The group wanted to collaborate more to reach goals and solve problems. I told them that one of the secrets of dialogue was teaching people to give up the need to be in agreement. Someone stood up and said it was an unwritten rule at the company to come to meetings already having agreed on decisions, and further, it was a rule not ever to disagree publicly. I said, "Do you want to harness the collective intelligence of your group?" Yes! "Do you believe that the best ideas come from a clash of different views and perspectives?" Yes again. "Does your way of interacting help you to reach goals and solve problems?" No. "Then why not test and amend these unwritten rules?"

Use Stories, Metaphors, and Examples. I usually (1) make a few distinctions, (2) use accumulation of argument, and (3) seal it with a story. The combination has a tremendous impact. When Steve Jobs was leading the first Apple Macintosh project team, he would often use metaphors to coach, guide, and instruct them in their work. According to Douglas Dayton, a designer from IDEOS who was on the team that designed the mouse, Job's teachable point of view was that the personal computer should be user friendly. The metaphor he used to get this point across was, "It should be as ubiquitous as an old bicycle lying against the wall of the garage."[9]

Invest Your Own Emotional Energy. Another key ingredient is to invest emotional energy, which allows you to connect to people in a deep way. To move others, you first have to be willing to be moved yourself. If you want others to be excited about your message, then you have to communicate your excitement so that it becomes re-created in them. This requires getting out of your head and expressing your communication through your heart, your gut, and your entire body. For example, if you have to give a speech, never write it out. Instead, take the main messages and write them on three-by-five cards. Then mill about the room speaking with edge—making distinctions, delivering your arguments, telling stories, using humor.

Passion makes communication easy; hammer a few simple powerful messages.

REFLECTION ASSIGNMENT

Getting Your Message Across

Write down in your journal the people or groups who you want to get your teachable point of view across to. What is the message? How will you use the following catalytic mechanisms to get it across?

1. Passion: Expressing the following emotions that are inside me.

2. These distinctions: between . . . and . . . , from . . . to. . . .

3. Accumulation of argument: If you agree with . . . , then what about . . . ?

4. The following insights, stories, metaphors, examples, demonstrations:

5. Person(s):

   Teachable point of view to get across:

   I will use the following to get my message across:

   I will talk to the person by:

6. Person(s):

   Teachable point of view to get across:

   I will use the following to get my message across:

   I will talk to the person by:

7. Person(s):

   Teachable point of view to get across:

   I will use the following to get my message across:

   I will talk to the person by:

There is a phrase in West Africa that means "deep talk." Often in a perplexing conversation an older person will offer a saying, metaphor, or parable and then say, "Take that as deep talk"— meaning that you never find the answer; you need to go deeper and deeper to find wisdom.

SEIZE "COACHABLE MOMENTS" EVERY TIME THEY ARISE

The best coaches are superb at recognizing the opportunity to transform small incidents into teaching opportunities. The best coaches never let such opportunities slip by. They approach them with relish.

For example, one day a top executive from Nordstrom's department store overheard a disgruntled customer who had picked out a dress she was in love with only to discover that it cost hundreds of dollars. The executive went right to the department manager, who was also in charge of the less expensive dresses, and asked her to do something to make the person happy. As soon as the board meeting was over, the executive bounded over to the dress area to find out how things had gone. The level of interest he showed conveyed something not only to the people in that area but also to many others.[10]

Another kind of coachable moment is the kind the coach generates himself or herself. A favorite example of mine is in Tom Peters's *In Search of Excellence.* A manager of a glass company found that sales were down. He suggested spiffing up the product design and creating some new stock. However, managers throughout the company didn't see any point in designing or building any new glassware until the large quantities of goods in the warehouse were sold. The executive had difficulty getting his message across, so one day he took a sledgehammer and smashed hundreds of crates of glass. The very next day the team began to design and produce a plethora of new, more fashionable designs, which as it turned out, sold at a tremendous rate.[11]

REFLECTION ASSIGNMENT
Recognizing Coachable Moments

Make notes in your journal about coachable moments you missed in the past few weeks. If possible, refer back to those moments and communicate to people your teachable point of view now.

EAGERLY SEEK COACHING YOURSELF—TAKE A REFLECTIVE STANCE

We have spent most of this chapter speaking about the coach as teacher. However, the chapter would not be complete if we did not also address the issue of the coach as learner. In my experience, the best coaches avoid lecturing from on high. Rather, they share the lessons learned from their own life experiences in stories. They personify through their personal sharing of their successes and failures what it is to be a learner who can transform "dirt" into "gold." Others are usually inspired by their example—especially their willingness to be vulnerable.

The best coaches, in my experience, also know their strengths and limits and eagerly seek coaching from others—whether it be their "boss" or a direct report or someone in their network. This could involve receiving coaching on leadership and managerial skills or technical and subject-matter expertise. When the coach asks for coaching from others, he or she is open to that person's teachable point of view; rather than debating it or needing to be right, he or she graciously seeks feedback and takes a reflective stance with respect to turning insights into real change.

At this point, ask yourself, With respect to my role, responsibilities, and mission, what are my strengths and limits?

PRACTICE ASSIGNMENT
Identifying Areas In Which You Need Coaching

Try some of the following as areas of focus:

1. Leadership and coaching skills: List strengths and limits.

2. Management skills: List strengths and limits.

3. Subject-matter expertise: List strengths and limits.

4. Technical skills: List strengths and limits.

(*Note:* **In 2000, Jossey-Bass will publish the *Masterful Coaching Inventory,* a 360-degree feedback process intended to assist leaders in assessing and developing their coaching and teaching skills.)**

THE MASTERFUL COACHING JOURNEY: A ROAD MAP

We are at the beginning of Masterful Coaching—The Method™. So far, we have been looking at the coaching process from the coach's point of view, providing a step-by-step approach. Another way to look at the coaching process is from the coachee's point of view.

Many people have never experienced coaching. At the beginning of a coaching relationship, providing the individuals or group with a coaching road map serves to clarify what they can expect. It can be both an adventurous and an arduous journey that demands a lot of people, individually and as a group. However, people generally have a much greater capacity for both accomplishment and growth than they know.

The pursuit of breakthroughs often brings us to where we can no longer make progress by proceeding step-by-step and we need to leap across the abyss. By referring to the road map when it seems appropriate, people can see where they are on the journey, where they are going, and what to expect from the coach at any given time. Along the journey, the coach shows the road map to the coachee.

THE COACHEE'S JOURNEY

MARKER 1   GETTING ON BOARD WITH COACHING

In this stage, we look at what a coaching relationship is and how it can empower the coachee to be successful. We agree on what impact coaching will have. The coach and the coachee or coachees bond by spending some social time together.

What the coachee might feel: "I'm intrigued." In this stage, it is normal to be both a bit excited about realizing your goals and a bit apprehensive about the fact that someone is going to be there to support and challenge you to move beyond where you have stopped.

MARKER 2   RELEASING PASSIONS, SETTING GOALS

Every worthwhile goal has an aspiration. Here we will look at goals that you passionately care about and how your life can be an expression of them.

What the coachee might feel: "I feel great. What a high." The coachee will probably find this stage exhilarating and see new possibilities.

MARKER 3   LOOKING THE DEVIL IN THE EYE

It is often important either before or after setting goals to be clear about the way things are now. Facing reality is a key to creating a readiness to change, setting goals that are realistic, and planning effectively. For example, if one's goal is to become a millionaire, one first determines how much difference there is between the present and the desired future.

What the coachee might feel: "I'm in the valley of despair." It is normal in this stage to feel despair at confronting situations that one has been avoiding. Once people face reality, however, they will generally feel much more empowered to create a new future.

MARKER 4   IDENTIFYING WHAT'S MISSING

Finding what's missing can catapult you forward. Here we will begin to look at all of the things that are missing to realize the coachee's goals.

What the coachee might feel: "I feel creatively inspired but overwhelmed by all the things I need to do." The coachee feels a mixture of excitement from the newfound clarity about what is needed and uncertainty about how to get from here to there.

MARKER 5　MOVING INTO ACTION

Here we start to break down what's missing into doable steps. We also are asked to develop good work habits. If we do that, good things start to happen.

What the coachee might feel: "It feels great to get some things done." Coachees start to see results and feel motivated to accomplish more.

MARKER 6　EXPOSING BREAKDOWNS

The coach may notice that the coachee has lost touch with the vision or isn't following through with what he or she said. This calls for some blunt feedback. Coachees are asked either to push past considerations and "just do it" or to plot another goal or another course.

What the coachee might feel: "This isn't what I expected!" Coachees feel stuck, ineffective, and confronted by the reemergence of old patterns they thought they had licked. They blame themselves and perhaps the coach. They want to quit.

MARKER 7　THE RETURN TO ACTION

The coach reminds the coachee of the vision and his or her promises, perhaps helping to come up with some alternative strategies that make things more doable, or breaking steps into smaller pieces.

What the coachee might feel: "I feel like I am generating some momentum." The coachee is past where he or she expected to be at this stage in the journey. Small inputs are starting to produce big outputs.

MARKER 8 BREAKTHROUGHS FOR PEOPLE, BREAKTHROUGHS IN RESULTS

Some results that were previously unimaginable have been achieved.

What the coachee might feel: "We've done it and it feels great!" Coachees marvel at what they and their colleagues have achieved and take time to acknowledge and celebrate.

RECIPROCAL GOALS OR INTERESTS

The coach joins with the coachee's sincere and honest goals and intentions. It also has to work the other way around. Mutual interest is the glue that holds the relationship together: realizing a higher goal, transforming the future, learning something new. Look after the interests of every person or team you coach, and request the same in return. For example, I always say to clients, "Let me tell you about the journey we are about to embark on. At some point, the waters will get rough and people will want to stop. I invest a lot of emotional energy in my projects, and I want to know that you will be there for me when this happens or I don't even want to start." To me, whatever the person says at this point is more important than any contract.

SUMMARY

Coming up with your teachable point of view as it pertains to various situations and people means taking time to mull it over and then articulate it. Remember:

1. Think about your mission.

2. Come up with a teachable point of view about how to accomplish the mission, based on key life learnings and by observing what has worked for others.

3. Come up with a few simple, powerful messages to hammer home and begin to communicate them with commitment, passion, and zeal.

As you communicate your teachable point of view, you will hone the articulation of it so that people can easily "get it" and so that it has an impact.

Wealth comes from relationships, not just productivity or efficiency.

STEP 2. INVEST IN RELATIONSHIPS

Building Powerful Partnerships

It is 7:00 a.m., two hours before the bell will ring signaling the opening of the New York Stock Exchange. It is May 1990 and Peter Lynch, who by that time had built Magellan into the biggest mutual fund in the history of the world, is having a coaching session with a group of new young Fidelity Fund managers.

According to George Vanderheiden, manager of Fidelity Destiny, Lynch preached and taught his money-making philosophy over a period of years, investing in a relationship with these rising stars and holding round-robin discussions of investment trends. This was supported from time-to-time by bringing in scouts from around the world who were part of Fidelity's research group.

Says Vanderheiden, "We were paid to learn from each other." More than a dozen of the young fund managers at the time went on to build mutual funds that would capture the attention of investors around the world.

This shared-learning environment stood in direct contrast to Fidelity's competitors, who were often secretive. When top Fidelity managers left the company, they would never do as well as they did at Fidelity, partly because the other firms lacked a coaching culture. By the way, from the time of this meeting in the late 1980s to when Lynch retired from his post, Fidelity grew from $100 billion in assets to $500 billion.[1]

Investing in a relationship between at least two people means that the value increases twice as fast as if you invest on your own.

Kevin Kelly[2]

INVESTING IN RELATIONSHIPS—CREATING PARTNERS

In the previous chapter we reviewed your personal coaching mission and began developing a teachable point of view to help you succeed with it. You now have an overall sense of what you want to accomplish in your job and a particular perspective from which to come as you interact with others. This should give you a platform to stand on, as well as a sense of confidence and power.

The next step in masterful coaching—*The Method*™—is to invest in relationships with others who can leverage your effectiveness in accomplishing your mission. In designing The Method™, we have taken into account that we are living in a network economy and that, to accomplish your goals, you may need to invest in relationships with your direct reports and other talented people or groups in the company, as well as with network partners.

It is also important to keep in mind that in today's talent-driven, knowledge-based world, everyone is a volunteer. You simply cannot lead, coach, and teach anyone without his or her permission—even someone who reports to you. Sure, you can use all the authoritarian, heavy-handed tactics you want to *make* people accountable for showing up and doing certain tasks. However, it won't make people *feel* responsible for the larger mission or be open to your teachable point of view. The idea is to inspire individuals and groups to produce extraordinary and tangible results, not to extract the results out of them.

The ability to accomplish your goals depends ultimately on investing in your relationships until you have built a powerful partnership that can move mountains. This means realizing your goals by helping others realize theirs. It means building your success by building the success of others. It means engaging in coaching conversations in which you support one another's growth and development, regardless of who reports to whom.

It starts with investing what is probably the most important thing you have as a leader and manager: *your time and attention.* It could mean helping a talented person find a way to link personal passion to his or her business goals. It could involve bringing your team together for a special session during which you both discuss business performance and learn about each other as human beings. It could mean taking the time to give someone meaningful feedback, thus building personal development. It could mean offering to be a thinking partner for a colleague.

A RELATIONSHIPS ORIENTATION—THE KEY TO SUCCESS IN A NETWORK ECONOMY

Before going further into the why's, what's, and how's of investing in relationships, ask yourself, Do I personally have a relationship orientation? Do I recognize that there is an enormous difference between *being* in relationships with other people so that I give them the gift of my presence and *having* a relationship with others the same way I would have an object? Do I tend to get things done by focusing on my own personal or group productivity and efficiency, or do I try to get things done by orchestrating new patterns of relationships and interactions with others? Would other people say that I was not only smart and talented but also emotionally well-developed?

The fact is that based on the direction in which the world is going, the "winners" will be those who have a relationships orientation. The "losers" will be those who slog it out on their own. Kevin Kelly of *Wired* magazine has pointed out that the central economic imperative of the industrial era was for managers to amplify productivity. In contrast, says Kelly, "The central economic imperative of the network economy is to amplify relationships."[3]

Today, productivity is often just a by-product of relationships. For example, it is no longer essential for a company like Dell Computer to make software or chips for its computers; it is essential, however, that they have relationships with companies that have that capacity. In the same sense, it is not necessary to stand over knowledge workers to make sure they are productive, but it is necessary that leaders create relationships with them and inspire them to give their best.

The key to being a successful coach today, in a network economy, lies in having a relationship orientation—and the skills and attitudes to go with it. Your effectiveness depends almost entirely on amplifying both the quality and quantity of economic relationships: between yourself and each of your team members, between each team member and other team members, between your firm and other firms, between employees and other firms' employees, between your firm and your customers, between your machines and customers, and between your customers and their customers.

One of the key coaching attributes is the ability to instill an attitude of collaboration, and one of the key skills is to learn to use technology to amplify relationships. As Michael Schrage has pointed out in *No More Teams,* "We need to shift away from the notion of technology managing information and toward the idea of technology as a medium for managing relationships."[4]

A coach using today's relationship technology can bring an extraordinary combination of people together from across the world in virtual teams to accomplish the impossible—cutting cycle time in half, building a breakthrough product, managing a complex customer relationship. As Tom Sudman, a knowledge management expert and inventor of "Knowledge Rooms," a virtual team technology, points out, "In face-to-face meetings, coaching is a nicety; in virtual space, it is a necessity."[5] As Kelly says, "Start with technology, end with trust."

Coaches must learn how to articulate goals and challenges in a way that inspires people to come together around a purpose larger than themselves. It is not just a matter of assembling the right group of people; it is a matter of improving the way knowledge workers think and interact to create innovation—building new products, cutting cycle time, amplifying and extending relationships with customers.

A relationship orientation is just as important in coaching individuals within a group. It is impossible to imagine people supporting a mission or being willing to be coached in the absence of a meaningful relationship. To make the relationship meaningful, it is important to emphasize shared meanings and goals and to deemphasize status and rank.

In previous economic eras, the smartest way to build a complex organization when information was scarce was to build a hierarchy: When information is scarce, people follow orders. However, when information is plentiful, as it is today, people relate as peers and counterparts.

Keep in mind that because a relationship usually involves at least two people who are invested in it, it increases in value at least twice as fast. The cost of switching relationships or abandoning them is high. Although friction is natural in relationships, a key coaching skill is being able to heal bruised relationships. This means not burying conflict under the rug but completing things as you move along.

The following is a list of coaching tips for investing in relationships. We will look at each point in more detail throughout the chapter. Also, the coaching caps to use in this step are shown.

Coaching Tips for Investing in Relationships

1. Decide which relationships to invest in that will leverage your effectiveness in accomplishing the mission.

2. Engage people by learning about their passions, goals, and aspirations.

3. Enroll people in coaching, holding out images of positive possibilities.

4. Look for openings to initiate coaching conversations.

Coaching Caps to Use for Investing in Relationships

- Put on your Assessment Cap to distinguish talented people and to recognize their talents and gifts. (See page 117.)

- Put on your Drawing Out Cap to get to know people. (See page 122.)

- Put on your Declaring Possibilities Cap to highlight opportunities that come out of connecting with others. (See page 115.)

Based on my mission, focus, or project, which relationships do I need to invest in that will allow me and my organization to create the future we truly desire?

DECIDE WHICH RELATIONSHIPS TO INVEST IN TO LEVERAGE YOUR EFFECTIVENESS IN ACCOMPLISHING THE MISSION

The next step involves thinking about the people and groups or networks with whom you want to invest in a relationship. The people you select will vary according to your position in the organization. If you are the CEO, for example, you will choose people to be on the general management team. If you are a business unit manager, you will choose different functional heads. If you are a project leader, you will naturally choose people with the talent and skills you need, or you may choose to invest in a relationship with joint venture partners. Consider people outside your immediate universe.

You may or may not want to invest in a relationship with all the people in your group. Instead of thinking in terms of jobs and the organization chart, think in terms of roles that must be filled to accomplish your core mission. As Eric Wilson of Cogos Consulting says, "The question of who to bring together to accomplish a goal or project is not who, but rather what talents, skills, and capabilities you need in order to accomplish your objective."[6]

The idea is not to select people based on their status, rank, or years of employment, but to select people with the knowledge and set of experiences to match what you have to achieve. Today knowledge work is generally done through collaboration, so it is important to select people who have enthusiasm and a basic attitude of collaboration, and who are dogged hard workers.

REFLECTION ASSIGNMENT

Decide Which Relationships to Invest in (Part 1)

Think about which people in each of the following categories you would like to invest in a relationship with. If you have difficulty, read the following section first.

To complete my mission, which people do I need to invest in a relationship with in each of the following categories?

1. Top talent on your team:

2. Knowledge specialists:

3. Support people ("glue"):

4. Free agents:

5. Alliance partners:

Identify direct reports who represent the top talent on your team. The first people to think about investing in a relationship with are those who represent your top talent, particularly your direct reports with leadership potential. Select people for special roles on merit, not on elitism. It starts with asking yourself as a coach, Who are the people on my team who can leverage my effectiveness in fulfilling the team's mission or mandate?

One of the issues I have with human resource and performance appraisal processes in many organizations is that they often lack what some leaders call "edge." They are too soft. People are not really assessed on breakthroughs in performance or development, but rather on fulfilling predictable goals and demonstrating predictable behaviors—such things as "takes initiative" or "gets along well with others."

Identify knowledge experts who have two to three work experiences that relate to the project. It is critical to identify people in your group or beyond it who have the necessary subject-matter expertise. Although "knowledge is power," it is only powerful when people share it. So select people who not only have the right knowledge and experience base, but who also have an attitude of sharing what they know. Use the Internet to find people in other parts of your company or in other firms whom you can borrow until your mission is accomplished.

Identify valued support people who are the glue of the organization. Joan Holmes, executive director of the Hunger Project, pointed out to me that traditionally leaders on the white horses are the ones we build statues of. She explained that Senators get the attention in the newspapers, but it is the Senate aides and pages who do most of the work, especially in making sure that key relationships are established, that key meetings happen, and that logistics are handled.[7] Every team needs leaders in this category. Make sure to invest in relationships with people in this area, and make sure that you offer to provide coaching and mentoring to them as well.

Identify free agents, alliance partners, or outsourcing groups that can add value at a minimum of cost and effort. The best organizations focus on their circle of competence and create alliances or outsource the rest. Determine what jobs, functions, and roles would be better filled by going outside. Who are the people or groups with whom you want to invest in a relationship? If your company is mainly involved in knowledge work, consider farming out anything that has to do with accounts payable, financial statements, compensation and benefits, and so forth.

Break the brick and mortar paradigm permanently. In knowledge work, the value of the knowledge produced is greater than the value of the objects produced. In the past, whether you could work for a company or not depended on where you lived. Today, with a Web-based work style, it depends more on your education and experiences. For example, executives working on "strategic issues management" could easily create a virtual mastermind group with other executives from other firms, R&D functions can be carried out by people who are not in the same location, and so on.

> ## It is not "who" to have on your team, it is "what" skills and capabilities you need.
>
> **Eric Wilson**[8]

REFLECTION ASSIGNMENT

Decide Which Relationships to Invest in (Part 2)

A. Getting the Coaching You Need

1. Given your mission or mandate, what are your areas of strength and areas in which you have gaps? Use performance metrics and developmental criteria, as well as 360-degree feedback.

2. Who in the company has done or is doing a similar job and has a strength in an area in which you need development, such as in finance, business operations, sales, or distribution?

3. Who has mastered some of the developmental areas you need to strengthen?

4. Are you willing to create a relationship with the person in which you ask for some coaching? Are you able to "request" coaching?

B. Coaching Direct Reports

1. Write a list of names of ten people in your group.

2. Beside each name, score the person's performance on a scale of 1 to 5. Be ready to explain why you chose each rating. Use the following scale.

   - 1's are people everyone recognizes as stars. These people consistently deliver on performance commitments and consistently live leadership values.

   - 2's do not meet all performance commitments but consistently live the leadership values. Their hearts are in the right place. They need coaching.

   - 3's meet performance commitments but do not consistently live the leadership values. They need coaching.

   - 4's neither meet performance commitments nor live the leadership values. They may need to be moved out of the group.

   - 5's definitely need to move out of your group.

3. Identify two people (1's to 3's) you think can perform and develop at an accelerated rate with coaching relevant to your mission.

   - Are they open to your teachable point of view?

   - Would you like to coach these people? What would be in it for you? For them?

   - How would you describe each person's strengths and limitations as well as derailment potential (fatal flaws)?

C. Coaching Your Group

1. Are you as a coach investing in creating a "great group" or do you mainly just delegate to individuals?

2. Have you articulated a shared, understood goal for your group that inspires them to collaborate? It must be big enough and significant enough for them to subordinate their egos to.

3. Do people in your group recognize that to reach the goals it will take the group, not just individuals?

4. Does the group spend time in focused dialogue on business issues? How well do people think and interact together? What needs to be different?

5. Is the group working on a collective work product—something that can be achieved in weeks, not months? Are people taking action around this?

6. What openings or opportunities do you have to coach the team?

ENGAGE PEOPLE BY LEARNING ABOUT THEIR PASSIONS, GOALS, AND ASPIRATIONS

At this point, you have identified the talented people or groups who can offer you powerful assistance in achieving your mission. They may be people from either inside or outside your company. The next step is to engage those people in a relationship and in the possibility of thinking and working together on a goal, problem, or project.

One of the first things to do is establish some kind of personal contact with the individual or group, whether face-to-face, by telephone, or through e-mail. The key to success is to be the kind of person who does not shy away from inviting a direct report or colleague to lunch to discuss his or her mission (or the other person's) and to get to know each other better. It is also important to pick up the phone and call a talented person, even one you don't know, for an introductory conversation.

Give People the Gift of Your Presence. One of the things I do when I am interested in signing people up for a mission or potential project team is to introduce myself, tell what my goals and plans are in general terms, and see what that elicits from them. Often my sense of curiosity and discovery takes over and I find myself asking one question after the next. It is important when having such conversations that you give people the gift of your presence. This means looking in their faces when they talk and really paying attention to what they have to say. The key is not to be *interesting* but rather to be *interested*.

If I am enrolling people who are already on my team, I ask questions that are designed to find out what their passions, goals, and aspirations are and to discuss what they see as their next developmental steps. Managers often make the mistake of assuming that people want to continue doing more or less the same thing. If I don't know the people as well, I again put on my curiosity and discovery hat and ask lots of questions about who they are, what they are passionate about, and what their goals, aspirations, and interests are.

I have found that asking people what they are passionate about, as well as what their talents and gifts are, can be incredibly empowering to them, especially if they have buried their passions as a result of being part of a "climate of resignation." It is by asking questions that you discover the potential links between your goals and aspirations and theirs. It is by asking questions that you begin to get a sense of how to enroll the people to bring their committed participation to a project.

Stay in an Open Inquiry Mode. It is important to discover not only people's goals, talents, and gifts but also their developmental edges or derailment potential (fatal flaws). If you can begin to get a sense of how a person or group could realize performance goals and accelerate experiential development by establishing more of a coaching relationship with you, you have the basis for building a powerful partnership.

For example, I was interested in starting an e-commerce consulting business. I met a very talented young manager who had previous consulting experience with McKinsey and Company. I asked the manager what he was passionate about. He told me he was passionate about "creating things" and that he had started four to five different entrepreneurial businesses—including restaurants, a mail-order clothing business, and a recording studio.

At that point, he said that he was really passionate about business, design, and technology and would relish an opportunity to be part of a company that allowed him to put these together. When I mentioned the possibility of an e-commerce consulting business that would integrate the three things he was passionate about, he was ready to jump on board. I asked him to tell me more about his strengths and developmental edges in order to find out what he might need coaching on.

You either care about people or you care about what they think of you.

ENROLL PEOPLE IN COACHING, HOLDING OUT IMAGES OF POSITIVE POSSIBILITIES

Let's say that you have identified others who can support you in realizing your mission. You have reached out to them and begun to invest in relationships with them by giving them the gift of your presence. The next step is to begin to enroll the players in the mission, whether they are new players or existing ones from whom you seek greater commitment.

One of the keys is to hold out not only the possibilities and opportunities in terms of the results you want—innovation, greater sales, process re-invention—but also the possibilities and opportunities for each person. Talented knowledge workers are looking for projects that are provocative, intriguing, and risky and for the opportunity to work with people they like.

This step is not only about enrolling people in the mission but about coaching them as well. Focus your coaching on a goal or problem in which people have something at stake. The ideal situation for coaching is when people are requesting it—indeed, when they are demanding it.

One of the things you can do to assist people in being open to coaching in actual practice is to clarify the different roles coaches play, as mentioned in Chapter One and listed below. From time to time, you can say something like, "Now I am putting on my leadership development hat" or "Now I am putting on my conversation partner hat," to remind them of your roles.

Roles of a Coach: (1) Leader who develops others as leaders, (2) performance maximizer, (3) thinking partner, and (4) master architect of creative collaboration.

Enroll people in your mission or the team's mission by holding out images of aspiration. As a masterful coach, help others to realize dreams beyond their grasp or to perform at levels at which they are not now capable of performing. According to Kouzes and Posner in their book *Encouraging the Heart,* "This starts with holding out positive images which create positive possibilities."[9] A classic example is when Steve Jobs was courting John Sculley, then head of PepsiCo, for the CEO position of Apple. Jobs asked, "Do you want to change the world or make sugar water for the rest of your life?"[10]

This applies not only to individuals but to teams as well. When Rob Manning, chief engineer for the Mars project, was recruiting young, talented engineers, he looked to people who watched *Star Trek* when they were young, read science fiction, made model airplanes, and were fascinated

> **The most powerful way to create a great relationship is to look for the best in people and help bring that best to its full potential.**

by the Apollo launch. He offered them the project of a lifetime: being part of a team to land a space probe on Mars, with a fixed deadline of July 4th, 1996.[11]

Enroll people in giving their best to the team based on what motivates them. It is often the case that a coach needs to awaken people's inner goals and aspirations to get them to give their best to a team. When Rick Pitino was coach at the University of Kentucky, he asked player Jamal Mashburn during his junior year, "Does it bother you that people are talking about drafting your teammates for the NBA and no one is talking about drafting you?" Mashburn replied, "I guess I just don't have the skills to play at that level." Pitino told him, "You have all the skills you need except one. That explosive first step off the ball and, if I were you, I wouldn't waste a minute being jealous. Instead, I would get to work on that explosive first step. I will be here and do absolutely everything I can to help." Jamal became Pitino's first truly great player at Kentucky.[12]

Show people how coaching can help them reach their goals faster. Enrolling people usually involves making some kind of offer. For example, Candice Carpenter, the CEO of iVillage.com in Cambridge, Massachusetts, has developed a concept she calls "radical mentoring," based on the idea that people sometimes don't grow as fast as the company may need them to. She suggests that senior leaders ask, "Who are ten leaders I can grow quickly, and what's the crash course that's right for them?" Then contract with them. Coaches have to be able to manage their schedule. Says Carpenter, "I can do this with only a few people at a time." Carpenter's concept of radical mentoring involves catapulting people forward with tough assignments, as well as being extremely blunt.[13]

1:1 COACHING ACTIVITY

Enrolling People in Your Mission and in Coaching

Think about some of the people in your organization who have high potential. Imagine them reaching their full potential. Create some positive images

for them. Use your imagination. (Or if you prefer, do the same thing in conversation with each person.) Then have an enrollment conversation with each person. Use the following guidelines:

1. Get to know people by drawing them out. Recognize their talents and gifts.

2. Hold out positive possibilities for people or groups through positive images.

3. Introduce the idea of people being on a team to accomplish a mission. Introduce the roles they could play in a way that gives them a sense of significance.

4. Offer to be a coach or mentor with a view toward helping others reach their goals faster, as well as helping them to be catapulted toward success.

5. Show people the link between coaching (being on the team) and moving from where they are to where they want to be.

6. Ask people for their commitment to the project and to the coaching relationship.

7. Say, "We will meet and talk about this again soon." Then follow up to see whether they are solidly enrolled.

GROUP COACHING ACTIVITY

Enrolling the Group

Use this activity to bring a group of people together around a purpose larger than themselves. Spend at least two to three hours on this activity.

1. State the possibility you are standing for or the mission. You will define specific goals in the next step.

2. Ask each person in the group to write a one-page business case explaining why accomplishing this mission matters. (This could be done as prework.) Share the cases with the group. Listening to each person's case will build shared understanding.

3. Ask each person to prepare and make a statement about why he or she is personally passionate about reaching the goal and whether he or she is willing to make a voluntary emotional commitment.

4. If someone cannot do this, reevaluate the mission and that person's role or presence in the group. (It is especially important in breakthrough projects to give people a choice whether to play.) Allow the person to deselect from the group.

5. Celebrate with a drink or a meal.

LOOK FOR OPENINGS TO INITIATE COACHING CONVERSATIONS

Once you enroll others in your team's mission, your relationships change dramatically. At this point you begin to share a destiny, even if the specific goals and objectives have not been completely defined. You are now, as the leader of the group or colleague in it, in a position to initiate coaching conversations, whether with individuals, groups, or network partners.

The best way to do this is to keep the coaching conversational in a setting that is both purposeful and social. Get the ball rolling by taking people out to lunch. Draw people out and talk to them about their passions, talents, and interests or about problems they are having. Offer to be a conversation or thinking partner. Also get the ball rolling by offering either to lead the next team meeting or to challenge assumptions and inferences that people make at the next problem-solving meeting.

It is important to develop a strong sense of self-awareness so that you balance your own desire or need to say something that makes a difference with another's desire or need for coaching at any given moment. Don't get stuck in "Shall I say this or that?" "Do I have permission to coach him?" or "I don't want to impose." Instead, look for openings or opportunities that present themselves to initiate coaching conversations that naturally occur in the process of working together.

REFLECTION ASSIGNMENT

Initiating Coaching Conversations

Think about openings for coaching that have recently presented themselves to you, then figure out which of the following coaching conversation caps would have been appropriate to put on.

Cap 1.   Declaring Possibilities

Cap 2.   Making Assessments

Cap 3.   Teaching or Advising

Cap 4.   Drawing Others Out

Cap 5.   Reframing

Cap 6.   Forwarding Action

Look for openings for formal coaching relationships with individuals. Think about the opportunities you have to coach others who report directly to you or who are on your team. Who enjoys being stretched? Who can deal with having her thinking challenged? Who has made a request for coaching? Who is asking for some new skills? Who is stuck on a key project? Who keeps repeating the same mistake? Also think about how you can use the coaching forums built into your job, for example, an upcoming leadership development program, strategy sessions, normal team meetings, performance reviews, or customer calls.

Possible Openings for Formal Coaching Relationships

- A strategy session after which people left uninspired and intellectually disengaged

- Performance reviews, product reviews, presidential reviews

- A special project that requires a focus on performance and development

- Someone asks for your perspective or advice on an issue

- People demonstrate blocked mental models or frames

- People in your group are missing goals

- People are repeating the same mistakes

- Someone requests to learn a new skill

Look for openings for informal coaching relationships. Informal coaching relationships are extraordinarily important for any company that wants to establish a learning culture. As Hubert Saint-Onge said, "Coaching is the way that we relate to each other across the firm with the intention of 'causing' each other's success . . . in a boundaryless way."[14] This starts with giving people the gift of your presence or being available when someone asks you for your perspective or has a question. It involves recognizing when someone else has half an idea and you have the other half. It involves formal and informal coaching.

Possible Openings for Informal Coaching Relationships

- On a business trip, you have a chance to put out the vision and your coachable point of view.

- An incident occurs between customers and employees that is an opportunity to teach values.

- Someone tells you his or her career is not fulfilling aspirations and requests mentoring.

- People request a "fresh perspective" from someone who is a senior in their work.

- A colleague requests some knowledge you have in solving a problem.

- Team members remain silent and hesitate to share their views.

- People in a meeting are avoiding hot or controversial issues.

LESSONS FROM GREAT COACHES—LEARNING FROM EXCELLENCE

A good example comes from the Great Plains software company in Fargo, North Dakota. At Great Plains they have developed a powerful informal "mentoring" system based on leadership skills or expertise. Since Doug Burgum, Chairman and CEO, joined Great Plains in 1983, he has placed a lot of attention on creating a learning culture wherein people are expected to demonstrate "boundaryless" behavior.

According to Jodi Uecker-Rust, executive vice president, "A lot of the mentoring happens laterally." How does it work? Every year, Great Plains holds its Pioneer Day and presents awards to people who are excellent in various dimensions of the business: a Jesse James Award for innovation, a Sodbuster Award for pioneering ideas, a Heritage Award for customer service, and others for excellence in various technical areas.

The people who win these awards are held up as mentors, and others are encouraged to learn from them, either individually or in groups. There is an extraordinary number of "coaching sessions" every day.[15]

GROUP COACHING ACTIVITY
Coaching Guidelines

One of the ways you can create a coaching relationship with your group is by intervening with the intent to transform how people think and interact at team meetings. The next time you are leading a meeting or have the opportunity to facilitate, post the following ground rules from Roger Schwarz's *The Skilled Facilitator*.[16] The ground rules are excellent, both in terms of offering groups a powerful assist in building new shared understandings and in terms of recognizing and dispersing defensive routines. Ask the group to adopt these ground rules as their own. Make it clear to the group that you will coach and intervene only on the basis that the group will stick to these ground rules. Ask the group to cofacilitate with you by holding themselves and others to the ground rules.

Ground Rules for Effective Groups

1. Test assumptions and inferences.

2. Share all relevant information.

3. Focus on interests, not positions.

4. Be specific—use examples.

5. Agree on what important words mean.

6. Explain the reason behind one's statements, questions, and actions.

7. Disagree openly with any member of the group.

8. Make statements, then invite questions and comments.

9. Jointly design ways to test disagreements and solutions.

10. Discuss undiscussable issues.

11. Keep the discussion focused.

12. Do not take cheap shots or otherwise distract the group.

13. Participate in all phases of the process.

14. Exchange relevant information with nongroup members.

15. Make decisions by consensus.

16. Do self-critiques.

REFLECTION ASSIGNMENT

Matching Coaching Assets to Coaching Relationships

Take a piece of paper and divide it into two columns. List your coaching assets in the first column; list your potential coaching relationships in the second. Now draw lines between the two columns to create matches. Have conversations with the people on your list to inquire whether they would be interested in creating a coaching relationship.

TO CONTRACT OR NOT TO CONTRACT?

The enrollment conversation brings up the issue of contracting. In fact, once people say they are enrolled in coaching, you already have the basis for an informal contract and may not need to take it any further. However, it is very useful to create a somewhat more formal contract so as to clarify expectations and avoid future misunderstandings. Some samples might be, "As a coach, I see myself as responsible for inspiring, empowering, enabling you to reach your goals, not as someone who is responsible for your goals and deliverables," or "It is my job to help you reach your quota of $10 million in sales by sharing my ideas and insights as a conversation partner. It is not my job to produce $10 million in sales."

ELEMENTS OF A COACHING CONTRACT

Use the following elements to design a coaching contract:

1. The coach, before entering into a coaching contract, makes every reasonable effort to ensure that there are opportunities for significant benefits to the coachee and that there are no real barriers to achieving these benefits.

2. The coach and coachee agree to work in a collaborative way that leverages both the coach's and the coachee's knowledge of their industry, businesses, situation, relevant new technologies, and problem solving.

3. The coachee is accountable for reaching the goals. The coach is accountable for empowering the coachee. The coach and coachee agree on the impact they want the relationship to have.

4. The coach and coachee clarify any other expectations. For example, the following statements could be applied to governing values: (1) the coach will supply feedback based on valid information and examples, or (2) the coachee will have a free and informed choice as to whether to change and which options to act on.

5. The coach and coachee agree on coaching sessions at regular intervals. They hold frequent informal and formal progress reviews as a pair and in groups.

6. If the coaching project involves group work, the coach and coachee seek to build a shared understanding at all levels on the nature and importance of problems, alternatives for solutions, and the pace at which changes should be made. They agree on the important stakeholders.

7. The coach and coachee agree on how long the contract will last. As it is not always possible to make certain in advance that the conditions exist to achieve the expected benefits, the coach or coachee agree that they are free to withdraw from the agreement with fair notice.

Use the coaching contract form on the next page for your own coaching opportunities.

A COACHING CONTRACT FORM

1. I, the coach, believe that there are opportunities for significant benefits to the coachee and that there are no real barriers to achieving these benefits. These benefits are:

2. We, the coach and coachee, agree to work in a collaborative way that leverages both of our knowledge.

3. We agree that the coachee is accountable for reaching the goals and that the coach is accountable for empowering the coachee. The impact we want this relationship to have is:

4. The governing values that we agree to operate by are:

Our expectations are:

5. We agree to have coaching sessions at regular intervals. The number of coaching sessions we will have and when are:

6. [Optional for group work] We agree to seek to build a shared understanding at all levels on the nature and importance of problems, on alternatives for solutions, and on the pace at which changes should be made. We agree to do this with the following stakeholders:

7. This contract will last until _____. Because it is not always possible to make certain in advance that the conditions exist to make the expected benefits possible, the coach or coachee is free to withdraw from the agreement with fair notice.

REFLECTION ASSIGNMENT

Applying Your Learning

1. Which individuals or groups that you are coaching should you contract with more formally?

2. With which individuals or groups could you share the coachee's journey (on page 159) to provide more context for what will happen during your coaching relationship?

SUMMARY

- Decide which relationships to invest in.

- Engage people by discovering their goals, aspirations, talents, and gifts.

- Enroll people in coaching by holding out an image of a positive possibility.

- Look for openings to initiate coaching conversations.

- Create a coaching contract, informally or formally.

- Share the coachee's journey with your coachee to create a context for your coaching relationship.

Stretch goals hold the possibility of breakthroughs in performance and development.

STEP 3. PLAN STRETCH GOALS COLLABORATIVELY

Declaring Extraordinary Results Possible

In the early 1990s, Jim Sacherman, who founded the Palo Alto Design Group (PADG), held a strategic planning session with his team. The company's ambitious goals were not being met and growth was stalled. Like most industrial design consulting firms, PADG sold time. The only way to generate growth was to work longer hours in an intellectual, artful sweat factory or hire more designers.

Sacherman challenged the group in the strategic planning session, saying that the whole "consulting" arena was designed for failure. Then someone asked a question: "How do we go beyond fee for service?" The group came up with a breakthrough solution they called "design for equity." They looked for clients who were willing to exchange stock options or royalties for PADG's design services.

Positive images create positive possibilities.

James Kouzes and Barry Posner[1]

One of these designs turned out to be the Pilot, a highly successful retail product for Palm Computing. In 1995, U.S. Robotics bought Palm Computing, and Sacherman and his team cashed in.[2]

SET STRETCH GOALS THAT CAUSE PEOPLE TO REACH FOR THE STARS

Until now, we have looked at the mission, the teachable point of view, and investment in relationships with others. The next step in The Method™ is for individuals and groups to set stretch goals that will foster both performance and development, for example, to be best in class, to get the new products in the pipeline, to increase sales, or to have a profitable year. There is no way to reach such performance goals without the individual and the group developing.

Stretch goals may be set in a collaborative way so as to ensure that they unleash personal and collective aspirations. In setting goals with both individuals and groups, it is often important to ask yourself or others: "What's really possible here?" instead of "What's predictable?" Also ask, "Is there enough opportunity in this goal for me (or for my team) to seriously pursue it?"

The following is a list of tips for planning goals collaboratively that will be discussed further in the rest of this chapter. The coaching caps to use in this step are also listed.

Coaching Tips for Planning Stretch Goals Collaboratively

1. Don't tell people what to do; be a thinking partner.

2. Together assess "where we are now" with respect to the mission.

3. Set stretch goals that foster performance and development.

4. Identify "what's missing" that will make a difference.

Coaching Caps to Use for Planning Stretch Goals Collaboratively

- A new possibility comes into existence because it is declared. Put on your Declaring Possibilities Cap to enroll people in a positive possibility or to set an extraordinary goal. (See page 115.)

- Put on the Assessment Cap to start the "where we are now" analysis. Then put on the Drawing Out Cap to see what people think. (See pages 117 and 122.)

- Continue with the Assessment Cap and record all that's missing. Then, as needed, put on the Reframing Cap and challenge orthodoxies. Come up with inventive solutions. (See pages 117 and 125.)

DON'T TELL PEOPLE WHAT TO DO: BE A THINKING PARTNER

Traditionally, managers said, "Here's the goal; come back at the end of the year when you have the result." Any coaching that was done was done not in a conversational way but rather by telling people what to do. It was often, "My way or the highway." In today's knowledge economy it is ineffective to use this method, as the coach often knows less about the goals or how to reach them than the knowledge specialist being coached.

The coach's role in setting and reaching stretch goals is therefore less to be the "boss" and more to be a thinking partner who can draw people out, challenge assumptions, or make suggestions. As mentioned in the introduction, if the mission is to "grow the business," the coach's job is to get every idea in the person's head out on the table, not to show off his or her own infinite wisdom.

When it comes to reaching stretch goals, the likelihood is that neither the coach nor the coachee will know the answers when starting out. If you find yourself in this position, instead of acting like an arrogant know-it-all, say, "I don't know the answers. Let's go out and discover them together." To do so, the coach and coachee need to engage in a collaborative inquiry over time. This means asking questions and staying with the questions until you have more results than answers.

It is not what people achieve in reaching a goal that is important; it is who they become in reaching it. Often this involves not just straightforward planning but also challenging deep beliefs and assumptions. On a more powerful and profound level, the coach and coachee are likely to come face-to-face with the fact that people will have to transform who they are in order to reach the stretch goal. I have discovered that there is a way of inquiring, of engaging in questions about reaching stretch goals, that is actually transformational with respect to the questioner.

For example, Joan Holmes, executive director of the Hunger Project and a person committed to ending hunger throughout the world, was previously a school teacher and psychologist. She told me that when she took a stand to end hunger, it totally altered the way she saw herself in the world. She had to reinvent herself many times over—from being a follower to being a leader, from being reluctant to appear in the spotlight to being a powerful spokesperson, from being an American in her style and approach to finally being a global person.[3] To transform who she was in the world, Joan relied a great deal on coaches and mentors who believed in her goal and who assisted her in closing all the escape hatches in her mind.

The coach plays a similar role in a group. It often starts with the coach articulating stretch goals that inspire commitment and collaboration, as well as acting as a thinking partner in creating a concrete plan. This involves drawing people out, challenging orthodoxies, as well as eliciting new ideas, fresh approaches, or innovative solutions. In the same sense that a coach offers individuals a powerful assist in transforming who they are in reaching the goals, they must also transform the group. If you ask people whether they have ever been a part of a great group, they will often say yes. If you ask them if the group started out as a great group, they will probably say no.

What makes a great group is often a leader or coach who brings talented individuals to the "moment of recognition" when they realize that reaching the goals is going to take a group thinking and working together—not individuals doing their jobs and throwing the results over the wall. One of the keys is not just creating a shared goal or plan but creating a focus on producing collective work products in a tight time frame.

Whether coaching an individual or a group, the key is staying in the relationship and continuing to have robust dialogue. Says Bob Mason, manager of Poland Springs, "It is important to let daily actions emerge from the coaching conversations as you take your plans and execute. It is not just a matter of saying, 'This is what I think,' but a matter of asking people, 'What do you think?' When people answer, they get involved."[4]

A THREE-STEP PROCESS: STRATEGIC PLANNING IN ACTION

People go to business school to learn elaborate methods for making plans. They develop all kinds of complex approaches to planning, such as scenario-based planning and "root cause analysis," but in reality, planning is something simple. It involves what I sometimes call "strategic planning in action": (1) Assess where you are now—in other words, face reality; (2) decide where you want to wind up; and (3) ponder, brainstorm, and decide the logical steps to getting there. The power of this planning process lies in doing all three steps. Often individuals or groups leave out one step, usually the first.

First, we will look at strategic planning in action for coaching individuals and then for coaching groups.

- *Together Assess "Where We Are Now" with Respect to the Mission.* Michel Renaud, an executive coach in Montreal who has reached levels of mastery in his coaching, says that the only way to create a powerful future is to have a profound understanding of the present—of everything that is working or not working. He calls this "looking the devil in the eye" or facing reality. In this stage of the process, it is important not just to give an arbitrary opinion about someone's performance or development or what is working or not working to date, but rather to back opinions with facts. This could include using things like performance measurement yardsticks, 360-degree feedback, or other tools.

- *Set Stretch Goals That Foster Performance and Development.* Start by setting a few reasonable goals that people can accomplish based on who they are today. Identify some goals to which people can make a contribution and have the experience of winning. Next, set a stretch goal that will really require a superhuman effort. Set a stretch goal that will foster high performance and development at an accelerated rate.

  It is important to frame the stretch goal so that it speaks to people's inner aspirations and needs, in order to ensure their internal commitment. It is also important to show the links between the performance aspects of the goal and the developmental ones. Say, for example, "This stretch assignment will be a catalyst for taking a powerful leadership position in the business. Here are some of the specific ways I think it will help you develop."

- *Identify What's Missing That Will Make a Difference.* Once you set the goals, you will discover in conversation that something is missing. It could be something obvious or it could be something that needs to be discovered. What's missing is different from what's wrong. What's missing could be very tangible, such as technical knowledge and skills, money in the budget, or tools. Or what's missing could be less tangible, such as leadership skills and capabilities needed to meet performance requirements.

1:1 COACHING ACTIVITY
Strategic Planning in Action

Use these steps to assess the coachee's readiness for future planning:

1. Set up a meeting with the person you are coaching, preferably in an informal setting in which you can generate a natural flow of conversation.

2. Review your Personal Coaching Mission—your mandate—and review, if possible, your Performance Excellence Scorecard. (In so doing, you are clearly communicating to the person the business results you have promised to achieve, and setting the stage for making some powerful requests of the person.)

3. Discuss in a general way the person's role and responsibilities on the team and the performance expectations you have of him or her. Make it clear that you will also be discussing the person's developmental needs to reach the goals you have set.

4. The stage is now set to discuss where the person currently is with respect to the performance expectations, as well as where he or she is in terms of development as a leader or manager. Act as a thinking partner, drawing the person out around the following three questions:

   - Where we are now with respect to the mission—or your performance?

   - What would be a stretch goal that would foster your performance and development?

   - What's missing that, if provided, would make a difference?

LESSONS FROM GREAT COACHES

Michel Renaud, the executive coach in Montreal mentioned earlier, told me a story about coaching an entrepreneur and his spouse who were seeking financial independence using the "strategic planning in action" method. The first conversation was about "where are we now." Says Renaud, "I tell people that we are going to look at how things are and whatever comes up about how things are."

"I also tell them that the only way they can act powerfully is to act according to a real understanding of how things are." He tells people in advance that although this conversation will be empowering, it will also be confronting. "There will be both good news and bad news," he tells coachees, "but whether you have the news in front of you or not, it's probably weighing on you. It is stressing you."

Renaud told how he started out by asking Joe, "How much are you spending today?" After some calculation, it turned out that Joe wasn't really aware of his expenses and was in fact spending $30,000 per month. He then asked Joe, "How much are you making?" Again Joe wasn't clear, but after some investigation it turned out he was only making $15,000 a month. His computer consulting service business, which had previously been very successful and had netted him $500,000 in savings, had gone down as a result of market changes. On top of this, Renaud found out that Joe and his wife had only $35,000 in the bank and were about to go bankrupt.

Joe knew he had been living in a dream world, expecting that his business would turn around and that they would get back to normal. As a result, he was in denial about his real situation. In that session, he looked the devil in the eye and faced reality. Says Renaud, "When he left my office that day, both he and his wife were green."

The next conversation involved setting an extraordinary goal. Michel said to Joe, "We need to get clear about what those goals are and to make sure that they are not too big or too small." Joe said he wanted to make something like $700,000 in the next year and $50,000 in the next two months. Renaud responded, "I don't buy that. How are you going to make that, given your starting point? That's pie in the sky. You have some good services, but you don't even have a relevant product." The conversation penetrated Joe's illusion and his tendency to be a victim of hope. Renaud then told him, "Let's choose a goal that gives you a sense of standing in a new future but which is also achievable." Joe chose an outrageous goal of $200,000 for the year or about $16,500 per month.

Michel then addressed what was missing, It is important to point out that what's missing is not what's "wrong." In Joe's case, what was wrong was that he was running out of money and needed cash; what was missing was a way to produce it. Says Renaud, "I asked Joe what he was doing to make money now and he told me he was selling his company's services in computer consulting. He said that, while the company had a strong product in the past, it had lost a lot of its luster due to technological change. It became clear that what was missing was a 'hot' product and sales." Also missing was a staff to help him develop a product. Joe thought he could do it himself, but he couldn't find the time. "When he said that," Renaud said, "I saw that he needed to develop some time management. He also needed to get into action on sales. So we went to work on that."[5]

REFLECTION ASSIGNMENT
Creating a Talent Performance and Development Plan

Take the following steps to create a plan for developing your talent:

1. Think of one of the talented people you decided to invest in a relationship with and coach. Reflect on and sketch out the answers to the following questions.

    *   With respect to your team's mission and general performance expectations, where is that person now? What developmental needs are showing up as the person seeks to reach his or her goals? What issues do you have with the person?

    *   What would be a stretch goal or assignment that would foster this person's performance or development? Think in terms of developmental needs to meet both today's and the future's performance requirements.

    *   Regardless of how well the person is performing today, what would be a meaningful role for him or her in the future? How would the person need to develop to fulfill it?

    *   What's missing that, if provided, would make a difference?

2. Schedule a coaching conversation with the person involved and ask the same questions.

3. Discuss both of your answers until you are in alignment.

4. Do everything you can to assist the person in reaching his or her performance and developmental goals.

STRATEGIC PLANNING IN ACTION FOR GROUPS

As I mentioned earlier, several years ago I spoke with Joan Holmes, executive director of the Hunger Project, an organization that is committed to ending hunger throughout the world but particularly in India and Africa. Joan told me how they apply strategic planning in action in their conferences to end hunger.

I use this example to illustrate how strategic planning in action is done with a large, diverse group. It shows collaboration at a level that most businesspeople are probably not familiar with but that I believe will be absolutely essential in the years ahead as people are faced with more and more complex problems that reach across traditional boundaries. At the same time, the strategic planning in action process can be used very successfully in any group, in any business.

The key to planning goals collaboratively is recognizing that to reach an extraordinary objective it is going to take a group of people. Then the question becomes, "Which group?" To solve problems of higher levels of complexity, the group is usually the work team with which you typically interact. To reach goals that involve the highest levels of complexity, the concept of team needs to be replaced with the concept of collaboration, as it will usually take a group of unlikely collaborators from around the block—or around the world. It is also likely that the group may have to meet virtually. (See the Tom Sudman interview in Chapter Thirteen for tips.)

BEING A CONVENOR

Joan Holmes says, "The greatest part of the work is not what happens at the meeting but what happens before it in convening everybody. This involves investing in relationships with many who are unlikely collaborators."[6]

A Hunger Project conference may include government bureaucrats, nongovernment organization managers, agricultural experts, scientists, artists, businesspeople, and poets, all of whom often have an attitude of polite hostility toward each other. Says John Coonrad, Holmes's chief of staff, "Our first job is to get people to come by speaking to their vision of ending hunger. Once people buy into the possibility of ending hunger and come to the conference, the stage is set for miracles to happen."[7] A shared vision and a focused dialogue begin to pull people beyond individual differences and harness the collective intelligence of the group.

To illustrate this process, I have chosen a Hunger Project initiative in Senegal, Africa.

WHERE WE ARE NOW

The Hunger Project had declared an area of Senegal in Africa a Hunger Free Zone. As part of making this come to pass, they assembled a small team of people in one of the regional villages to plan a conference on ending hunger. In preparation, someone did a complete factual analysis of the condition of chronic hunger and poverty in the region. The report, which was to be presented for discussion, included everything that was working and not working with respect to the possibility of ending hunger.

One of the "what's so" conditions they listed was that even though it is women who often suffer the most from hunger and women who bear primary responsibility for health care, education, and nutrition (90 percent of the farmers in Africa are women), they had never before been involved in any decision-making conferences and had traditionally been left out of leadership roles. Interestingly enough, the night before the conference, one of Holmes's colleagues called the African area manager to say that the women who were invited to the conference were not coming. Never having participated in such a conference, the women believed that they would not be listened to. The Hunger Project considered these women to be an integral part of solving the problem of hunger and, with some convincing, they did attend.

Other current issues the Hunger Project discovered were that the land was becoming a desert and that the young people were leaving the villages for the cities.

Set a specific goal that will keep your mind focused. It is the first step in accomplishment.

OUR EXTRAORDINARY GOAL

Every vision has a goal. The next step in the process, as already mentioned, is to create an extraordinary goal against the background of "what's so." The key is to base your goals on your vision of what's possible and on your individual and collective aspirations, not on your immediate resources. It involves what Holmes calls "making a declaration and belief without evidence." At the same time, the goal cannot be too outrageous in light of what's so. In this case, people at the conference aligned around the goal to end hunger in this area of Senegal. A subgoal was to keep the young people from leaving and moving into the city.

WHAT'S MISSING THAT WOULD MAKE A DIFFERENCE

Once people aligned around the goals, they began to work on distinguishing what is missing that, if provided, would make a difference. One thing missing in this case was women who were involved in the project. The group also discovered that in some cases people had food but did not know how to combine the food in a way that nourished them (such as rice with beans).

It was also discovered that the land would grow certain foods but people did not have the right seeds. So the Hunger Project, at a relatively low expense, brought in a nutritionist who taught people new ways to prepare food, and an agricultural expert to teach them which seeds to plant. They also found an agricultural division of a big company to donate the seeds.

Another thing that was missing was vegetation to protect the soil from erosion. The group came up with the idea of planting fruit trees to protect against soil erosion and to provide irrigation in conjunction with a Swiss nongovernment organization at low cost.

Today this area of Senegal is a successful Hunger Free Zone. The land is green and flourishing, people are no longer hungry, the level of poverty has been affected, and the young people are no longer leaving the rural villages for the cities.

LESSONS FROM GREAT COACHES—ORIENTEERING

A similar kind of process is used for strategic planning in many businesses. For example, Peter Jackson, director of marketing for Royal Insurance, uses a metaphor to describe the strategic planning process. He calls it *orienteering.* Jackson recounted to me, "I am a very simplistic person and I have said many times there is nothing complex about planning. Planning only involves three questions: Where are we now? Where do we need to be? and How the hell are we going to get there? There are all kinds of programs out there to make this simple thing complex when what we really need to do is make the complex simple.

"A good metaphor for it is 'orienteering,' which is like hiking and is a very popular European sport. You go into the woods and say, 'Three valleys over and past all those pine trees is the mountain that I want to get to.' So you set the compass off the mountain and say, 'That's five degrees off of due north,' and you go down into the valley. In the valley, you lose sight of the mountain, but before you start walking you pick a pine tree that is also five degrees off of due north, and you go there. Arriving at the pine tree, you stop and say, 'Where am I now? Where do I want to be and how am I going to get there?' Well, I still want to get to the mountain. How I am going to get there is that I am going to walk to that rock, which is also five degrees off of due north, because I still cannot see the mountain.

"You need to stay the course, until you can see the mountain, making any corrections so that you finally arrive at your destination. But the only way you can get there is to know where you are today. I have observed in all kinds of planning that the very simple, basic problem is that people don't figure out where they are today. Everybody assumes that they know where they are today, and they charge off and lose their way. For example, if I asked you how you drive to Stockbridge and you tell me you get there by going north, I will say, 'No, you get there by going south.' The reason that we have two different points of view is that we will be starting from two different places."[8]

GROUP COACHING ACTIVITY
Strategic Planning in Action

Bring your group together around a positive possibility, a mission, or an area in which you want to have an impact. Make sure that everyone has a shared understanding of what that possibility or mission is and that the people involved have something at stake in achieving it. Make sure that all of the people you believe should be involved are there.

1. Do a "what's so" analysis that determines where you are now. Ask people to come prepared to do a complete factual analysis of the possibility. Look at everything that is working and not working that is pertinent to the possibility. Ask people to take a scientist's view of where they are now, rather than an emotional view. Separate facts from interpretations.

2. Come up with a strategic intent or stretch goal in the group. Choose a stretch goal that has transformational potential and that people are passionate about. Choose a goal that creates a focus.

3. Ask, "What's missing that will make a difference?" Look at what is needed and wanted to reach the goal. Look at what is missing that will produce what is needed and wanted. Focus on the most high-leverage items.

SUMMARY

Whether you are coaching an individual or a group, collaboratively plan goals by asking the following questions:

- Where are we right now in terms of reality?

- What is our strategic intent or extraordinary goal?

- What's missing that, if provided, will make a difference?

CHAPTER NINE

STEP 1.   DEVELOP YOUR COACHING MISSION
           AND A TEACHABLE POINT OF VIEW

STEP 2.   INVEST IN RELATIONSHIPS

STEP 3.   PLAN STRETCH GOALS COLLABORATIVELY

STEP 4.   FORWARD THE ACTION

STEP 5.   PROVIDE FEEDBACK AND LEARNING

The spirit to win and the will to excel are measured one stroke at a time.

STEP 4. FORWARD THE ACTION

Breaking Down What's Missing into Doable Projects and Actions

Once people have faced reality, set goals, and identified what's missing, there is a feeling of optimism. They are standing in the new future they are creating with a coach who believes in them and who can empower them in reaching that future like nobody else can. It is like the beginning of the baseball or opera season, grade nine at school, or a new calendar year. The conversations in people's head are all about possibilities. It is like spring training, the time of year when every team is flushed with the possibility, no matter how remote, of going all the way. It is the time when every play on Broadway will be the next **Les Misérables.** *It is when all our dreams have the potential to come true. Part of the reason for this is that people haven't done anything yet or tried to perform under stress and pressure. Their skills and capabilities have not been tested by reality.*

Our dreams will be dashed and our feelings of hope will be short-lived unless we begin to move from thinking to doing. Soon the grand plan will start to look overwhelming, like something that is hard to fit into all the other things that are happening, such as the fact that the boss has asked you to work on a big customer proposal or you have a week-long conference in Hong Kong, then a sales meeting in Seattle, after which you need to attend your cousin's wedding.

FORWARD THE ACTION

The next step in The Method™ is for the coach to interact with the coachee in a way that forwards the action, taking into account that people are always in the middle of their lives and that there are always lots of other things going on. What we are talking about here is the difference between elaborate strategizing, planning, and preparations and actually making something happen. The job of the coach is to generate action. This often involves looking for a place to start, especially in reaching breakthrough goals or solving complex problems.

Soon after signing on as marketing director of Royal Tire, Reg Stalley walked into a meeting with his staff to discuss the shift from "selling in" tires to coaching customers to "sell out" or getting them off the shelves. He said, "Guys, what we have in front of us is a huge ball of twine that we will eventually unravel, but today I am just looking for a loose end—some place to start. I would like to spend this conversation searching a little while until we find the right place to start. Once we've got that, we will jump into action."

The rest of this chapter will go into more detail about the following four coaching tips for forwarding action. Also listed are the coaching caps to use in this step.

Coaching Tips for Forwarding Action

- Break what's missing into a few small projects.

- Focus on doable steps.

- Encourage people to use action language.

- Review progress: What happened? What's missing? What's next?

Coaching Caps to Use for Planning Stretch Goals Collaboratively

- Put on your Drawing Out Cap to generate options, then put on your Assessment Cap and ask people if they would like a suggestion. (See pages 117 and 122.)

- Put on your Conversation for Action Cap to find the critical path to the result. Use action language to create specific promises and requests. (See page 127.)

BREAK WHAT'S MISSING INTO A FEW SMALL PROJECTS

Now that you have faced reality, set stretch goals, and looked at "what's missing," the question that will naturally arise is, What do we do now? The answer lies in looking at what's missing and breaking it down into small projects and doable actions that, once taken, will result in building momentum and a sense of success.

Start by going back to Step 3—Plan Stretch Goals Collaboratively—and look at all the things that you put down that were missing to reach the goal. If you are working on a breakthrough goal, the more complex the problem is, the longer will be your list of things that are missing. The idea is not to try to do everything at once, but rather to select from that list those things that are the most high-leverage in reaching your goals, and then to transform them into small projects that will allow you to spearhead a larger breakthrough.

Let's say, for example, that you are coaching an executive whose goal is to develop the top talent of your organization in order to fill the leadership positions here and around the world. Let's assume that without these leadership positions being filled your company will not be able to seize the growth opportunities that are in front of it. In effect, there is a high level of urgency to meeting this goal. Now let's look at all the things that are missing that could make a difference.

1. A talent marketing strategy to bring in people from outside

2. Internal leaders involved in coaching and teaching other leaders

3. Ways to link business strategy to leadership development

4. Leadership courses offered at your corporate university or business school

5. More people who have been developed through adverse and diverse experiences

6. A more effective 360-degree feedback program for all managers

7. A mentoring program to develop and retain your present staff

8. Professional coaches for high flyers in your company

9. The latest leadership books available for managers.

Although some or all of these things might be missing in the leadership supply process, the question is, Which of these things could executives turn into a small project that they could take action on in weeks, not months? Which things on the list would provide the most high-leverage results and are doable? Which of the things on the list could be started in a small way and then used to build momentum in other areas? Again, the idea is not to try to unravel the whole ball of twine but rather to find a place to start.

LESSONS FROM GREAT COACHES—COACHING ONE-TO-ONE

Michel Renaud coached Joe, the entrepreneur from the last chapter who had few sales and poor products and was running out of cash, to address everything that was missing. He asked questions like, Who is your customer? Which of your products will give you a future that is stable and powerful? What is your marketing material like? Renaud then coached Joe to break down what he needed to do into projects, approaches, and doable actions that would build momentum.

According to Renaud, "First, I attacked the issue of the product because I knew if he did something powerful here it would sustain his image of a new future. It involved designing a new computer training program. I told him, 'Set aside two hours in your agenda and write the first draft of the first module.' I made it clear that I wasn't going to meet with him the following week unless this was done, as it would serve no purpose. He came to the meeting with a totally different energy." Joe had written two modules.

Renaud continued, "I also said, 'Okay, you want to make $100,000 in sales. That's ten clients at $20,000 each.' Then I asked, 'Who are you going to call?' and he got a bit scared and overwhelmed. I said, 'I think we can accomplish this with just twenty conversations a week.'" Joe agreed that was doable, so Renaud coached him to list his twenty best prospects, call them, and make four appointments for the following week. Each day Joe was to call other prospects and make more appointments, so that when he had finished his initial round of meetings and had made one sale, he would have sixteen more appointments set up. Renaud explained to me, "I knew Joe might not make a sale and that this could lead to him getting discouraged or paralyzed, so we prepared a next step." The next week Joe closed not one but seven new sales.[1]

PRACTICE ASSIGNMENT

Forwarding Action

The following steps will help you to forward the action.

1. Think about the goals of one of the people you are coaching.

2. Write down the list of everything you see as missing for that person reaching the goal.

3. Select from the list those things that are missing that are the most high-leverage.

4. See which thing the people you coach could transform into a small project.

5. Ask yourself whether you are willing to coach them on that project.

Design small projects to spearhead a larger breakthrough. A breakthrough project is an excellent way to make a dent in a larger goal. I call it "spearheading" a breakthrough. It involves taking a look at what's missing that's high-leverage and providing that by breaking it into a project. In a breakthrough project, you start small to do big. It is important to accomplish something significant in a short period—weeks, not months. The idea is to create a success and then expand that into a widening circle of successes.

I sometimes refer to this as the Breakthrough Technique and I wrote about it in *Masterful Coaching.*[2] It is an extraordinary tool for leaders at all levels to generate momentum in a larger project with a group. Here are some excerpts:

Get people to focus on what they can do with their existing authority, resources, change readiness. Instead of people saying, "That's not realistic," or "We tried that," you want people to say, "This is what we have all been waiting for!" Just as important, if not more so, is to have people focus on what they can do with existing resources and authority.

Most groups say they would like to get better results, but they often start out with the same statement: "but first . . . ." This usually means the boss has to change, they need a bigger budget, or the corporate culture has to be transformed. The coach has to have the confidence to say, "Yes, I can see how getting all of those things sorted out might lead to better results, but possibly there are some things that you can do on your own."

Define a project to get started based on some razor-sharp goals. Although it is important to keep the larger mission or stretch goal in mind, the next step is to suggest that people select something from "what's missing" to turn into a small project. Which one of the things that the individual or team has identified would they most like to try? Where could they make the most progress with the least amount of effort? This is not just to get people to do something but to have them break out of the "I can't" mind-set and into the mind-set "I can." It is important to create some razor-sharp goals that are challenging but attainable.

Produce results in weeks, not months. After this kind of dialogue, the coach might ask the team to select a concrete first-step goal that could be achieved in a matter of weeks. The very act of carving off something that they can commit to, where success is near and clear, and not giving themselves any "outs" creates a bit of excitement. Team members will look at one another like they are about to invest themselves in something that they know will require initiative and risk.

Each success leads to a widening circle of successes. An early success will build momentum, creating additional readiness for change. People will then feel ready to set new, more challenging breakthrough goals. To encourage people to greater heights, a coach might well say, "You know, that product improvement is something our customers will appreciate; it gives me an idea of how we can do the same thing across the whole product range."

Elicit commitment, passion, and zeal by building in "zest factors." The breakthrough technique is based on designing each project for success. These automatically elicit the fun and excitement of high-performance teams. They include

- A sense of challenge and risk

- Urgency

- Near and clear success

- Cutting through bureaucracy

- Fun and excitement

The greatest potential to affect desired results is to exist at the point where action takes place.

In *Masterful Coaching* I also described an implementation technique. Excerpts follow.

The Four-Step Breakthrough Technique—Implementation Model.

1. *Find a sponsor who identifies a performance opportunity.* The sponsor takes a stand for the opportunity and brings a team together, giving the team the confidence to skip up and down levels or move across traditional functional boundaries to get the job done. The sponsor

   - Identifies what performance is today

   - Presents the opportunity for a team to see whether they want to go for it

   - Reviews team's short-term goals and work plan and removes obstacles

2. *Choose a team leader and team.* Team members are selected based on their knowledge and capabilities, not on their personalities or status. Team leader and member qualities

   - Have a proven record of performance

   - Know how to get along with people

   - Treat everyone on the team as a colleague

   - Have demonstrated necessary and relevant knowledge and capabilities

3. *Design a breakthrough project by creating an urgent, short-term goal.* The next step involves setting a goal that is clear-cut and attainable, as well as one that represents a significant step up in performance. The goal must be

- Razor sharp and measurable

- Accomplished in two to twelve weeks

- Have clear conditions of success—who, what, by when

4. *Convene a one-day kick-off session and coaching follow-up.* During the kick-off day, the coach helps the team create a written work plan. The coach then meets with the team on the second, fifth, and eighth weeks to see if the project is on track. After the project is completed, the coach meets with the team to harvest the insights that have been gained and to see how they could be applied to expanding the scope of the project or to institutionalizing the success that has been achieved. The coach

- Makes sure goals are razor sharp

- Assists in creating the work plan

- Ensures that the work plan includes diverse views and perspectives

- Monitors progress in weeks two and five

- Harvests opportunities with the team in week eight

GROUP COACHING ACTIVITY
Designing Breakthrough Projects

After your group has done the strategic planning in action and come up with a strategic intent or goal and discovered what is missing, bring the group together to design some breakthrough projects. Do the following:

1. Design a few breakthrough projects that represent some high-leverage areas and that will help provide what is missing.

2. Pick projects with an eight-week to twelve-week completion time.

3. Put together the project team and leader.

4. Design a work plan with accountabilities.

5. Meet every two weeks with the teams to monitor progress.

LESSONS FROM GREAT COACHES—COACHING TEAMS

Tom Kaiser is the president of a Zurich American Insurance Strategic Business Unit called International Accounts. Kaiser is a masterful coach who exudes positive energy and optimism that is contagious. He also treats every person on his staff as a colleague and expects that the person makes a powerful contribution. People who work for him soon start to believe that both they and the team can win, and Kaiser has developed a coachable system that is bankable. He likes to bypass elaborate planning and focus on the real mission.

Kaiser observed early in his career that so much time was spent in making mission statements and complex planning that people would get lost in the process and forget what the real mission was. So he developed a coachable point of view that was contrarian. "I break complexity down into very small, bite-sized pieces that people can readily understand. The first thing I talk to people about is a very simple concept: business is all about getting and keeping customers at a profit.

"It is great to have a vision that sounds good, like 'We will be the best of the best.' But what does that mean? It is hard for people to focus on that on a day-by-day basis. But when I say to people, 'Okay, getting customers—what does that mean?' They intuitively know it means targeting, planning, following through. So out of the simple idea of 'getting customers,' intuitively come all of those things that are written about in management books. It is not a plan but a protocol for action, something to focus on today. Then there's the retention side of it. You are not going to grow a business profitably unless you retain the customers at a profit."

Kaiser believes that he should "never waste a lunch. I take key people from the business out to a restaurant and talk to them for two hours about whether they are doing the things that are basic. For example, if they say, 'I have a population of five hundred possible customers,' I say, 'Let's break it down into something manageable. Who are the ones who are most likely to buy? Who are the best fits, based on the quality of the company and the buying habits of the buyers?' After that I talk to them about targeting. I work with people to come up with an individual plan about how we are going to go after a certain piece of business. First, I listen to their ideas, then I add value from my own perspective.

"Then I might talk about what they are doing to invest in relationships with the buyer and develop a compelling sales message. I act as a sounding board, assisting them in coming up with ideas to build the relationship, and honing their message. I often tell people that generally the first year you work on a client you are not going to be successful, but if you keep calling on that client over a three-year period, you will develop an unbelievable conversion rate.

"One of the biggest mistakes people make in sales is that they are so focused on getting the order that if they don't make the sale the first time they never go back and take advantage of the fact that they have built goodwill with that customer. Instead, they tend to narrow their market to those customers they can be successful with, or they get paralyzed and head for the bunkers. They stop taking action. My focus is to keep people in action by creating a successful road map for them to follow and identifying the high-leverage steps they can take."[3]

You can't manage the scoreboard. You can only manage what people do.

FOCUS ON DOABLE STEPS

You can't manage the scoreboard. A coach can work with people to set stretch goals but cannot simply point to the scoreboard in the heat of the game and say, "Make the score go up." To do this is to set expectations that not only will overwhelm people but also will doom them to failure because they may not know what to do to make the score go up. A masterful coach realizes that although people can't manage the scoreboard, they *can* manage what they do. This means looking at the goal or project and asking, "What in this is doable?" In breaking things down and identifying what is doable, the coach creates an opening for action.

I spoke to John Reingold, who at the time was leading a group at Microsoft responsible for the development of Microsoft's project management software. Reingold and his team had been very ambitious in redesigning the product. To achieve the goals of making the software usable, they rewrote large sections of the product and fundamentally changed the way it worked, creating a lot of instability.

As they began to test the software, Reingold and his team discovered hundreds of bugs. As they fixed one bug, another would pop up; soon the number became overwhelming and morale began to fall. Reingold came up with the idea of fixing the old bugs first. He created a project called "zero old bugs" by a certain date, which was seen as doable. Then new bugs were less overwhelming to deal with and they made their release date.[4]

> **Obstacles are the frightful things you see when you take your eyes off the goal.**

It is essential to stay focused on doing the things that represent the critical success factors for the individual or the group. It is very easy for most people to become sidetracked and lose their way. A scorecard can be an extraordinary tool for supporting people in creating a focus. Let's go back to Renaud as he coaches Joe: "Okay, one project is to have a successful preview seminar with at least ten potential customers of your new computer training program. To do that, you need to talk to twenty to twenty-five people. That's just four conversations a day. Is that doable?" This is the perfect opportunity to set up a scorecard using a large index card. Each day Joe creates four categories on his card: (1) people called, (2) how conversation went, (3) outcome, and (4) learning. This sounds simplistic, but it works amazingly well. The scorecard keeps people doing the things they are supposed to do—and good things do happen.

1:1 COACHING ACTIVITY

Developing a Review Sheet
Based on Success

Work with the person you are coaching to select a key goal or project. Break it down into doable actions. Have the coachee use the following scorecard to track progress. (This process can also be done with a group.)

Date: _____   Key goal or project: _____

Daily action 1 _____

Outcome _____

Learning _____

Daily action 2 _____

Outcome _____

Learning _____

Daily action 3 _____

Outcome _____

Learning _____

Daily action 4 _____

Outcome _____

Learning _____

Daily action 5 _____

Outcome _____

Learning _____

Empower, don't manage. I have observed that although most people enjoy being coached or empowered, they abhor having someone hovering over them and managing them. To be sure, there is nothing more irritating than someone who is always catching people dropping something out or doing something wrong. Coaches are responsible for empowering people to take successful action by nurturing positive thinking and identifying high-leverage actions. The coach is *not* responsible for managing people's days or checking up on them to make sure they are doing the things they need to do. When you are managing people's time or day-to-day actions, you are not coaching.

ENCOURAGE PEOPLE TO USE ACTION LANGUAGE

After you have broken down what's missing into a few small projects and identified some doable steps, what is required next is for people actually to commit to doing something. A powerful tool for making sure something will actually happen is to encourage people to use *action language*. There is a type of language that leads to action, and another type of language that leaves people sitting on the fence.

Coaching people to use action language starts with getting them to speak their commitments. This means that after you have clarified what a goal or project might be or the steps that people might take, you now have to listen for whether people are willing to speak their commitment to take action on something or whether they hem and haw. Generally, the more sincere people's commitments are, the more action will follow. The less sincere their commitments are, the more you will hear reasons and excuses later on.

Getting people to speak their commitments—promises versus predictions. For example, there is a difference between someone saying, "I *promise* to do this project or take these steps" and someone saying, "I will try," "It all depends," or "That's a definite maybe." Also, the coach has to listen not only for whether people are making a sincere promise but also for the explicit conditions of satisfaction that go along with it—what exactly are they agreeing to do and not to do? If when I'm coaching someone I hear him or her making an insincere promise, or if I hear the person being vague about what he or she will actually deliver on, I stop the conversation and say something like, "I don't understand what you are saying."

Making requests versus complaints. As a coach whose job it is to empower people to produce breakthrough results, you are often in the position of pushing people past where they stop. This means you have to be able to make powerful requests of people. Recall the story about Jack Welch when he discovered that GE CAT-scan tubes produced only half as many scans as the competition. He made a powerful request to the manager in charge of the CAT-scan tube business to not only double but triple the number of scans the tube could produce. Then he coached him on a weekly basis to forward the action.

It is also extremely important to encourage coachees to make powerful requests of others rather than just complain. For example, many managers complain that they don't get the quality of coaching they want, but they never go and make a power request to someone who can give it to them.

Offers versus wishes. There's a big difference between wishing you had more talented people on your team and looking those people up and making them an offer they cannot refuse. Similarly, there is a difference between people you are coaching telling you they "wish" they had a more meaningful role in the organization and people identifying an opportunity and going to the appropriate person and offering their services.

Is there power in the person's speaking? This is something you can immediately pick up on. You can tell who people are from what they are saying and whether or not they will be able to create a new future, have an impact on their world, or energize others. In most cases, these people will be using action language—declaring possibilities, making powerful promises and requests. By contrast, you can also tell when someone comes to you and there is no power in his or her speaking. You can tell that the person will probably be in the same place months from now, having little impact and driving others away. Their speaking is usually a string of "definite maybes," wishful thinking, and endless complaints.

In coaching others, one of the most effective tools you will have for empowering people to act is to support them in transforming tales of resignation into declarations of possibility, predictions into promises, complaints into requests, and hopes, wishes, and dreams into offers. This can have a powerful and immediate impact not only with individuals but also with a group.

I can remember doing a team-building session with Adidas. The managers in one unit said they were resigned to being beaten by the competition, who had a larger advertising budget. At the same time they seemed to hedge on promises and complain endlessly about each other's departments. This was resulting in low morale and a lot of lost energy. It was clear that the team-building session would be a disaster unless people started speaking in a different way.

So I intervened and said, "New ground rule: Don't say another word unless it is a declaration of possibility, a promise, a request, or an offer." In thirty minutes or less this had an amazing impact on both individuals and the group. It totally transformed the way people in the group interacted with one another and the results they were able to produce.

REFLECTION ASSIGNMENT

Using Action Language

Try using action language to get results from coachees.

1.   When do you need to hold someone accountable to a promise they made? When will you talk to them?

2.   Where do you need to coach people on making promises? When will you talk to them?

REVIEW PROGRESS: WHAT HAPPENED? WHAT'S MISSING? WHAT'S NEXT?

As people begin to take action on their projects, they may discover that things have changed and that the plan needs to be adjusted. At the same time, people may not always be successful in taking effective action and may wind up with unintended results. Or the team may have stayed on course for a while with the direction that was set but that has now started to drift.

In effect, the coaching doesn't end at the planning stage; it begins there. Though this seems glaringly obvious, it is actually the opposite of what many managers do, especially those who rely on management by objectives; in other words, "Here's the goal, come back and see me at the end of the year." Perhaps the most important part of the coach's job is to coach people in action as they move from planning to execution. To do that, a cultural clearing needs to be created in which people understand the coach's intervention to be support, not interference.

Thus, the next part of The Method™ is to establish a protocol for being able to review the progress the individual or group has made, assessing breakthroughs, as well as breakdowns. To keep it simple, I use a weekly coaching protocol that involves asking three questions: "What happened? What's missing? What's next?"

For example, I might say to an individual, "What happened since we last talked?" Are people doing what they said they were going to do, when they said they were going to do it? If results are not what I expected, the next question I ask myself or the person is, "What's missing that, if provided, would make a difference?" If someone is stuck or ineffective, pondering this question can lead to new ideas, fresh approaches, and innovative solutions. Then, once both the person I am coaching and I are clear about this, I ask, "What's next?" which is a question designed to get people back into action. The following paragraphs take a closer look at these questions.

Weekly Coaching Protocol

1. What happened?

2. What's missing?

3. What's next?

WHAT HAPPENED?

Once people start to take action, virtually anything can happen, but one thing that you can usually expect is change. I call this the "hour of the unexpected." There can be a shift in the strategic plan of the organization, the competition may have made inroads with a key customer, or the other department of the organization that was expected to cooperate may seem not to be cooperating at all. At the same time, the team that the individual is working on may be coming apart at the seams. Finally, the individual you are coaching, and with whom you spend so much time working out projects and action steps, may have done absolutely nothing.

For example, Michel Renaud told about an entrepreneur he was coaching who made an agreement about accomplishing something and broke that agreement three times: "Each time he broke the agreement, I asked him, 'What happened?' The first time, he gave me a reason, the next time, an excuse. I sensed something was off but I didn't say much because I didn't want to become his manager. The third time it happened, however, I knew I had to go further. I said, 'Something is missing. What is it?'"

As Jimmy Ballard, a great golf coach who coached Curtis Strange in his two U.S. Open victories, once told me, it is easy to find the fault, it is harder to find the cure. In other words, as soon as the coach recognizes that there are unintended results, he or she must then investigate what will allow people to adjust their actions and produce intended results for the first time.

WHAT'S MISSING?

I have discovered that asking the question, "What's missing?" provides a much more powerful framework for this investigation than "What's wrong?" The question, "What's missing that, if provided, would make a difference?" leads to new openings for possibility and action, whereas the question, "What's wrong?" tends to result in dwelling on what happened or often leaves people stuck in despair. It also tends to evoke feelings of blame, shame, or guilt.

Quite often, if people are not taking the doable actions they agreed to, the first thing to look at in terms of what's missing is if there is a sense of ownership. The first thing I look to is whether or not I, as a coach, have "polluted the goals," meaning I found them exciting or thought they made logical sense but they didn't really mean enough to the coachee to call him or her to action. In this case, what's missing might be to adjust the goals.

The next thing I look at in terms of what's missing is whether the approach that was offered fits the coachee's personal style. For example, if you have suggested that someone market his or her product by making a lot of sales calls and the person equates selling to begging, there is a good chance that the problem lies in the approach. What's missing in this case might be supporting the person in breaking through fear or more realistically trying a different approach—in this case of business development, direct mail.

Let me add that in many cases the question, "What's missing?" requires more than simply adjusting people's goals, approach, or action. For example, it may require the coach to help people to view things from a new angle so that they can see new openings for successful action that they didn't see before. Or it may require a deeper level of feedback about who people are in the world—their thinking or attitudes. Or it may mean dealing with the upset that someone has about what someone else said or did and getting them back into action. This often involves helping them look at what happened in a way that is more inspiring, empowering, and accurate—as opposed to invalidating.

WHAT'S NEXT?

Once you discover what's missing, the next step is to take whatever actions are necessary to produce what's missing by asking, "What's next?" The idea here is not only to adjust goals and the approach so as to get people on the right track, but also to get them back into action. There is always a next step that can be identified at this point—again, a small, doable step or series of steps that people can act on.

1:1 COACHING ACTIVITY

What's Next?

Have a coaching session with someone you believe is stuck or having some trouble accomplishing what needs to be accomplished. Use the following protocol to guide your interaction:

1. What is happening?

2. What is missing that will make a difference?

3. What's next?

SUMMARY

• Break what's missing into a few small projects.

• Build good work habits based on doable steps.

• Encourage others to use action language.

• On a weekly basis ask, "What happened? What's missing? What's next?"

CHAPTER TEN

STEP 1.	DEVELOP YOUR COACHING MISSION AND A TEACHABLE POINT OF VIEW
STEP 2.	INVEST IN RELATIONSHIPS
STEP 3.	PLAN STRETCH GOALS COLLABORATIVELY
STEP 4.	FORWARD THE ACTION
STEP 5.	**PROVIDE FEEDBACK AND LEARNING**

Make sure feedback is around every corner.

STEP 5. PROVIDE FEEDBACK AND LEARNING

Framing Feedback So That It Stretches, Corrects, and Builds Self-Esteem

Someone once asked the legendary Ted Williams of the Boston Red Sox about goals. Williams said, "It is important to have lifetime goals, not just weekly and daily ones. Mine is to have people say, 'There goes Ted Williams, the greatest hitter who ever lived.'" Williams took action on his goals every day in the batting cage at Boston's Fenway Park and was the last player to bat .400 for the season. What's not commonly known about Williams is how open he was to feedback.

I am not going to coach you on a million things. I am going to coach you on the one or two things that can make a difference to you.

He frequently invited the best hitters from his own and opposing teams to watch him hit balls and to give him some ideas on how he could do better. He would take whatever tips they had to offer.[1] This story captures the essence of this chapter.

FEEDBACK AND LEARNING

Thus far, we have set aspirations, planned, and forwarded action. The next step in Masterful Coaching—The Method™ is to observe people as they make committed attempts to perform, and then to assess what happens. It is inevitable that when people are committed to high performance, there will be breakdowns in the action. Coaching is a committed attempt to anticipate these breakdowns and to intervene with the individual or group so as to produce intended results.

The role of a coach is to step back from the front lines and the heat of the action and be a different kind of observer than anyone can be "on the field." No matter how much talent you and I have, we cannot see ourselves as others see us, or detect and correct our own errors. The coach's observations and assessments provide feedback that allows people to eliminate the breakdowns and take successful action.

Coaching Tips for Providing Meaningful Feedback and Learning

- Be courageous, compassionate, and relentless.

- Frame feedback so that it stretches, affirms, and corrects.

- Encourage learning while working.

- Customize challenging experiences that promote accelerated development.

Coaching Caps to Use for Feedback and Learning

- Put on the Declaring Possibilities Cap to affirm people. (See page 115.)

- Put on the Making Assessments Cap to determine where people are now in relationship to their goals. (See page 117.)

- Put on the Reframing Cap to support people in being able to think or act differently. (See page 125.)

When people change how they are being, it automatically alters what they are doing.

BE COURAGEOUS, COMPASSIONATE, AND RELENTLESS

The most powerful feedback is given in the context of coaching people to fulfill their dreams and aspirations, especially when it involves achieving extraordinary and tangible results. Coaching people to produce an extraordinary and tangible result requires feedback that is more powerful than that given in annual reviews held behind locked doors. It involves something more than the usual 360-degree feedback—more than the same predictable questions and the same predictable answers.

A masterful coach provides feedback with a commitment to producing breakthroughs in results and breakthroughs for people. This involves going beyond conventional wisdom as well as conventional practices. It may involve coaching people in a way that reminds them of their possibilities or it may mean leaving them in despair about current reality. It may involve speaking loudly or softly, or providing feedback that is tough or compassionate. It may involve being deadly serious or using crazy wisdom.

Some managers may not understand where the masterful coach is coming from and say, "I don't like your style." These managers often have no idea what it takes to coach others to be extraordinary. I have often seen managers whose intention to "look good" is so strong it displaces their intention to "be good" or to produce results. They tend to be more concerned with style than with substance, more concerned with political correctness than with speaking with openness and candor, more concerned with reasonableness than with coaching people to take bold and unreasonable action.

Some of these people have natural ability as coaches, but it is never utilized because of their considerations: "I don't believe in raising my voice," "I need to be nice," or "I need to be tough." What's worse is that they inflict these considerations on others in their environment.

Whenever you see leaders who *are* capable of coaching people to get extraordinary results, they don't follow the rules. For example, many would consider Ben Zander, Bill Gates, or Bill Parcells crazy or fanatical.

What are the implications for you? Discovering your own ability to be a masterful coach may involve a shift in who you are being, not just in what you are doing with respect to providing feedback and learning. It is not just a matter of technique. You will never be able to expand people's capacity to produce extraordinary results if you are stuck in *being* ordinary (settling for less of yourself and others), *being* polite, and *being* reasonable.

Again, this requires a "transformation," not a "change," a leap, not a step. Let's say you're playing it safe by not setting high goals for others and by carefully watching what you say in coaching conversations. Then you receive some 360-degree feedback about this and you start playing a little bit less safe, and then less and less. That's a "change"—step-by-step.

Then imagine that one day you have a conversation with a mentor and you talk about the feedback people are giving you about playing it safe. The mentor helps you get to some underlying beliefs that tell you that in order to succeed you should play to avoid losing rather than play to win. With your mentor's help, you get in touch with various times in your life when you used this approach to protect yourself. The mentor helps you to see that your world is a shadow of what it could be.

You feel a gut-wrenching pull of regret for playing so "small" in your life and you make a commitment to go for what you want. Something transformational has happened, and you make a leap in regard to your ability to be at risk. You find yourself daring to dream big dreams not only for yourself but also for others. You find yourself being relentless in your ability to hold up a standard, courageous in your speaking and listening. You find yourself being truly compassionate with people about what they need to go through to fulfill their own possibilities. To sum it up, by transforming how we are as coaches, we also transform what we do. We become able to enter into coaching conversations with others that allow them to discover who they are and what they are magnificently capable of. These conversations are not just conversations about possibility (pie in the sky); they are about action aimed at accomplishing extraordinary and tangible results.

In many ways these conversations are like a dance in which the coach and coachee respond to one another against the music of the background situation. Each step the coachee takes reveals something—either a smooth, harmonious movement or an awkward, interrupted pattern. Each misstep becomes an opportunity for the coach to provide feedback that alters the person's way of being and calls for the action that is needed.

LESSONS FROM GREAT COACHES—BENJAMIN ZANDER HAS A DREAM

Benjamin Zander's dream includes putting a recording of Beethoven's Fifth Symphony into the hands of every man, woman, and child in the world. Zander, the much admired conductor of the Boston Philharmonic, enjoys the distinction of being the only conductor who leads an orchestra that was created expressly for him.

Previously the conductor of the Boston Civic Orchestra, Zander was let go for insisting on playing music that was "too difficult"—namely, that of Gustav Mahler and Anton Bruckner. The entire orchestra resigned in protest and formed the Philharmonic, where Zander has been for the last thirty years.

Zander possesses some of the qualities of a masterful coach and teacher. He has the proven capability to take talented young musicians and transform them into shining stars and to inspire audiences at his preconcert appearances to choose to live their personal and professional lives consistent with their real possibilities.

I called Zander to talk to him about our mutual passion for coaching and teaching. He invited me to attend one of his classes for graduate students in Brown Hall at the New England Conservatory of Music. Zander is passionately holding out the possibility that each of the students in the room will become a great musician, suggesting that they radiate that possibility from this day forward rather than see themselves on the rung of a classical career ladder. Most of the students had not yet learned to express fully in the music who they are, even though they are technically excellent.

Zander believes that a leader should never doubt the capacity of those he leads to realize the possibilities he has dreamed for them. The combination of his personal commitment to making those possibilities a reality, his let's-get-to-work attitude, and the relentless but compassionate commentary he gives as people perform their pieces produces transformational results.

On the day I visited, Zander started the class with a special message for Lukasch, a cello player. Zander explained, "At the end of the last class, Lukasch played very, very beautifully. Later in the car, Vikram Savkar [Zander's assistant] commented to me that Lukasch gave everything to the performance except himself."

Zander then pointed to the blackboard that he had divided in half by a white line, on either side of which he had written contrasting words that represent different ways of being. The words on the left side described the place from which many of us live our lives: *ambition, competition, comparing ourselves with others, feeling cornered, being comfortable,* and *being observers.* On the right side were written the words *full self-expression, being joyous, passionate, loving, engaged,* and *participating 101 percent.*

"Lukasch." Zander focused on the student. "Please play again, except this time give yourself to the piece." Lukasch picked up his bow and started to play. He looked scared and stiff, but Zander interrupted and said, "Ask for some comments from the group." People tried to be encouraging, but one woman responded, "I don't know what to say." Zander said smilingly, "That's your problem, Lukasch. You are not reaching her. At the same time, I know you have it in you to do so."

Zander, who stands for what's possible for people, is entirely capable of telling it like it is. He is alternatively tough-minded and loving, even physical with his students. "Please look up at that board, Lukasch," he said, pointing to the words on the left side (*not fully expressed*). "You see, from where we normally stand, we can't play Bach. When we play music from over here [pointing to the right], from passion, from courage, there is no doubt in people's minds."

He asked Lukasch, "Tell me what is on your mind before you give a performance." Lukasch answered three things, each of which is technical. "Lukasch, if I wanted to give a great performance, I wouldn't be thinking about any of those things. I would think about being spiritually alive. I would think about reaching people with my passion, the beauty of the music."

Lukasch tried again, but the inspiration Zander was looking for was still not there and he stopped the performance after a few bars, addressing Lukasch and the entire class with his teachable point of view. "Look, right now, you are a great professional musician. Even today you could get a job with a major symphony orchestra making a healthy living. You could get a little house with a white fence around it. But Bach didn't write his music for people who wanted to play it safe. He wrote it for the glory of God, so that people could experience what it is to be spiritually alive in the adventure that we call life."

Lukasch smiled and picked up the cello to play again, not waiting to be asked. Suddenly, there was light in Lukasch's eyes and his entire face became radiant. His body began to follow the shape of the music and suddenly the music was liberated, soaring as if in flight.

The class burst into applause. "That was the difference between playing notes perfectly and truly understanding and projecting the meaning of music. What you just did was a transformation. Not an incremental step, but a leap."[2]

REFLECTION ASSIGNMENT

How Do You Have to Be?

1. How do you need to "be" different to give feedback so that it has an impact on people? For example: more courageous, supportive, challenging, or relentless?

2. To whom have you avoided giving feedback? What do you need to say to the person? When will you do so?

FRAME FEEDBACK SO THAT IT STRETCHES, AFFIRMS, AND CREATES

Let's look at how to prepare for feedback before looking at the issue of how to frame it. Preparation starts with assessing where people are going, where they are now, and how they need to adjust. A masterful coach always begins with the end in mind: (1) realizing what's really possible for people in terms of their aspirations, (2) achieving an extraordinary and tangible result, and (3) mastering a particular discipline or skill. If coaching is not grounded in specific accomplishments, it tends to become meaningless. Research with thousands of managers at all levels of organizations and from all walks of life shows that results-oriented coaching consistently produces more satisfying outcomes for coach and coachee than behaviorally oriented coaching.

Making an Assessment. Once you establish people's desired destinations, carefully observe them in action and assess whether they are on course. If you determine that people are off course, it is important that you assess what needs to be altered in order for them to adjust. There are three questions I ask at this stage, beginning with the end in mind and taking into account where we are now: (1) How does the person need to be different? (2) How does the person need to think differently? (3) How does the person need to act differently? (See the triple loop learning model in Chapter One, page 22.)

Communicate with just enough edge to remove the blinders from people's eyes.

Creating the Opening for Coaching. In preparing to give feedback, it is important to consider (1) your own tendency to avoid giving people honest feedback, and (2) what Fernando Flores, the Chilean business guru and linguistic philosopher, calls the "phenomenon of blindness." People often see unintended results and see how others contribute to unintended results, but they *do not see how they themselves contribute to them.* Give people the kind of straightforward feedback that will allow them to see how they contributed to unintended results.

This often requires moving beyond the usual social virtues and speaking with enough edge to penetrate people's illusions. You communicate in this way out of your love and respect for people, not because you do not love them or respect them. René Jaeggi, Adidas chairman, was once a student of a judo master in Japan who frequently told him, "I love you, so I have to hurt you," before delivering some very blunt feedback.[3]

 Never forget that the person you are coaching is a human being.

Frame Feedback as a Gift. Why do some leaders give people feedback in a way that brings out the best in them, while others give feedback in a way that brings out the worst? Why do some people give feedback in a way that others gladly accept, while others only put people off? The answer has to do with how they frame the feedback they give. Masterful coaches I have observed in business, sports, and the performing arts consciously and intentionally frame their feedback, and there is a pattern to it. They also tend to provide the feedback in a conversational manner after looking for openings. The following tips for giving effective feedback are explained in more detail in the coming section.

Coaching Tips for Framing Feedback

1. State the person's name and offer coaching feedback. Make it clear that it is the person's decision as to whether or not to receive the feedback right now. Also, it is the person's decision as to whether or not to agree or disagree with the feedback or do something with it.

2. Affirm people's possibilities and talents, and what's working. Start your feedback by positively affirming what's really possible based on the person's talents and gifts. Also assess

what the person is doing that is working with respect to the goals. This sets the stage for offering corrective feedback.

3. Point out one or two things to correct that will make a difference. This is because people can focus on improving only one or two things at a time. Also, frame feedback in a way that is goal oriented, not evaluative. For example, "To reach your goal of [fill in], here's one thing I see that is missing," or "Here's what I see that is working [or not working]," not "Here's what you are doing wrong."

4. Stretch people by giving them a star to shoot for. After talking honestly about problems with as much edge as necessary to reach the person, refocus on new images of aspiration that will inspire the person to make necessary adjustments. Look at further actions the person can take to make these adjustments a reality.

5. End by saying "Thank you" and "You're welcome." This may seem obvious, but it is the step that most people overlook and it is an important piece in bringing the conversation to closure.

Note: It is not necessary to do these steps in the exact order given. For instance, if you want to have more edge in order to get through to someone, give the correction first and the affirmation after.

Always speak in a way that empowers rather than diminishes.

GROUP COACHING ACTIVITY

The Hot Seat

This activity is very good when you want the group members to create stronger relationships with one another and when you believe that the communication in the group needs to be more honest so they can work in a more productive way. We have noticed that the productivity of groups skyrockets after doing

this activity. To start the exercise, have the group gather around a table in a room that is fairly private. One person sits in the "hot seat" and the rest of the group (one person at a time) gives that person feedback using *exactly* **the following protocol:**

1. One thing I appreciate about you is. . . .

2. Where I have difficulty with you is. . . . (or one area in which I could see an improvement is. . . .)

3. What I would like to create with you is. . . .

The person receiving the feedback just listens (whether agreeing or disagreeing) and does not respond. When everyone has finished, the person who received the feedback can make a comment, not justifying or explaining the feedback but letting people know that it was heard: "I heard what you said," or "Thanks for the feedback."

This exercise takes some time, depending on the number of people involved. Your job as the coach is to see that people do not rush through the exercise because they are uncomfortable, and that there is a good quality of listening. The atmosphere should be respectful, without joking that might be intended to deflect the feedback.

LESSONS FROM GREAT COACHES—RICHARD PERRY'S BEST TEAM PLAYER

Richard Perry from Peregrine Design Group told me that a goal he had when he came to his company was to develop a coaching style that would make people want to be in his department. He shared with me a story about one of his coaching successes: "The only way to be the kind of coach I wanted to be was to develop relationships with people in which I was not just their boss but a partner and coach. I had read in *Masterful Coaching* about the importance of giving people the gift of your presence. To me this meant engaging in dialogue with people and really listening to them. Second, it meant to give them a courageous response, if I disagreed or had some honest feedback that I wanted to give them to make it possible for them to succeed.

"A manager is always being presented with what you call 'coachable moments' that we can either seize or let go by. It is very easy to let these go by because giving people a courageous response can be uncomfortable. So much of being a good manager is having the courage to be honest. It is tempting not to make a coaching comment when you should. We all have certain social virtues, like being 'respectful,' that result in being just a little dishonest in relationships because its good manners. These social virtues are absolutely appropriate in a social setting, but in a work setting we need to interpret them in a different way so we are able to have the tough conversations with people."

Perry continued: "There was a young woman, a high-potential employee. She was extremely bright and extremely talented. She was also extremely ambitious, so much so in fact that she was perceived by all her colleagues as a self-serving opportunist who would crawl over everybody else to get to the top. She had crashed and burned in several job assignments within the company already. Nobody wanted to work with her. Personnel asked me to hire her on special assignment in my area and coach her. I built the relationship with her by asking her to do a couple of projects for me, which allowed me to observe her and make an assessment.

"In truth, Kathy had her vision of the mountain—to be in senior management and to progress within the company. The tree she was headed toward on her way to the top was called superstardom. She thought that to reach her goals she had to be an individual superstar, to stand out, to be in the limelight a lot, to be perfect at everything. This was getting her in trouble. I needed to help her refocus on the right tree, which was to become a team player.

"One day I approached her and said, 'I have some things I want to share with you. Are you open to coaching feedback?' She responded, 'Absolutely, I have heard around the building that you are one of the good coaches.'" Perry began by affirming Kathy. He said, "Here's what I see about you right now. I see a bright young businessperson, loaded with talent and ability, who does a hell of a lot of things right. And if you keep doing those things, you will have a great career ahead of you. Let's talk, though, about the one thing that can really make a difference to you, and that is becoming a team player."

Next Perry began framing his feedback with the intent of helping Kathy correct her course: "I agree with your vision about senior management. You've got the right backpack, hiking boots, and staff. At the same time, I have to be honest with you. Do you want to know about it?" She agreed. He said, "Your compass is not quite set in the right direction. You are not seen as a team player. You are perceived as being so ambitious that you will step over other people." He offered some examples.

At first Kathy didn't fully accept the feedback because she didn't realize how she was perceived. She actually thought she was a team player. Perry continued: "We can't see ourselves as others see us. Also, you can't change if you don't know the things you are doing that aren't working." It started to sink in and her eyes misted up. She slowly said, "I had no idea." Perry said, "That's why it is really good we are having this conversation."

Then Perry began to frame his feedback to stretch Kathy by setting an aspiration designed to alter her way of being, thinking, and behaving. He said, "Now you have two more months with me. I want you to forget about having perfect spreadsheets. I want you to forget about dotting all the I's and crossing all the t's. I want you to concentrate on one thing. I want you to concentrate your efforts on being the best team player in the building."

Talking and brainstorming together, Kathy and Perry created a vision for her and an action plan. Perry said, "Instead of being the star who gets the job done first and best, go and offer to help others. Let others shine at meetings. Don't jump in at the beginning of the meeting and always be the first one to give your opinion. You don't always need to be in the limelight. You are very well perceived, so ease up a bit. Let others shine; become more of a team player."

In the following year, Kathy progressed from being a person no one wanted to being an assistant brand manager. Says Perry, "She is perceived as one of our rising superstars, and people are saying, "If I could only get Kathy on my team."[4]

ENCOURAGE LEARNING WHILE WORKING

Bob Tulgan interviewed hundreds of managers for his book *FAST Feedback*. (FAST is an acronym for "fast," "accurate," "specific," and "timely.") Says Tulgan, "One of the most regular complaints is that feedback takes place long after the performance that is being critiqued occurred. The once or twice a year evaluation is a creature of the workplace of the past. Today's business leaders expect workers to be project driven and results oriented."

That doesn't fit with the old model of reviewing performance every six to twelve months. Says Tulgan, "Many successful companies are trapped in this 'annual review' mode because they have so many well-developed systems to support it."[5] There are no systems for day-to-day engagement with workers, for example, setting aside a certain amount of time each day for giving feedback, and using a variety of means to deliver it: face-to-face, e-mail, and voice mail. The shorter the time between performance and learning, the better.

One of the concepts that is very powerful and innovative is the concept of coaching people in action. This involves the coach interacting with the players in a way that actually fulfills their human potential, helps them to perform at a higher level, or builds a new skill. Because it is difficult for people to learn under stress and pressure, the practice field or rehearsal hall metaphor, introduced in the *Fifth Discipline* by Peter Senge, is very useful.

As mentioned earlier, today's business leaders need to embrace, as part of their responsibility, the idea of continually moving people back and forth between the performance field, where they have to produce results, and the practice field, where they can build new skills and capabilities necessary to succeed. This means showing up at practice sessions and getting involved in the "drills," rather than leaving it to human resources or outside consultants.

Think of *learning while working* rather than looking at learning as a separate activity to be done in abstract training programs. Think about how you can create a climate or atmosphere for people to learn in while working in your area. For example, allot an hour a day for scanning on the Internet for things that are work related or for reading a business book. Encourage people not to be shy, to ask questions, and to seek out others who can provide valuable points of view on a subject. For example, if people are developing a strategy in a complex situation, they might pick someone who is more cerebral and introspective to talk to. If they are ready to take action, they might seek out people who are very action oriented.

GROUP COACHING ACTIVITY
Designing Practice Fields

Take an inventory of the three most important skills you would like the people in your area to develop, and devise a practice field once a week—followed by beer and pizza. For example, have a practice field on telemarketing, running software tests, or packing a case of important equipment.

CUSTOMIZE CHALLENGING EXPERIENCES THAT PROMOTE ACCELERATED DEVELOPMENT

Most leaders, if they take the time, have at least some ability to give feedback that shows a person's strengths and limitations. They may also be able to discern what developmental steps would allow the person to reach present goals and take the next career step. Traditionally, at this point managers tend to throw up their hands and delegate the job of actually helping people make those steps to human resouces, the corporate university, or the training department, based on the notion that people develop from taking classes.

John McCall, a professor at the University of Southern California, has done extensive research showing that few successful managers say that the biggest factor in accelerating their development was a classroom experience. Almost all say that they developed into successful managers as a result of challenging experiences, often those in which they had to produce results. For example, some of the experiences managers identify as having developmental possibilities are as follows:

- Being coached by a demanding leader

- Working at one's first managerial job

- Shifting from a staff job to a line job or vice versa

- Taking stretch assignments—getting in over one's head

- Being placed in a job in a different culture

- Taking on a fix-up or turnaround situation

- Being assigned special projects or being on a task force

In coaching others, your job doesn't stop with providing feedback that shows strengths and areas of improvement; it also includes customizing challenging experiences that will result in breakthroughs in results and breakthroughs for people. The idea is not to eliminate the classroom or other developmental tools, such as 360-degree feedback, because each of these has an important role. Rather, it is to make these experiences challenging as well.

The selection of top talent goes hand in glove with coaching and creating challenging experiences. If people are provided with challenging experiences without coaching, they may well fall back on old strategies—attitudes and behavior—to "survive" them. When you provide talented people with a combination of challenging coaching and mentoring experiences, accelerated development occurs.

At least four times a year, review each person's performance and give meaningful feedback. This is a good opportunity to create or review talent performance and development plans. Engage people in conversation about how they see their next developmental steps. What kind of attitudes, skills, and capabilities do they need to develop to take the next step in their careers? Also, what kinds of situations do they want to be able to handle more effectively at the present time?

Arrange to have another conversation the following week in which to talk about next steps. This gives you time to ponder what learning experiences will meet the person's particular developmental needs. When you meet again, outline different ranges of options that will allow the person to meet his or her goals—giving a choice, if possible, as to how to proceed.

For example, some options for developing top talent might include exposure to external thought leaders, stretch assignments, or a special course that gives people accelerated experiences—such as a strategic planning simulation module. Another option might include gaining access to internal leaders as coaches, role models, and so forth.

This is really an opportunity to make learning creative and fun. John Burdett, a consultant in Toronto, is a world-class expert in designing challenging experiences. Burdett designed a leadership program for AlGroup—a $48 billion diversified industrial firm with headquarters in Zurich, Switzerland. Burdett believes that leaders are developed based on a balance of head, hand, heart, and spirit.

Most programs, he believes, do not focus enough on the real ingredients of leadership—spirit and heart—and focus too much on head and hand—knowledge and skills. When designing a program for a group of leaders, he noticed that they were too much in their heads. Instead of talking to them about leadership theory, he sent them to a class on tap dancing to build spirit. He has designed other programs that included challenging experiences, such as bullfighting in Spain and Formula One auto racing in Florida.

The following coaching activity will assist you in thinking about how to customize learning experiences for accelerated development.

1:1 COACHING ACTIVITY

Challenging Experiences for Accelerated Growth

Try these ideas to help your coachee grow:

1. Think of a person you are coaching. State the person's developmental priority in terms of a situation he or she would like to be able to handle well.

2. How many different experiences—such as exposure to thought leaders, assignments, educational opportunities, or projects—can you think of that would force the person to learn that ability?

3. Which experiences would be the most powerful teachers? Rate them from 1 to 3 in terms of their power.

4. Create a powerful combination of the above.

GROUP COACHING ACTIVITY

Action Learning

One of the keys to being able to lead an effective group to reach a high goal or complete a complex project is reflection in action. I first heard about this idea from Sallie Hightower, principal consultant at Conoco University. It provides a solid method for achieving extraordinary results, while at the same time promoting personal feedback and team learning. (It is a variation on the theme of the plan-do-act check cycle.)

1. Identify a significant business-building idea or issue, for example, changing leadership, finding a new supplier, opening a new market, or speeding up a process.

2. Bring together a group of high-potential people around the idea or issue. Offer the group education they need to have an impact on the matter, as well as 360-degree feedback.

3. Have each group analyze the issue and create a concrete plan within two to fourteen days. Tell the group to look both personally and collectively at what they want to do.

4. Have the groups reconvene and present their plans to potential senior management, who coach and decide whether to go forward.

5. Ask the group to implement a key project over the next two to twelve weeks. Hold reflection in action meetings weekly to review accomplishments and insights, issues and dilemmas, and next steps.

6. Ask the individuals in the group to look at themselves and reflect publicly on what they have learned personally; then do the same for the group.

7. Repeat the process every seven to fourteen days until the project is completed.

LESSONS FROM GREAT COACHES—SYDNEY LUMET COACHES PAUL NEWMAN

There are several stories I picked up from Sydney Lumet's book *Making Movies* that embody the notion of learning by working. Here is one that illustrates a masterful coach in action. Lumet was coaching Paul Newman on the film *The Verdict*. One day, they ran through the whole script. Things looked quite good, but somehow Newman's performance seemed rather flat. Lumet tells the story: "I asked Paul to stay after the rehearsal. I told him, while things looked promising, we hadn't hit the emotional level we knew was there in David Mamet's screenplay. I said his characterization was fine, but hadn't evolved into a living, breathing person. Was there a problem?

"Paul said that he didn't have the lines memorized yet, and that, when he did, it would be better. I, however, didn't think it was the lines. I told him that there were certain aspects of the character that were not particularly attractive that were missing so far. I told him that I wouldn't invade his privacy, but he could choose to reveal only that part of the character or also that aspect of himself. I couldn't help him with the decision. We lived near each other and drove home together. The ride was silent. Paul was thinking. On Monday, Paul came to rehearsal and sparks flew. He was superb. His character and the picture took on life."

Lumet went on to say, "I know that the decision to reveal that part of himself was painful for him, because Paul is a shy person, but he is very dedicated. Yes! He's a wonderful actor and a wonderful man."[6]

Feedback Tips for All Occasions

Here are a few tips about giving feedback that can really make a difference in almost any situation:

• *Give valid information.* If people feel your feedback is valid, they will be much more willing to accept it and embrace change more easily. Find two to three solid examples that back up every assessment you make.

• *Emphasize free and informed choice.* Make it a practice to give people the power of choice with respect to providing feedback. Are they open to hearing it? Are they willing to change? Do they want your help in doing so?

• *Look for internal commitment.* If people have valid information and free and informed choice, they will have an internal commitment to change.[7]

• *Provide feedback in a conversational manner.* Too many leaders confuse feedback with paperwork. "Filling out a form is an inspection, not feedback," says Kelley Allan, senior associate at Kelley Allan Associates, a consulting firm in Ohio. "If you use forms as the basis for your meeting about performance, you change only one thing—what might have been a natural, helpful conversation turns into an awkward, anxious inspection."[8] The most valuable kind of feedback involves daily interactions between leaders and the people who work with them.

• *Get out from behind your big desk.* Instead of talking to people about their performance in your office, go someplace more social (neutral) that naturally lends itself to an easy conversation. Many coaches, such as Tom Kaiser of Zurich Insurance, have found that lunch is a good setting for collaborative discussions of goals and tactics.[9]

• *Don't let the thought that people may react to feedback make you shy away from giving it.* First of all, people react to feedback, no matter how well it is framed. They may react by treating it too scientifically, as if it had nothing to do with them. They may react with negative emotions. They may react positively and gratefully, and they may react by not reacting at all. These are just natural responses. A masterful coach never lets the thought of how people might react deter him or her from giving feedback. Coaches consider it hostile (uncaring) not to give people feedback that can help them grow and learn. At the same time, a masterful coach is willing to alter feedback so that people are more able to take it. "Okay, this isn't working for you. Let me see if I can put it in a way that will be more empowering, not diminishing."

COACHING OTHERS THROUGH THE FOUR STAGES OF CAREER DEVELOPMENT

Often managers say, "I know I should develop managers, but *how* do I develop them?" In our courses on masterful coaching, we have designated four stages of development that business leaders and managers go through. The coaching model presented next tells managers what attributes, competencies, and results people need to develop to move from one stage to the next. Advancement is based not only on certification of knowledge or skills, such as degrees or jobs held, but also on the ability to produce results. A manager may have one attribute or competency with different people at different stages at different times. Here is a simplified version of the process.

STAGE 1   WHO AM I, WHAT CAN I DO?

This stage involves coaching and mentoring people to identify who they are and what their passions, talents, and interests are, as well as what education and basic skills they need before pursuing the career of their choice. People are ready to move on to the next stage when they have not only identified but also actually acquired, the direction, education, and technical skills that match their choice of jobs. Coaching people through this stage is useful not only for younger employees with basic education, but also for managers in midcareer who want to make a lateral career change.

STAGE 2   GETTING THE JOB DONE—TECHNICAL COMPETENCE

In this stage, job holders learn to take the knowledge and skills they have acquired and apply them to getting a job done on their own. At this stage people usually gain competence or master a particular technical skill, for example, a software designer writing code for a particular application, a call center phone person placing an outbound sales call and getting an order, or an assistant editor at a publishing company handling the logistics of assembling the author's work, coordinating with copyediting and graphics, and making sure that the whole package goes to the printer on time.

People are ready to move on from this stage when they are consistently able to achieve a desired, specific result on their own with a minimum of supervision and have perhaps begun to develop the necessary attributes and capabilities for the next stage—management.

STAGE 3   MANAGING A GROUP

This stage starts when people are able to take over responsibility for motivating, planning, and organizing a group of people in carrying out a set of tasks, whether those tasks are simple or complex. People at this stage must let go of the tendency to do the work themselves and begin to empower and enable others to do it. In this stage, the person becomes a coach and mentor to others. People in this stage are usually business unit heads with profit responsibility, function heads, team leaders, or front-line supervisors.

People are ready to move on from this stage to the next when they are consistently able to produce the desired results that are expected. Moving on also usually requires broadening their experience from one function to the next—for example, from accounting to sales or from running a function to running a business unit or complex system.

STAGE 4   ENTERPRISE LEADERSHIP

At this stage, the person has the leadership, business, social, and technical skills to manage an entire enterprise. He or she is able to pioneer new possibilities and bring about significant change, as well as manage other managers. Great expectations are placed on people in this role, such as the CEO of a company or the head of a major division. They must have a high level of proficiency in managing strategic issues, stakeholder issues, legal issues, and so on just to keep their jobs.

REFLECTION ASSIGNMENT
Mentoring People's Development

1. Select two or three people in your group with the greatest potential.

2. Assess at what stage they are in their professional development.

3. Identify any performance or development gaps. Use 360-degree feedback to help. Focus on people's ability to produce desired results, not just desired behaviors.

4. Engage each person in a coaching conversation about his or her career development at least four times a year. See whether the person agrees or disagrees with your assessment.

5. Discuss what the person needs to do to advance his or her career and move to the next stage. Address any competency gaps.

6. Create a personal learning plan and provide access to learning resources. (See Chapter Two, page 44, Figure 2.3, on the PULL Approach to Leadership Development.)

SUMMARY

Masterful coaches always give feedback in the context of enabling people to realize what's possible and achievable—world's best hitter, great musician, entrepreneur, and so on. When feedback is given in this context, it is generative and usually well received. Giving feedback in this context is different from giving feedback that is merely evaluative—which is usually not well received. In a generative context, where positive possibilities have been declared consistent with people's inner goals and aspirations, evaluations do have a place and are seen in a much more constructive way.

Seven Guidelines for Providing Feedback

- Focus on coaching people to achieve extraordinary results through doable projects and actions.

- Reflect on how you are *being* as a coach, not just on what you are *doing*.

- Frame all feedback so that people walk away feeling empowered.

- Talk to people on a regular basis and ask: "What's happened? What's missing? What's next?"

- Communicate with the intention of having an impact, not just to he heard, with enough edge to take the blinders off and penetrate illusions.

- Coach people in action until both desired results and learning are evident.

- Celebrate the goals that have been achieved and how people have transformed who they are in the process.

CONCLUSION: MASTERFUL COACHING—THE METHOD™

If you have read these five chapters carefully, you will be able to fulfill the promise made at the beginning of this section. You will be able to say to yourself "Yes! I can do it." If not, go back and read any sections that you are not sure about. If you still have questions, contact us at <masterfulcoaching.com>. We will do our best to answer any questions you have.

If there were one more step in the method, it would be this: Celebrate! Celebrate all goals that have been reached and celebrate who the person has become in the process of achieving them. To be sure, the person who has been coached for any period will not be the same person you started out coaching. If you have been successful, the person you started out coaching no longer exists. The person who is there now did not exist before.

In the next section, you will read about masterful coaches in various arenas of practice and the results they have achieved.

PART III

MASTERFUL COACHES ON THE FRONT LINES OF BUSINESS

Matching Coaching to the Job

I have discovered that although it is important to create the business case for coaching and to have a method or model that is universally applicable, coaching is always grounded in a given community of practice. One does not go to a sports coach; one goes to a ski coach, golf coach, or tennis coach to improve one's game.

The same applies to coaching in the world of business and in organizations of every kind. For every community of practice or job function—marketing, sales, production, or whatever—there is a distinct body of knowledge and there are professionals who have built up this knowledge through rolling up their sleeves and getting the job done. The best coaches and mentors are those who not only have knowledge on a tacit level but also can make that knowledge explicit for others.

In this section of the book, we move beyond generic aspects of coaching and feature masterful coaches who can provide insights you need about how to coach people within your specific profession or occupation.

The masterful coaches presented here are widely known and admired in their respective fields, are excellent communicators, and have proven track records of success. Each one is a thought leader in his or her respective field. You will notice that they have reframed a traditional function with new thinking that has led to new vocabulary. They possess the ability to put their ideas into words in a way that makes it possible for others to think outside the box.

The following six coaches are brought to life in the next seven chapters:

Tony Jimenez, Coaching Senior Management. Jimenez, an internal consultant for Chevron Oil, has a knack for coaching busy executives on the run, for saying the one thing that can make a difference. He does this with wisdom, compassion, and humor. You will find invaluable ideas, tools, and methods for coaching executives and managers, especially if you are a human resource (HR) manager or a consultant.

J. Mays, Coaching Design and Innovation. Mays is progenitor of the new Volkswagen Bug and chief designer of Ford Motor Company, in charge of all brands. He provides insights on building a brand through distinctive design, innovating new product ideas, and bringing out the best in talented people and groups. This chapter is especially for coaches who are designers, product developers, or brand builders.

Tom Sudman, E-Coaching Teams in a Virtual Age. The interview with Tom Sudman is essential for people developing the leadership skills necessary to manage virtual organizations. His ideas can be applied to coaching any group to come together as a team and produce extraordinary results. Sudman, an expert on virtual coaching, shows how any global company can leverage its highly talented people more effectively by assembling teams to work on local issues independent of time and distance. The chapter is especially of interest for coaches who are in knowledge management, faster innovation, operational excellence, customer care, or distance learning.

Chris Higgins, Coaching Successful Projects. Higgins, acclaimed by *Fast Company* as Bank of America's "Mr. Project," provides in-depth insights, tools, and methods on how to coach any business project, large or small. Higgins provides some high-impact ideas, such as identifying and focusing on what's core rather than on the bells and whistles. This chapter is especially for coaches who lead projects in technology, operational excellence, or customer service.

Hubert Saint-Onge, Dragon Slayer of Human Resource Myths. This breakthrough interview shows how to leverage your position as an HR manager to a strategic level. Saint-Onge provides a fascinating model for integrating structural, human, and customer capital. You will see how to transform people from dependents to owners, as well as how to transform training into learning. This should especially interest coaches who are CEOs, CIOs, or strategic planners, or in HR, organizational development, and training.

Jay Abraham, Marketing Genius and Money Maximizer. Abraham, who according to the *Wall Street Journal* is a "certifiable marketing genius," provides powerful, dynamic, high-impact ideas and methods to maximize every marketing dollar. This chapter is especially for coaches who are CEOs, product innovators, marketers, or small business owners.

Art Wilson, Coaching Large, Complex, Team-Based Sales Across Boundaries. Sales departments now are usually multidisciplinary teams from one or more organizations working together in collaboration with customers. If you are looking for a way to coach people to strategically plan and leverage big account sales and cross-sell to turn low-margin customers into high-margin customers, you will find lots of insights here. This is especially for CEOs who believe in creating a company in which "everyone is in business development" and also for coaches who are in marketing, sales, and distribution.

CHAPTER ELEVEN

TONY JIMENEZ

COACHING SENIOR MANAGEMENT

Tony Jimenez is a masterful executive coach with a day job as a leadership development consultant at Chevron Oil. He is known to ignite strategic insights by asking a single question that is both powerful and sublime. He also uses what the Buddhists call "crazy humor" to get managers to stop taking themselves so seriously. Jimenez only has one arm. When people ask him where and how he lost it, he answers, "San Francisco." Then, depending on who he's talking to, he says, "I lost it in a coaching session," or "I lost it working on an oil rig." Invariably his answers come with a chuckle or an outright howl, and they elicit the same in return.

Jimenez is smart and sophisticated yet he comes from a world of people who grew up on the coal face—drilling wells, running refineries, and marketing their products. These are people who are on the run and have little patience with elaborate management theories. At the same time, they call Jimenez again and again for the savory bits of wisdom he can serve up in short conversations, as well as for the hors d'oeuvres he dishes out from the leading business thought leaders of the day. His knowledge of business books and business savants is nothing short of encyclopedic.

As people talk to him about their goals and problems, he shares information, asks questions enthusiastically, and listens as a way of calibrating what he is going to say. His specialty is the off-the-cuff idea, joke, or remark that can help people think creatively or extricate themselves from the reality in which they are lodged. He often begins his comments with, "Let me say this, and maybe that will trigger something in you"; or more challenging, "Let me throw this spear in your side," or "Have you read this latest article?"

In this chapter on executive coaching, written by Jimenez, he shares from his fountain of knowledge and insight.

Coaching Senior Management—The Art of Strategic Whispering

BY TONY L. JIMENEZ

Imagine someone leaning over to another person and giving him a strategic whisper. Coaching managers and executives is more like strategic whispering than the popular image of someone shouting on the sidelines.

Strategic whispering uses simplicity and ingenuity, and it is practical for the executive or manager receiving it. Strategic whispering is short, satisfying, and saves time. The highest form of the strategic whisper unleashes the creativity of the executive to achieve his or her results. We will approach this topic with simplicity, ingenuity, and in a practical way.

"One can't communicate in a word—the whole person goes with it," is the old saying. Each person develops a coaching style over time, consciously or unconsciously. My style is highly metaphorical, playful, informal, sound-bite sized, short-story based, thought triggering, conscience disturbing, hors d'oeuvres sharing, visual, and behavioral. I share this with you because my attempt will be to discuss critical issues in coaching using my "normal" style. What I am missing is your reactions and facial expressions for me to use to adjust my thoughts to you.

For the past twenty years, my coaching of all levels of management has been on the way to dinner in a car, in hotel rooms, at dinner tables, in elevators, car garages, conference rooms, private offices, hallways, and yes, even rest rooms. Informal settings may be where most coaching for managers occurs. Formal settings take on a whole life of their own, and most of the time they may inhibit coaching a person who is supposed to have all the answers.

My opportunities for coaching all levels of management come from upward feedback sessions, advanced management courses, coaching on formal and informal presentations, preparing managers to lead discussions with other managers, consulting, and organization development work.

I feel extremely fortunate to have seen and worked with some of the brightest, most hardworking, and trustworthy senior managers in many stages of development. My observations will attempt to add to your knowledge in this area without destroying the confidence these people have frequently and honestly given me in good times and bad. I will sprinkle concepts, experiences with clients, and concerns for the coach into our conversation.

ACTION! START DOING! STOP DOING! DO MORE! DO LESS!

As a coach, I try to get my clients to *think like a person of action* and *act like a person of thought*. One action-oriented manager was rushing out to do something that was against his own interests and I could not get him to think until I told him the following story:

A manager went to visit a foreign country. The manager was visiting a shrine and his guide took him to a light burning on a type of altar. "That flame," said the guide, "has been burning for a thousand years." The manager leaned over and blew it out. "Well, it's stopped now; you don't have to worry about that problem anymore."

The manager had a pained look after he heard my story, and he stopped the action that was going to hurt him. A coach should be able to get clients to start doing, stop doing, do more of, and do less of certain actions.

A blinding glimpse of the obvious—most of our clients are driven by time, action, and results, and personal reflection time is scarce. Coaches who are strategic and creative, who help clients with time, action, and results, are truly appreciated.

COACHING AS A STRATEGIC PROCESS

Framing coaching for senior management as strategic whispering brings to mind private, hushed tones, short, delicate, and high-leverage responses for only one set of ears. Strategic whispering brings to mind being able to say the one thing that can make a difference to a person.

I view coaching as a strategic process that leads to a sustainable, competitive advantage for the individual. Effective strategies with an individual act as a bridge between the past and the future. Effective strategies are opportunistic, planned, spontaneous, and creative. Effective strategies involve a wide variety of actions. Many of my management clients are preoccupied with strategy and its execution. Working with senior management has many issues and has to be strategic.

Stuart Wells, in a current book on strategic thinking called *Choosing the Future,* gives questions to consider in the strategic thinking process. His questions mirror the coaching process.[1] He asks:

- What seems to be happening?

- What possibilities do we face?

- What are we going to do about it?

These three simple questions provide a coaching framework.

A GREAT QUESTION REACHES DEEP INSIDE AND PULLS YOU OUT!

A great question can bring great value: (1) Reach in and pull out the potential of your client, (2) move your client to the highest leverage point, and (3) tap client creativity for better solutions.

One client was struggling and second-guessing himself on a decision. All it took was for me to say, "What would you do in this situation if you were the president of the company?" This question pulled out his self-confidence and he was able to make an effective decision.

A question in the form of a strategic whisper helps the client move to the highest rung of the ladder in the situation. For example, "What option has the highest leverage for you?"

The following example illustrates a subtle and creative shift in the thinking of one of my clients when I was using a strategic whisper.

My client was using old language that stuck him in old patterns, so I suggested a "what if?" question. A "what if?" question takes the client to a creative place. "What if instead of referring to what you are creating for your clients as tools (the word *tools* is an old metaphor that comes from the factory age and limits your thinking), we use a more current term?"

A question cannot only help people be more creative, but it can also help them reframe their thinking so they can be more effective. Jerry Hirshberg, in *The Creative Priority,* says that the most penetrating question for an auto manufacturing company is, "What is a car?" The form of the question itself contains both the limits and the potential character of the possible answers. Thinking about a car as a people-mover suggests an utterly different set of possibilities from framing it as a mode of personal transportation, an expression of individual style, or a mobile pollution device on four wheels.

"Creative questions . . . are often disarmingly simple and . . . are particularly effective in jarring 'The Known' loose from its all-too-familiar moorings . . . the thick, dead underbrush of old associations and assumptions, allowing for fresh light on a subject. And the potential for the growth of new ideas."[2]

MENTAL MORSELS

Coaches create or discover what I call "mental morsels." A mental morsel can be a short story, a thought, a valuable chunk of insight, a small bit of practical wisdom you can apply right away. An example from Peter Drucker's *The Effective Executive* has helped me with my clients and may help you.

Courage rather than analysis dictates the truly important rules for identifying priorities:

- Pick the future as opposed to the past;

- Focus on opportunity rather than on problems;

- Choose your own direction rather than climb on the bandwagon; and

- Aim high, aim for something that will make a difference, rather than for something that is 'safe' and easy to do."[3]

DEVELOPING A UNIQUE CLIENT PERSPECTIVE

The art of coaching requires a certain touch and feel and a talent for perspective. Bernard Baruch once defined this as the ability to walk around a big issue the way a photographer walks around a subject he's going to photograph, saying nothing, mulling things over. Finally he says, "We'll take it from this angle."

The coach needs to truly understand the world of his client. This is the rare and precious ability to see, sense, and feel from the other person's point of view.

An executive once said to me, "You have to develop antenna. If someone tells you that you did something wrong as an executive . . . it's too late." He was giving a glimpse of the environment many executives face.

Executive obsolescence may be the most hidden fear many struggle to hide. Often I have joked, "The race is between obsolescence and retirement—which one will win?"

The need to be perfect or not make mistakes, the need to avoid obsolescence, the struggle with internal and external competition creates a serious cycle for some.

While one executive was fretting about competition, I shared with him the story of two hikers being chased by a grizzly bear. While on the run, one of the hikers reaches into his backpack and pulls out a pair of jogging shoes. The other hiker glances over and says, "Why bother? This bear can outrun you even with those on." His partner responds with, "I don't need to outrun the bear, I just need to outrun you." The executive laughed out loud and we were able to break the serious cycle.

WHAT AREA HAS THE HIGHEST LEVERAGE POINT FOR THIS PERSON AND THE BUSINESS?

One of the fundamental issues in coaching executives or managers is the standard I am using to measure them against. Edgar Schein, who wrote *Process Consultation,* talks about artifacts in corporate life, such as a list on a wall stating the attributes of a role model executive or manager that sound good in theory but aren't the real measures—they are only professed by many.

The standard by which to evaluate the person receiving the coaching may come from a combination of sources: the boss, business requirements, self-assessment, and peer and employee assessments. The difficulty begins if there are too many measures or they seem to be too conflicting and confusion occurs.

The easiest areas to identify may be problem behaviors to correct. But which areas have an impact on the business? What area has the highest leverage point for this person and the business?

The best scenario is fewer standards or criteria to coach and measure results, affecting the person and the business. The worst scenario is a coach following a personal image of a perfect executive or manager and then picking up a list of professed attributes that aren't the real measures.

STRATEGIC WHISPERING IN DIFFERENT FORMS OF COACHING

There are many forms of coaching, but here's a short list:

- Leaders coaching leaders

- Coaching for innovation

- Problem solving

- Targeting selected behaviors

- Coaching the manager and team simultaneously

I will highlight briefly the first two forms. Over the years, in senior management courses I have coached leaders to coach other leaders. Leaders coaching leaders is an extremely high-leverage activity. Noel Tichy in *The Leadership Engine* creates new excitement and raises the bar on this important topic. Organizational culture and priorities, rules written and unwritten are passed when leaders coach leaders.

Leaders who continually borrow ideas from others without investing their own thinking and reflection have difficulty with "a teachable point of view." Leaders who are confused about their values have difficulty making it work. As a coach I have whispered to these types of individuals to find out, "What really matters to you?" Leaders with unclear values require help sifting, sorting, and getting in touch with values they can demonstrate.

Coaching for innovation is helping a client develop a new product, a new system, a new organization, or a new approach to something that does not currently exist. Coaching for innovation is taking individuals or teams into unexplored territory. This feels like running in the dark and not knowing what you are going to hit. I call this the world of "what if?" The world of "what if?" breaks with the past dramatically. The world of "what if?" is exciting, scary, full of possibilities, and requires courageous travelers.

My strategic whispers help to break with the past. For example, What if these policies didn't exist? What if we started with a clean sheet of paper describing our organization and the reporting relationships?

Strategic whispers you use in coaching for innovation may not be logical. I would suggest that coaching for innovation is an extremely creative process. Conventional wisdom may not apply. For example, some coaches work hard to have a clear outcome.

I would like to disturb your conscience and suggest it's certainly true that if you don't know where you're going, you'll end up someplace else. But it is also true that if you always know exactly where you are going, you have no chance of discovering someplace new. Sometimes in coaching with your clients you have to take mental detours to stimulate the creative process.

For example, sometimes when I am working with a client, we get too serious about the issue. I suggest that we take a mental detour. Sometimes the client looks puzzled. I explain that we need to break our serious pattern because it's blocking our creativity. Then, out of the blue I pull out my list of country and western song titles:

- My wife ran off with my best friend and now I miss him.

- We honeymooned on a waterbed and now we're drifting apart.

- You said you couldn't live without me so why aren't you dead yet?

- You're the reason our kids are ugly.

- Every time you go outside, I hope it rains.

Usually the client will laugh and it breaks the pattern of seriousness. But you have to be careful when you create a mental detour because your client could assume you are a little crazy. Mental detours require a good set up.

COACHING NEEDS TO BE FRESH, NOVEL, AND USEFUL

Often in my coaching, I use classical and current hors d'oeuvres to stimulate or trigger the thinking of my clients. Coaching needs to be fresh, novel, and useful. The philosopher Alfred North Whitehead says that knowledge must be either new or invested with some novelty of application to the new world of new times. There must be a certain freshness. "Knowledge does not keep any better than fish."[4]

To stay fresh, novel, and useful, a coach must experiment. Experienced coaches start to experiment with ways to influence their clients with a base of knowledge and experience. One simple example of experimenting: As I coached clients in the upward feedback process privately, poor listening habits would come up in coaching with all levels of management. Prior to going into a session with direct reports, I would coach the manager to describe his or her listening habits to me using simple metaphors. My listening is like a rushed train trip, a mechanical process, a tennis game, a black hole, a valuable exchange, a clogged up strainer, an accounting process, a political campaign, and so forth.

My clients, with a little assistance, would come up with a novel or striking way to describe their listening issues. We would laugh and gain insight. This is a simple way to add freshness and creativity to an old issue we all struggle to master.

PLAYFUL INTERVENTIONS

A senior manager once said to me, "What is all this empowerment crap? Isn't it like turning the prison over to the inmates?"

I said, "No, it is more like turning the farm over to the farmers." This is what I call a playful intervention with my client. Playful interventions unleash the creativity of the client for his or her results. Playful interventions have great potential to be effective or to be misunderstood, not necessarily in that order. Playful interventions point out new possibilities. They may or may not be humorous, but they add a new perspective.

A playful intervention is my contribution to interventions. Edgar Schein describes fundamental interventions in his classic book, *Process Consultation.* He lists the following:

1. *Exploratory Interventions:* Reflect the intention to make as few assumptions as possible about what may be going on so that the client can get out the story in whatever form it needs to come out.

2. *Diagnostic Interventions:* The focus shifts from just trying to find out what the client wants to getting the client to begin to think about what might really be going on.

3. *Action Alternative Interventions:* The focus shifts to actual new behavior that the client might want to consider.

4. *Confrontive Interventions:* These shift the focus to the client's possible areas of resistance.[5]

THE TECHNOLOGY OF FOOLISHNESS

To stimulate your creativity, I want to share an early influence that led me on the trail to playfulness. In *The Technology of Foolishness,* James March explores ways that organizations can make room for creativity without permanently disrupting systems, procedures, or assumptions that give order to individuals and groups inside.

March defines playfulness as "the deliberate, temporary relaxation of rules in order to explore the possibilities of alternative rules."[6] He suggests five new rules for injecting playfulness:

1. Treat goals as hypotheses.

2. Treat intuition as real.

3. Treat hypocrisy as a transition.

4. Treat memory as an enemy.

5. Treat experience as a theory.

After reading James March, I heard a lecture by Paul Watzlawick, who is with the Mental Research Institute in Palo Alto, California. He was discussing paradoxical interventions he used in Brief Therapy. His book *The Language of Change* is still available and is a useful reference. His interventions were brief, amusing, and effective. He raised the issue of getting dramatic results in the shortest amount of time, helping me to develop my thinking about strategic whispering.

Then a group of senior managers and I spent a week with the late, renowned philosophy educator Abraham Kaplan at the Ojai Leadership Labs. Kaplan was the quickest, funniest, and most profound individual; he used playful interventions with incredible skill. It really helps to see a great coach in action or someone who can intervene with great skill.

STRATEGIC WHISPERING REQUIRES QUICKNESS AND COURAGE

Quickness and courage are helpful attributes in working with senior managers as a coach—quickness for framing or reframing interactions and courage to hold your ground and make a difference with strong personalities.

One time a senior manager got the best of me in an elevator. I was giving him some feedback in front of another senior manager, which is not a good practice. He kept canceling at the last minute my invitations for him to be an evening guest for a management program that would require him to spend four hours answering tough questions from another management group. When I was giving him the feedback, he quickly reframed the interaction and humorously suggested that if I had invited him out to cook for the group, he would have been there immediately—because cooking was his greatest skill, not answering questions.

I share this example with you to help you become continuously alert that your client can quickly reframe interactions. Some people believe quickness cannot be taught. I believe you develop quickness by being constantly with quick people.

Whether one is an internal or external coach, your courage will be tested over and over. A strategic whisper brings different responses from senior managers with strong personalities. Fainthearted coaches will find the strongest personalities shouting in their faces like the coach on the sidelines. I have allowed managers to shout and vent all over my shoes until the whisper finally registers.

BLIND SPOTS

Blind spots are the greatest opportunity for senior management, internal coaches, and external coaches for change and development. If you go in and point out a senior manager's blind spot, it's like throwing cold water in someone's face when he or she is asleep. The challenge for the coach is to encourage people to throw cold water on their own faces to revive and wake themselves up.

There are many creative ways to point out blind spots either directly or indirectly. One indirect way that I use is to suggest that someone doesn't have the complete picture of the situation. That leads me to bring up the question, "What am I missing here?"

This is the question I help senior managers ask themselves. You would think I asked them to swallow an apple whole. For people who are bright and all-knowing, this is a difficult question. It encourages humility, learning, and calibration.

"What am I missing here?" also applies to internal and external coaches. Watching internal and external people succeed and fail with managers is an education in itself. I have seen many coaches and consultants shoot themselves in the foot, reload the gun, and do it again. External coaches will be wise to remember they are like a guest visiting a family. The family may or may not reveal the secrets that really matter. Is the family comfortable or used to visitors dealing with family business? Is the coach credible with the family? Internal coaches are family members who may or may not know the family secrets that matter. If they have credibility with family members, they can help.

The more you are around senior management, the more you see them as real people. They have at their command many resources, and time is one of their scarcest resources.

How much time does it take to trigger strategic and creative whispering?

Time management expert Alan Lakein's latest book, *Give Me a Moment and I'll Change Your Life,* talks about managing and making moments matter. In a moment:

- You can add a plus.

- You can add a purpose.

- You can add an action.

- You can add an activity.

- You can add an attitude.

Lakein even created a new word: *mome* (rhymes with home). A mome is a shortcut that shapes and enriches a moment.

Remember strategic whispering when working with senior management; your greatest value may come in small moments, triggering the creativity of your clients to achieve their goals.

My last whisper to you is that the line that is always left off of the favorite Einstein quote may be the most important. He said, "For while knowledge defines all we currently know and understand, imagination points to all we might yet discover and create."

Tony Jimenez can be reached by e-mail at <tlji@Chevron.com>.

CHAPTER TWELVE

J. MAYS

COACHING DESIGN AND INNOVATION

Innovative design is the mark of today's leading companies, as quality is the price of admission in today's marketplace. Those who have the ability to coach talented people to create fashion-forward, new products will be in increasing demand in the years ahead. This type of work involves creating something that never existed, while at the same time working within the constraints of human buying habits, desires, and tastes.

One night, while driving home from the airport, I looked up and saw a billboard that grabbed my attention. Lit up against the night sky was a picture of the new Volkswagen (VW) Beetle. It was one of the most distinctive looking cars I had ever seen. I said to myself, "I want to talk to the person who designed that car."

Shortly thereafter, we contacted J. Mays, who had since left Volkswagen to become Ford's vice president of corporate design, responsible for eight brands, including Ford, Ford truck, Mercury, Lincoln, Jaguar, Aston Martin, Mazda, and now Volvo. "Those brands and the products that are delivered under those brands are my responsibility in terms of the styling content and visual messages the vehicles give off," Mays says. His background includes fourteen years in Europe at VW

Audi. Mays told me, "When I left Audi, I was director of design worldwide. Highlights of my career include the Beetle and the Audi Avus (a show car) as well as the A4, A6, and A8."

In 1994, Mays left Ford to become an independent consultant for Ford and others in terms of how to position automobiles and products in the marketplace visually, and how to communicate to the customer through design. Today, as a full-time employee, he coaches the designers of every one of Ford's cars and light trucks.

The Millenial VW Bug

INTERVIEW WITH J. MAYS

Why did you decide to join Ford Motor Company as head of design? What are your responsibilities?

I came to Ford Motor because it gave me an incredible palette of possibilities as a designer. We have sixty-three different nameplates here at Ford, and last year we sold almost seven million cars. There are huge overall possibilities and responsibilities afforded to me.

In the automobile business, a product is made up of *functional attributes* and *emotional attributes*. The functional attributes are more than being well taken care of by my boss, Richard Perry Jones, who is driving product development.

It is my job to deliver the emotional attributes, which are everything that is part of a sensory experience when you look, touch, smell, hear anything that an automobile does. Emotional attributes are the "why buys" for customers. It involves more than the styling of an automobile—[it involves] the entire automobile.

How important is design to making buying decisions today?

It is one of the most important criteria. There is so much information out there at our disposal that it is impossible for us really to process it all. How we cope is by using visual signals or visual receipts that a product gives off.

An example of that is if you went into a doctor's office, you might not know anything about that doctor, but you would decide for yourself whether the doctor had any credibility by how the diplomas were hung on the wall, whether the magazines were in order, whether the waiting room was clean and tidy. If they were, you would probably think this is a fairly trustworthy doctor.

On the other hand, if the diplomas were all askew and the magazines were all over the floor and the upholstery was shredded, you probably wouldn't think the doctor was trustworthy. That is how we communicate as a society. This is a very simple example, but it brings to mind the importance of focusing on the need to communicate very clearly and very simply with the customers.

Let me shift the conversation to you as a coach. What did you do to challenge people when you arrived at Ford?

I did two things. I laid down the gauntlet for our one-thousand-strong design team around the world by setting some goals so that we would have clarity about where we were going. The goal was that in four years' time we were going to be considered the number one automobile design group in the world, bar none. That is a massive undertaking for us, but it is a goal that we are sincere in reaching. We are saying that to the press, and we are saying that internally as well.

When I laid out this goal for people, I said, "This is possible and I will lie down in the tracks to get there, but we are going to do it in a very specific way—by creating very focused vehicles under each one of the different marques [brands]." In order for that goal to be realized, each group has to be clear about where it is going so that it can operate independent of me. This is essential, as we have nine studios around the world—two here in Dearborn, one in California, three in Europe (Italy, Germany, and Britain), one in Hiroshima, and one in Melbourne. We have to have a clarity of where we are going, because I cannot be everywhere at once.

I also set the goal that we were going to separate, clarify, and amplify each of our brands into what I call a "power brand," a brand whose product you recognize from the first second you see it. You can put a name to it and understand by whom that product is made and understand the emotional and functional significance of that product. The reaction to these goals was very positive.

We have a couple of good examples of what I am talking about in the company, one of them being the Jaguar. There is no Jaguar on the road today that is not instantly recognized as a Jaguar. Ford trucks are another that we are very strong in. The truck stands for "tough," "durable," "trouble proof." Those are the attributes that people look for in a Ford truck.

Creating a power brand was happening by intuition at Jaguar and at Ford truck. But there wasn't that same clarity of intuition in the Mercury, Ford car, or Lincoln, or other brands. My main goal was to alert the designers to the possibility of improving in those nameplate areas. Not to say that we were not doing some fine Lincolns or fine Fords. We were. But to bring clarity to the individual marques was very important.

What is your teachable point of view about design and innovation?

Well, I am a manager, but I am still a designer. Part of my management responsibilities are to my teachable point of view—how I coached the design teams at VW and later here at Ford on the Thunderbird are applications of it. I think they are parallel stories, with similar thought processes. Let me put this in context by backing up a bit and telling you how cars have been designed over the last forty years.

A designer goes to art school, graduates with honors or distinction, and is hired by a car company. The person is put into a studio where his or her talents are used to create a product that ultimately speaks of that individual's own styling, direction, and taste. That product gets a badge on it, bearing the name of the company. This approach works very successfully on a nameplate by nameplate basis, but it doesn't create the type of consistency necessary to instill trust in the hearts of the buyers of a particular marque.

One of the things that I am trying to do, in addition to creating some year-by-year consistency, is to create a vocabulary of design for each of the marques—a visual vocabulary that is instantaneously recognizable by the customer. If you deconstructed three-dimensional design into its individual elements, you would have shape, color, material, and texture. Design is a process of discovering what shapes, colors, materials, textures are consistent with the values of a particular marque and the values that customers are aspiring to when they buy the product.

How do you coach people to design a distinctive brand that is connected to customers?

I use the word *marque.* It is the old word we used to use before someone came up with the word *brand.* In my field, it is the distinctive marque of automobiles. For example, the Jaguar, Lincoln, and Ford trucks are all great marques with strong traditions. By deconstructing their design into shape, materials, color, and texture, and so on, you can start to develop a design vocabulary for that marque.

This vocabulary provides a palette for again constructing a new design that, while taking tradition into account, is fresh and original. It is very important as the design elements go back together that the product communicate a very focused set of values that connect almost umbilically, if possible, with the customer.

At Ford we are taking a really hard look at who the customer base is that we are trying to convert. We are looking at key *customer groups,* which involves exploring generational attitudes, lifestyles, and life stages. This allows us to start to get a perspective on whether a particular customer is a fit with a particular brand—to determine whether we want to design a product for that customer and whether there will be an emotional connection back to the brand.

For example, if we know that our customer base for Lincoln has an income of $130,000 a year and a median age of fifty-two to fifty-five years old, we probably wouldn't be designing a four-wheel-drive, extreme-youth off-roader for that brand. We would place that kind of vehicle under a brand that would be a more natural connection with the customer and would design a more luxurious four-wheel drive for the Lincoln line.

How did you apply this thought process to the development of the new VW Beetle?

In 1990, VW sales were down to 43,000 cars a year in the United States. Basically, they were out of business. The problem was that there was a disconnect between what the people thought a VW was and what VW was selling. You could have asked anyone on the street what a VW was and they would say that the VW was the old Beetle. They would say it represented a simple, honest form of transportation that was trustworthy.

I got the whole team interested in the question of how to represent *simple* and *honest* visually. We did some brainstorming. To communicate accurately with the customer, you have to be able to create visual language and without ever doing an advertisement be able to sell people through the visual payoff.

The whole idea of simplicity was paramount, and the forms were very geometric. They were very simple. In fact, they were all circles, which is the most simple of geometric shapes. The VW Golf was very boxy looking, but the original VW Beetle was actually quite bulbous, very circular.

What was interesting for me was not that the old vehicle was circular but that circular was the visual definition of simplicity for 99 percent of the people. If I were to ask people to lay out a spectrum of shapes from simple to complex on a table, 99.9 percent of the time the spectrum would start with a circle, with the more complex shapes far to the other side.

The shape of the VW is made up of three concentric circles. The large circle of the passenger compartment and two smaller circles that make up the front and rear wheels. The VW design is so simple that, if you asked a child to draw a car, that is what it would look like. I believe that sends an intuitive message to people, a subliminal connection between simplicity and honesty—the exact values people saw in the original Beetle.

How did you make that simple shape so compelling—by thinking differently?

If you look at a lineup of cars next to each other in a parking lot, you will see a parking lot full of rectangles. This little circle would pop its head out of all those rectangles and become immediately obvious to anyone who might look at it.

People gravitate to this car because it is different and because it embodies the values of simplicity and honesty. The third reason is that it reminds them of the old Beetle, which reminds them of all the great times they had in life—either they had one or their friends had one, and that is really icing on the cake.

It also looks like it came from the future, suggesting a different era from the rectangular cars of today. I might add, the futuristic look has very little to do with the actual purchase decision. The "why buy" of that vehicle is that it makes people feel all warm and fuzzy and remember their childhoods.

Can you tell me how you are applying your coachable point of view to the Ford Thunderbird?

We are just putting the final touches on the new Thunderbird. That vehicle has a totally different set of values for people. We pulled our design team together and sent them out to ask car buffs and customers what the most important Thunderbird was to them.

Most people said '55 through '57. A few people said '61 or '62. It was intriguing when we asked people to explain what it was about those vehicles that made them so interesting. It turned out that the T-Bird exuded the confidence and optimism of postwar America, which connected powerfully to the driver's sense of possibilities. The car also portrayed a very relaxed type of sportiness, as opposed to a more overt sportiness that we find in our culture today.

Those became verbal metaphors for how we could start to visualize a product—optimistic and at the same time relaxed in its sportiness. And it would give off a feeling of being bold and confident in a way that much of postwar America was at that time.

We asked ourselves how we could convey that in a design today, so we looked at other products of the same era as the T-Bird that had a similar feeling. The Harley-Davidsons are a great example. They conveyed a visual message. If you look at a Harley-Davidson and the way you sit way down on that vehicle, leaning back, there is a relaxed sportiness about it, as opposed to a new Japanese motor bike where your rear end is up in the air and you are leaning forward, ready for action. It is a much more overt sportiness.

Interestingly, if you look at automobile design now, as opposed to the 1950s, a lot of the vehicles have higher rear ends. We call that in the automobile industry "a wedge," which signifies and conveys a more overt sportiness. So one of the designing cues we found for communicating relaxed sportiness is to have the tail end of the Thunderbird be lower than the front end, trailing off toward the back. So the weight of the seat shifts back, not unlike that of the Harley-Davidson. It gives off a much less overt sporty cue.

To the confident and optimistic side of the design, I coached the team to study our vocabulary of design cues. One thing that was associated with the confidence and optimism of the postwar era was the jet planes used by the military. In fact, the design of the tail lamps of the original Thunderbird were from the afterburners of those jet planes, which signified a very high confidence and optimism. So we decided to create head lamps and tail lamps that, although very simple in shape, convey a sense of power. I think we have recreated that in a much more graphic, simple way on the new car than on the original.

We are not just taking old design elements and reapplying them to the car; we are taking new, graphic, modern design elements and portraying them in a way that makes you think back to those vehicles you loved in the 1950s.

How do you coach a team to meet the design values, once you have decided what they are?

I will give you an example of that. Design is a very intuitive profession, and designers make a lot of mistakes until they come up with a great solution. If they didn't use intuition, the design would become a formula, which is not something we're trying to do.

We are trying to take the verbal information we know about the customer, give it a visual definition, then measure what the designer comes up with against that. If I am coaching a team toward "relaxed sportiness," I can tell by looking at a car that a design team is proposing just how far up the spectrum of relaxed sportiness they have come. If it is too overtly sporty or too sedate, then it doesn't make the cut.

It is important for the head of a design group to maintain a coachable point of view over time to preserve the integrity of the marque. For example, Thunderbirds that were produced in the 1970s actually got less sporty, less relaxed, and less distinct.

How do you coach people when you visit one of your design centers?

I make a point of talking to designers about the fact that we are living in what I call an overcommunicated society. I say that there are three things you need to communicate a product's attributes. *It needs to be simple*—so simple that the average Joe on the street can understand the moment he looks at the product what the message is. *It needs to be credible.* By credible I mean it needs not to promise any more than it can possibly deliver functionally. The visual and the functional attributes of the vehicle have to be in line. And third, regardless of the income of the consumer, *the vehicle has to be aspirational,* whether its a $13,000 entry-level product or a $130,000 luxury vehicle. But if it is an entry-level product, it can be a very ordinary product, but it should be done so extraordinarily well that it has an aspirational value. At the point that there is no aspirational value, we are back in the commodity business and we might as well be producing sausages.

When you are coaching people about a specific vehicle, what kinds of things do you coach them on?

I usually ask three questions: (1) Are the visual values of the car design true to the marque that you are designing it for? (2) Do the values of that design differentiate our product from the competition? and (3) Do the values of that design have any meaning to the customer?

If they can answer those three questions, then we are well on our way to creating a foundation from which to work. If none of those questions can be answered, then it is back to the drawing board. When I work with a team, I go much deeper into the design process, but I use these crucial design criteria as a general rule of thumb.

Could you give me an example of this?

I tell my designers that we want to create a fair product for a good price, but we are not designing to a price, we are designing to a standard. And that standard is directly in line with a particular marque that we are selling. You have to give off the same message with consistency at any point of contact with the customer. If it is a luxury vehicle, like the Lincoln, I want every detail of the product to reflect luxury. I want the brochure to reflect luxury. I want the buying experience to reflect luxury. I want the dealership to reflect luxury, so that there is a consistency of message at any point of contact between the Lincoln and the purchaser.

I will give you a specific example from this morning. We were looking at the design of a new Lincoln key. The team came to me with a black plastic key with an impregnated Lincoln badge on it. And my question to the team was, "What separates this key from the entry-level Ford product?"

If I were looking for an American luxury car, the kind of key I would imagine would be a metal finish or something made out of titanium, a nice aluminum, or chrome. It would have a beautiful enameled badge on the key, signifying the luxury aspirations of the kind of vehicle the key goes to.

You are producing a luxury vehicle, so the key you put in your pocket should have those exact same values applied to it. If you don't pay attention to such details, even on small aspects of the design, there will be a disconnect there for the customer. We are talking about the key, but keep in mind that this is only one of more than four hundred visible elements on the product.

The implications for us internally are that by building a consistent message throughout our marques, we will start to garner more trust and brand loyalty, because customers will know when they walk into a Lincoln dealership or a Ford dealership exactly what they are going in there for and exactly what they can expect to drive out.

Any final comments?

The message I would give to anyone coaching designers is that you are really not designing a product, you are designing a relationship with the customer. There is a huge significance to that that is often overlooked. If you see yourself designing in terms of creating a relationship with a customer, then every single thing you do becomes a way to enhance that relationship.

It is not unlike a relationship you would have with your wife or girlfriend or that a woman would have with her boyfriend or husband. You do things to enhance that relationship, just as much as you possibly can, and when you do that well, you obviously create loyalty there.

CHAPTER THIRTEEN

TOM SUDMAN

E-COACHING TEAMS IN A VIRTUAL AGE

Communities have always formed around the places of commerce—where ships touch the land, railroads touch natural resources, and the Interstate touches the strip mall. Today, as we begin to make the shift to e-commerce, communities can also be formed around the places where enterprising souls can reach out and touch the World Wide Web. The center of commerce will no longer be New York, London, or Tokyo, but nowhere and everywhere.

Tom Sudman, founder of Digital AV and inventor of **knowledge rooms,** *a virtual space that allows far-flung collaborators to do mission-critical projects over the Internet, says, "The world is shifting from places to spaces. As more enterprising souls get connected, they will discover that the Internet is not only good for sending e-mail and buying books and other sundries. They will discover that they can think and work together in groups without having to go to an office or step on an airplane. They will see that they don't have to go to the city to work. They can live on a mountaintop or in a pastoral village. They won't have to put the kids in day care."*

Sudman is not only the prophet of this new era but also an ingenious and practical implementer. His clients include Disney, FedEx, and International Paper. Sudman hails from the burbs of the

Smoky Mountains of Tennessee. He and his group design the Knowledge Room according to the nature of the mission, coalesce the group, and coach them to produce extraordinary and tangible results independent of time and distance. For example, one Fortune 500 company that couldn't beat a two-year new-product-development deadline for a decade stepped into the Knowledge Room and cut its time-to-market in half. Sudman has also had outstanding results working on supply chain issues and customer relationships.

Sudman practices what he preaches. Several years ago, Sudman collapsed Digital AV's forty-thousand-square-foot office with a hundred or so people to ten thousand square feet and created an almost totally virtual organization, with employees who work in Knoxville or on the winding, mountainous roads of the Smokies. The result was a 30 percent fixed-cost reduction at a time when business had increased 200 to 300 percent. Says Sudman, "There are a lot of people who have all the dazzling new technology to do what we do, but they have trouble because they tend to be one-dimensional."

The secret to successful virtual collaborations lies in integrating the technology of collaboration, masterful coaching of groups made up of extraordinary combinations of people, and focused dialogue—the kind that leads to new knowledge and creative and innovative solutions. Sudman is also working with me to create the world's first virtual university in which Knowledge Rooms, e-coaching, and communicating on-line will be an essential part of the core curriculum—all essential skills for the twenty-first century. This interview captures some of his key ideas, methods, and techniques.

E-Coaching in a Virtual Age

INTERVIEW WITH TOM SUDMAN

Would you please say a bit about your background?

My teachable point of view comes out of the fact that for over fifteen years we've been looking at groups and how they work together to carry out something that is bigger than the individual. Since the 1980s, we have been doing group design with respect to live projects with technology enhancement.

In the 1980s, we were looking at assisting groups that were face-to-face, operating more and more independently of time and distance over private networks. Two things have changed this: the ubiquitous nature of the Internet, which has given everyone access to the group; and a natural evolution of groups working much more virtually. I would characterize Knowledge Rooms as a natural evolution of our company's use of virtual project teams to conduct our own work. It also takes into account the shift from projects to a wider spectrum of processes that use knowledge.

What is your teachable point of view about virtual organizations and knowledge management?

Today, relationships are the key to the creation of business opportunities, as well as to the creation of value. Now, if relationships are the means by which people create and sustain value, those relationships that we consider meaningful—such as customer relationships—usually lead to the formation of a multidisciplinary group thinking and working together with a clear goal or problem-solving focus over an extended period of time. The dialogue that results from these relationships usually focuses on the creation of new knowledge.

Although it sounds counterintuitive, virtual space often provides a superior medium for sustaining such relationships and group dynamics compared with a face-to-face medium. For people to meet face-to-face requires that they make their time and attention an issue, overlapping on a particular time and place, which often involves interrupting their normal thinking patterns and work flow. The result is that, if you operate solely in face-to-face meetings, there is a high degree of likelihood that the relationship (group) or project that you are working on will experience some kind of discontinuity due to time and distance constraints. E-mail has proven to be a highly effective medium for sustaining relationships, but it breaks down in terms of ongoing group dialogue.

Virtual space not only allows people in a group to sustain their relationship independent of time and distance, but also allows them to keep the conversation going about a particular goal or project without the usual time that is lost scheduling meetings and waiting for days or weeks to pass before they get back together. In order to sustain the project and the group dynamic, there needs to be a "space" for people to stay in focused dialogue with one another. The Knowledge Room, on the other hand, is not just an empty space, but rather a space designed to make it easier for people to share knowledge and create new knowledge specific to their goal or task.

Think about all of the times you have gone to conferences in big hotels, where people put up flip-chart paper with bullets, or displayed objects such as project prototypes, or played a video. Now think of the discussion that ensued around these objects and all the emotional and intellectual energy people invested in these objects. Then all of a sudden, it's three o'clock on Friday afternoon and people look at their watches. It's time to break down the room and tear the charts off the walls. It's time to catch a plane. So you schedule the next meeting and leave, and when you finally get back together months later, you discover that a lot of the intellectual and emotional energy you put into the topic are lost. Okay, so now think about what would happen if you could not only sustain the relationship with the people and group, but you didn't have to break down the room.

Imagine what would happen if you could create such a special Knowledge Room for every key customer, for every new product innovation or supply chain issue. Imagine if you had one place where everyone involved could come together synchronously or asynchronously and participate on a day-in-day-out basis on any key project. And imagine if you could, through the Knowledge Room, expand people's capacity to think and interact while dramatically compressing the time it takes to get the job done. We have discovered with some companies, for example, that it takes approximately three weeks of actual meeting time to bring a new product to market, but it takes two years to actually have the meetings.

We have also discovered that in a virtual medium people will usually not jump at the first good solution, the way they often do in face-to-face meetings due to time pressure. Rather, because it is possible to keep the Knowledge Room open, people will tend to abide by "the solution after the next" principle, which often leads to a breakthrough solution.

How effective is virtual coaching versus face-to-face, and how does it work?

The same thing I have said about virtual space often being a superior medium also applies to coaching. If I am the team leader and the group is going to have a face-to-face meeting between nine and eleven and the boss unexpectedly calls me into his office to handle a customer emergency, I've missed the meeting and any coachable moments that occurred in it.

If, however, I am operating in virtual space, I can rejoin the meeting at eight o'clock at night, look at the threads of conversation, and then still perhaps do some coaching by entering my comments to the others who were involved. It is also important to point out that a lot of the group dynamics issues that would apply in a face-to-face context—such as goals, dialogue, and deadlines—apply also in virtual.

Now, as we move deeper into the knowledge economy, what you are starting to see is the whole shift into virtual space and the importance of coaching. In the manufacturing and industrial era, there was this concept called *management*. You managed and supervised people in order to move a bar of steel into a finished product. Just like the new space is virtual space, *the new concept of management is coaching.*

The coach's role is to help articulate goals and challenges that inspire people to collaborate rather than hide in specialist silos. The coach's role is also to make the knowledge workers more productive—individually and collectively—not simply to get people to perform routine tasks. The coach needs to orchestrate the process of knowledge creation, taking into account that the knowledge produced as a result of people's work is more valuable than the objects they produce.

For example, when people used to make steel from iron and coal, the ersatz material was more valuable than what people learned in making it. Yet when people's job was to design the Web, the knowledge that resulted from the work process was more valuable than the objects that were the immediate results—hyperlinks on diskette or a few new network servers.

Many people feel that coaching is not necessary in a Knowledge Room, but I strongly disagree based on the experience of walking through hundreds of Knowledge Rooms a week. Let me use a metaphor. Let's say you have a factory, a machine, and people. I can put all three of these elements together and get nothing. Unless someone assumes the role of manager, you will not get a finished product. In the knowledge era, when value is knowledge, you basically have the same situation. If you just put people in virtual space and give them a tool called Lotus Notes or a chat room discussion, you get nothing.

What other elements are important besides coaching in a virtual environment?

There are basically three design elements that need to be brought into play in order to create the new knowledge. To use a metaphor, they are like three Olympic rings: (1) a coach who can assist people in articulating a goal or challenge; (2) a group of far-flung collaborators, each of whom has a particular perspective or knowledge of an issue; and (3) the intersection of real dialogue with an object (or shared work space).

Let me explain what I mean by this third ring. One of the things we are able to do with the Knowledge Room is give people the opportunity to place an object in a room—like a set of bullet points on a virtual flip chart or a three-dimensional object or a set of patient X rays—and then move back and forth between the object and the dialogue or stream of conversation that is posted on the screen.

For example, people may want to make notations on the bullet points for a big presentation to the board, or alter the shape of the 3D CAD CAM object, or make comments about the patients. This investment of emotional and intellectual energy transforms the object from information into a knowledge artifact. It is the intersection of the different views and perspectives of the people in the group through dialogue with the object that results in the creation of new knowledge.

For example, it could be three different kinds of doctors from different parts of the world making notations about what spots on an X ray of someone's broken hip might mean and then, through dialogue, coming to a shared understanding about what the right surgical procedure might be—something that they might never have come up with on an individual basis.

What are some of the basic steps in coaching virtual teams?

First, *establish a shared goal that brings people together around a purpose larger than themselves.* We've found that when you start with that as a given, you are going to improve the success potential of the project dramatically.

One of my defining moments in a group arises when they agree that there is an overall mission that is bigger than any individual in the group. Until people experience that moment of recognition, what you tend to have is a bunch of individual superstars who deliver suboptimal performance.

Here's an example. In working with the UPI [United Press International], before we could talk about how technology could enhance their process, we had to talk about the importance of creating a group. Here's the scenario: We have a photographer in the field with a breaking photograph—a premier being assassinated or someone just winning a Nobel Peace Prize or Michael Jordan scoring a game-winning basket. Besides the photographer, the process includes the photo editor, a newspaper editor who has budgeted a hole on the front page for a breaking story, an editor who is writing copy around the photograph, a newspaper publisher, and all of the counterparts in the newspaper who have to make judgments as to whether the story and the photograph warrant the space, and a finite amount of time.

We first got that group to recognize the goal of getting headline-breaking news photos in the paper faster, and then got the group to recognize that it was a group. For example, the photographer in the field can shoot a great shot, but the photo editor has to recognize the greatness of the shot, and an editor at a newspaper has to want the picture for the story. Then there has to be the technology to make it happen, which involves a lot of other people. Unless all of those things happen, it doesn't end up on the front page.

Second, *design the ideal group, not the practical group.* The question is, What group? Now you start to get into the really significant cultural issues. Suddenly, as you start to define in virtual terms, the ideal group of people to solve a problem in the Knowledge Room is probably not the same people you would pick when confined to the restrictions of time and space.

Up until now, when the question of who should be in a group was asked, the issue would have been, What's the *practical* group, not the *ideal* group, to put together? As we move into a world of virtual organizations, you no longer have to build a group from the people who are in the next set of office cubicles; you can build the team from the most talented and knowledgeable people you can find anywhere in the world. This may well mean inviting people to join who don't work in the same building, or for the same company.

Today it is clear that the great breakthroughs come from multidisciplinary teams, and that breakdowns usually result from some kind of fragmentation. This was the crux of the problem with the International Paper project we did. To be competitive, they needed to speed up their time to market by 50 to 60 percent. In order to come up with a new product design, a meeting was needed with a plant manager together with a design engineer in specialty chemicals, a marketing manager, a CFO, and others. We discovered that with everything else that was on their agendas and the number of times they had to get together physically to discuss a new product, the challenge of getting those people to schedule a meeting was the decisive factor in defining the product development cycle.

In other words, the product development cycle was not defined by the time it took to create the knowledge necessary to move from concept to market. It was defined by the time it took to schedule eight diverse people from eight locations into a common space. That's what took most of the time. It probably never took over thirty days to develop a new product, but it was taking significantly longer than that because of the difficulty of bringing everyone together.

Now, when you ask most people how to form a virtual organization, they think of a collaboration software product and in most cases walk right over all the fine lines of distinction that we have been talking about: (1) articulating a goal that inspires collaboration, (2) creating the recognition that it will take a group, and (3) designing the group based on what's possible given the new technology of collaboration, not just what's practical.

Third, *decide what medium of interaction the group needs to use—virtual space, face-to-face meetings, or both*. Once you decide who is in the group, you can then design which medium you want to use. My feeling is that anything that can be done face-to-face can be done virtually. Over time people start to recognize that once they define the problem and look at the ideal group (beyond two), the idea of working in virtual space begins to make sense.

I maintain that we've been working in virtual space for a long time; we just don't recognize it. When I fax you something and we talk about it on the phone, then we have "intersection," we have dialogue around an object. However, as the group becomes larger than two and the documents we need to look at become more complex, the telephone and the fax begin to reach their limits as vehicles for the creation of new knowledge. That's when a Knowledge Room becomes the medium of choice.

I want to emphasize, however, that for effective knowledge transfer and creation, you often need *multiple* media (as opposed to multimedia). The coach plays a key role in deciding, at any given point, what kind of media can best support the dialogue. The coach should think of himself or herself as an orchestra leader who calls on different instruments as appropriate. A great conductor would never try to create a symphony with one instrument. So as a coach I pay attention to the threads of conversation that are posted in the Knowledge Room. At a certain point I may decide that the group is becoming too divergent and we need to have a conference call that will lead to more convergent thinking around a particular issue. Or I may send everyone in the group a video to watch before a certain date. From virtual space I can schedule and link to multiple media, including face-to-face.

What does a Knowledge Room look like?

The Knowledge Room is not just an off-the-shelf, virtual team-room product. It is designed for each client around the necessary ingredients needed to transfer knowledge and create knowledge (not just exchange information). The Knowledge Room is not just a meeting place devised to create social structure, nor is it a status symbol to show how big a boss I am by how big a conference room I have or how many important people I can put in it. This kind of false mission we associate with brick and mortar.

What has to go on in the Knowledge Room is basically the things that are important for that group to create knowledge. One of those is dialogue, which we deem to be the seed of knowledge. You have to support dialogue strongly in all ways, shapes, and forms. The Knowledge Room should support however we want to communicate the next thing we have to accomplish. If that is voice, then it should support voice or we should use the telephone. If it is video, then it should support video. If it needs to be synchronized so that you and I are doing this at the exact same moment, then it needs to be synchronized. If it doesn't and it can be any time, then it can be any time. Probably the correct solution is some mixture of all the things we have mentioned, and not getting stuck in the issue that any one of those is any better than any other one.

Once we have a space that supports dialogue between knowledgeable people, we consider what kind of objects we want to put in the room. If in fact it is a retail chain and this room is about moving sales forward in a region, then maybe on the wall of this room there is a dynamic tote board that shows what the ongoing sales results are for that region. Or if it is about a particular store, then maybe there is a dynamic tote board that tells anyone who walks into the room at any time the sales, costs, inventory, or whatever. Anybody who is doing some kind of important task has something to look at that gives a flavor.

What are some key tips for coaching people in Knowledge Rooms?

When you go into a Knowledge Room and observe threads of dialogue, you may pick up various things that the group needs to be coached on.

First, *state the shared goal or focus in one sentence.* A coach might begin a session by asking, "What is the shared goal or interest that has brought everyone together? If possible, ask the group to state the answer in a complete sentence, which allows for the creation of shared understanding. Saying something like "revenue growth" doesn't.

It is important for the coach to create a certain amount of focus around the goals throughout the dialogue and not just allow it to wander off in all directions. You have to do this through a loose-tight approach and not by become overly controlling.

Second, *coach to maintain a sense of recognition that it takes a group.* You are always looking for whether the participants believe that the shared goal is going to happen not just through an individual but through a group. You can tell a lot about this through language. Watch for patterns of words, choices of words, changes of words. For example, someone goes from *we* or plural words into *I* or *me.* Or some people shut down. Those are the types of tipoffs you look for. This is usually a sign of grandstanding or of one person trying to dominate the group or lurking to find out what other people say so they can go tell the boss. I may make some public postings that focus on the idea that it takes a team effort. Or if I feel I need to coach someone, I may separate what I post to that person from the thread of dialogue. I can pull up your name and look at your posts in the last forty-eight hours, then present them to you and ask you what you think is going on.

Third, *observe whether the group is building shared meaning.* In face-to-face meetings, coaching is a nicety. In virtual space, it is an absolute necessity. In face-to-face meetings, people seem more able to balance divergent and convergent thinking to build shared meaning and come to a decision. In virtual space, the thinking tends just to keep diverging. The coach may need to intervene in this. It starts again with picking up on the language people use in their postings. Is the conversation drifting off in all directions with no focus? Are people asking each other questions to explore more about their points of view, or just expressing their positions and disagreeing? Are they building on what the others are saying? Are they stuck in disagreement? If the conversation is too divergent, the coach might put some postings such as, "Let's focus on the topic at hand" or "What are the things that we agree on?" or "What would be a good working decision for right now?"

Fourth, *use breakthrough thinking—the "solution after the next" principle.* For example, one client in the trucking industry wanted to be able to tell customers where their shipments were at any time. The solution the group came up with in the first session was to put that information on a private network. I suggested that instead of adopting the idea wholesale, they should apply the solution-after-the-next principle, which usually involves *looking for a solution at a higher level of impact.* The result was putting the information on a Web browser, which opened up this benefit to all customers and thus became a competitive advantage. They never would have come up with this solution in a face-to-face meeting format, because people would have had planes to catch and it would have been hard to get back in contact as a group again.

Fifth, *focus on collective work products.* People can talk about teamwork all day, but the experience of being a team often comes from working on and accomplishing something together. The coach needs to create a focus on producing a collective work product—such as a plan, product prototype, or process model. We have discovered that the only way to know whether the group has a shared understanding of the solution is when they set out to design, build, and test something.

Good questions to ask are, What are we trying to design? Is there a way to create a rapid prototype of that? Can we test the solution?

Any closing thoughts?

Again, to operate as an effective team in virtual space you need those three Olympic rings: (1) an extraordinary combination of people, (2) dialogue around an object, and (3) coaching.

Tom Sudman can be reached by e-mail at <tsudman@digitalav.com>.

CHAPTER FOURTEEN

CHRIS HIGGINS

COACHING SUCCESSFUL PROJECTS

Chris Higgins, thirty-six, launched his career as a lieutenant helping an elite battalion of Army Rangers get ready for battle. Today Higgins is a senior vice president at BankAmerica's Payment Services Project Management Division in Virginia, where he has been called "Mr. Project." His job is to coach project leaders and their teams in a division that manages the bank's largest technology infrastructure projects.

Higgins understands from firsthand experience that multidisciplinary projects that are provocative and risky have replaced uniform, repeatable tasks. "Project leaders are accountable for results, even when they have little direct authority over the resources they need," he says. "They need to coach others in a collaborative way to be successful."

Project leadership is a vital skill for everyone in management today—and I could find no better mentor. Higgins's own story bears this out. He joined the bank to run a team of 8 project managers. Within three years he was running a team of 140 project managers, with a combined budget of $100 million. Then he developed a training program, which 300 of the bank's project managers have gone through.

Higgins is a very bright, down-to-earth person who has a clear point of view about how to run projects and a remarkable ability to communicate it for a broad variety of applications.

Project Coaching with BankAmerica's "Mr. Project"

INTERVIEW WITH CHRIS HIGGINS

What is your coachable point of view about project management, and how did you develop it?

I believe in keeping projects focused and simple. It starts with focusing on the fundamentals. For example, when I first came to BankAmerica's Payment Services Project Management Division, I found 130 projects in various stages of completion. I gathered our top project leaders and handed them each a stack of blank index cards. I asked them to write the name of every project they knew about on one side of a card and a few sentences describing it on the other side. When the leaders showed me their cards a week later, we reached a conclusion that 30 percent of the group's projects were duplicating work being done on other projects.

I got a camera, stood on a chair, and took a picture of the table with the cards on it. The photo became our work program. The job was a matter of looking at the different technology projects, finding the common building blocks, and then focusing on those projects that would allow us to "architect" these building blocks. There are always certain utilities that can serve multiple applications. Once that was done, everyone was eager to get to work on one or two major technology projects, but I asked the team to devote time to evaluating business requirements, choosing the team, and anticipating technical challenges—all before we wrote a single line of code.

I believe that most groups would benefit if they spent more time planning and less time doing. Project teams are often too quick to act and too slow to think. If you spend enough time planning, execution time can be very short. If you work on the fly, you can do things fast, but you may do the wrong things, which slows down the project. This kind of planning isn't about creating a blueprint from A to Z or figuring everything out right up to the last steps; rather, it's about figuring out what is essential.

What life experiences led you to this coachable point of view?

I first learned this principle in the Army, when I was in charge of supplying the Ranger battalion stationed at Fort Lewis, Washington. I led a unit of 120 people that supported 650 Rangers.

We had to supply diverse missions in four different climates—mountain, tropical, desert, and arctic. The goal was to have the support group airborne, headed to meet the Rangers with the right equipment, within eighteen hours after receiving our orders. Under the previous leader, the unit never made that goal. Its best time was seventy-two hours. My team eventually did the job in twelve hours. How? The previous leaders always framed the job in terms of what was different for each project. I focused on what was at the core, or the same.

First, we inventoried everything we had in terms of equipment, then we wrote down the scope of the mission and the challenge it presented, and we began to formulate plans about how to succeed. People's reaction to the challenge was, "Oh my God, how are we going to pack for these different environments in eighteen hours?" What I did was turn the tables around by reframing the challenge: "Rather than focusing on what's different, let's focus on what's the same."

We found that 80 percent of the material was basically the same. For instance, we would have to bring a tent wherever we went. Now, whether we would bring a liner or a stove or mosquito netting was mission specific. So we began to formulate our plans around what was common. We took our "primary," packed it, uploaded, got it certified, and got it on flatbed eighteen-wheel trailers ready to go.

Then we packaged everything that was mission specific in modular form and also loaded it onto flatbed eighteen-wheelers. So, if I got a call that said we were going to support Arctic, I would just go to the trailers with my primary already packed on them and to the trailers with the Arctic gear and get everything onto the aircraft ready for takeoff. I learned an incredibly powerful lesson in terms of understanding the art of managing projects—that everything is built from the fundamentals, from what is "core." It also reinforced the notion of building blocks, which is how we architect our technology.

So you make finding what's core phase one of any project you do?

Yes, I learned that this is the most important step. In coaching project leaders, I suggest that the project manager step back and get an understanding of the full scope of the mission, then go back and focus on what's core. To explain to people what's core, I often use the analogy of the tent from my military experience. It is what I had to bring everywhere I went.

Understanding what is core is very difficult and it requires planning and learning—whether it is a new software application, operations, or building a new facility. The mistake is that people try to put their arms around a redwood tree, which is an impossible task. They try to put in all of the bells and whistles, and the project gets too big for them to handle. They start out trying to do everything. As a result, a lot of time and effort are lost and they wind up whittling everything back, because the project was overly complex to begin with.

Typically, what happens is that the executives who sponsor the project in the first place have a very short attention span. If you can't deliver something to them in six to nine months, they've lost interest, and you've lost their attention. It is impossible to deliver a highly complex solution in six or nine months, but what you can deliver is the core business functionality.

Do you act as a thinking partner in helping managers get to what's core?

I usually engage in a coaching conversation about what's core, because most people don't take the time to find this out. I ask the project leaders to ask themselves and their customers, What is your vision of the future? What are you attempting to do in the long term? and then, What is most fundamental and critical to that vision's success?

I tell the project managers that by listening well they will understand what is core about that vision. Other questions are, What are you trying to do long term? What is the most important thing to do short term that can be used as a building block for future things? What are the logical functions you want something to perform?

How do you ask questions so that the project manager takes it in the spirit of inquiry, not as an inquisition?

I interact with them as a coach, not as a boss. I ask them questions, but I don't shine a light in their eyes. I operate much more like a thinking partner. The first thing I do when I am trying to teach a project manager to figure out what is core is to accompany him or her to a business meeting with our business partners (or clients).

Typically, I try to coach a project manager to first come up with the requirements definition. At the meeting, we ask the business expert, "What are the requirements? How does this system need to operate in order for the project to be successful?" What usually happens is that the business expert will try to bundle up two hundred different requirements for that project. We need to make it clear that while it may be true that it will take all two hundred components to make that business tick, you cannot deliver all of those components in six to nine months. We need to find out what's core.

A junior project manager will usually jump in and presuppose that because they have a little knowledge about the business, they actually know the ten to fifteen requirements that are core. They will cut off the business experts right in the middle of the conversation and tell them what these requirements are, although they are often wrong. Also, the fact that they don't listen really ticks the business experts off.

The real art is letting the businessperson speak, describing the end-to-end process, and then helping the businessperson get down to what is core for him or her. It doesn't do the project manager any good to say, "Here are the twenty core fundamentals," or "Here are the five to eight basic logical functions that are being performed." The business person has to grow to understand and accept the functions that will become phase one of the project.

Do you have any processes that help the project managers elicit what's core from the business partners?

I have an exercise that I take people through, after they have had a little trouble identifying what's core. I hand a yellow pad of stickies to the business experts as they are describing all of their two hundred functions and ask them to write one or two words on the yellow stickies as to what each function is. As they are describing the basic functions, we write down two to three words and we take the stickies and put them up on a wall.

Once they are done and we have all of the stickies on the wall, we ask the businessperson to help us organize these business stickies: "What functions exist together?" We challenge the businessperson to organize the stickies into five to eight buckets. What we are doing is walking that business manager through a process to get to the core process.

When we have the five to eight buckets of yellow stickies stuck to the wall, we then say to the business manager, "Help me out. What are the three to five most important functions within each of these buckets?" And they will go through it and look at it and inventory forty, and they will pick three to five and we will stick them on a different wall. What we end up with are five to eight core functions, with the three to five most important things in each.

How would you know one of your project managers is not a good listener, and what do you do about it?

I know that first by looking at the business requirements they have submitted for a project—they are very long and very extensive. And second, they have not gotten down to core functionality.

When I have asked the question, "What are the core functions for this particular project?" they probably will not be able to answer. Then I say, "Okay, let's do this together." It may be that the project manager is not a very good listener. Typically that's the case, but you don't want to rush in and assume that the project manager is not a good listener. It may be that the client is really ornery.

In coaching the project managers, I try to put them in the customer's shoes by translating into an everyday situation: "What if you bought a new appliance and got it home and plugged it in and it did not work. So you called the 800 number and they asked you to describe the problem, and every time you tried to describe the problem they would cut you off and say, 'Oh, go check this, go check that,' and they never allowed you to get a whole description out. What would your reaction be?"

Then I would say, "Okay, now let us apply it to our client meeting the other day. Did you let the client tell the whole story, or did you try to shortcut that conversation and do some damage in the process?" It is a lot of hard work. I even find myself cutting people off sometimes. It takes a lot of discipline to keep asking questions and keep listening and trying to understand what people are saying.

What is the next step in terms of managing projects successfully?

Step two involves thinking about who you want on your team based on what is core. You can go back to your business partner and reiterate the five to eight things that are core and what in each function are the most important items to do, and then say, "We need to have these individuals work on the project team." The next step is to take that team of technological experts and create a very logical "to do" list, which is called a project plan, clearly delineating who is responsible for what.

It is important to make the project plan logical and simple—first things first. Does one task or activity follow another in a logical sequence? You should be able to pick up the project plan and, without talking to anyone, understand the process and path that this project is going to take; and by looking at who is responsible for these activities, you will know who is involved.

One of the mistakes a project manager makes is to try to be involved in doing too many things. If the project manager's name starts appearing multiple times on the project plan, then that person is not really a project manager but a project "doer." The person has not really involved the experts who have the right skill sets. What that will do is alienate people with those skill sets, who are paid to do those jobs. For example, the project manager's job is not to be the lead designer but to say, "All right, Doug, you are the lead designer; this is your responsibility on this project. You need to pull together your own team and resources and deliver a system design over the next six weeks."

How far out do you plan? I have heard you mention an eighty-hour rule.

One of my little rules on a "to do" list is that no activity should be over eighty hours. So I am not going to give Doug six weeks to give me a finished systems design; I am going to want to see the first cut in two weeks. No task should be more than eighty hours. I learned that the hard way. Doug is usually going to come back to my weekly project team meeting and I am going to say, "Hey, Doug, how are you doing on the systems design?" At week one, he will say, "No problem; it will be there in another five weeks."

The next week he will say, "No problem, it will be there in another four weeks." And that continues until about week four or five, and he will say, "Chris, we really have got to talk. I have not started on this because this other project over here was consuming all of my time." Now the whole project is at risk because one of the designs is not ready. It has pushed the whole timetable back. If you make Doug report on it every two weeks, you may have lost two weeks, but that is better than losing four or five.

What tools should a project manager use?

There are three basic tools that a project manager needs to utilize.

The first is *project tracking,* a logical "to do" list in two-week increments. I lay these out using Microsoft Project. I just use the basic format—the milestones, the tasks, the activities. You can organize groupings of tasks and it is really easy to cut and paste.

Second is an *issue tracking system*. You have to be very disciplined about tracking issues that come up. Issues are questions that come up about the project, distinct from things to do. We use our own in-house database to track issues and to follow up on questions, but you could use just a good notebook with a calendar built in. I have been responsible for projects for which the project plan consisted of three thousand tasks, and I have had 1,500 issues. You might think that is a very bad project, but actually that is a very good project because it means we are getting through the massive number of questions everybody has.

You also need a *financial report card*. We create a simple financial tool using an Excel spreadsheet. If the project is budgeted at a million dollars, we know that all of the various components equal a million dollars, and that goes down the left side. Across the top are the months for the duration of the project and we track what we spend each month, so we can project what the project will actually cost.

How do the weekly meetings work? Is there any standard agenda?

Let's walk you through a weekly project status meeting. First of all, the meeting should last for no more than an hour. Any meeting more than an hour is a workshop, not a meeting. The purpose of a project status meeting is to find out the status on the project, and to do this the project manager needs to follow a standard agenda. The first thing the project manager does is pull out the project plan, the logical "to do" list, and ask for reports on everything due that week. Is it done or is it going to be done?

Next, the project manager asks people to look at what is due two weeks out, double checking with team members to make sure those activities are on target. If they are not, the project manager asks, "What do you have to do to get things done?" or "What is causing you problems?" It may be that they need extra resources or help. It is important to make sure that projects due within the next two weeks are properly resourced and are actually going to be finished. This may mean people on the team helping in areas outside their expertise.

Once we have gone through the logical "to do" list, the project manager reviews all open issues, basically starting at the top of the list and recording the issue name and number, the issue description, and the questions. Issues always have to be stated in question form. We need to understand what the impact is, why this is an important issue, how it will be resolved, and by when the answer is needed.

The project manager goes through all of the issues that are open and then goes around the table asking, "Does anybody have any questions that we need to answer about this project?" And as the questions pop up, the project manager says, "A question has been raised. Who is going to own this issue?" And if it is in the systems area, he'll say, "Okay, Doug, you are the systems representative on the team; you own this issue. Next week when we come back, you need to report where we stand." The project manager needs to make sure that Doug understands the issue, knows that it is due in two weeks, and will prepare an update for the next meeting.

After all of the open issues have been reviewed and new issues have been added, the next important part (and this is a little trick I've learned over the years) is to understand what issues you can close out. That means that you have understood the question, people did the research, and a decision has been made.

How does the person who is responsible handle the issue?

Handling an issue may require calling an *issue-working session.* Doug may say, "I understand the question; now I need to pull in six different people from six different departments and we are going to have a conference call." The key in an issue-working session is to make sure you are framing the issue properly. Ask yourself how it can be stated in a question. If it cannot be, it is really a task or activity that needs to be put on the project plan. The group will then research the issue and come up with a working decision.

What is a working decision?

Back when I was managing projects, I saw that people were really good at collecting facts around a question. In one of my projects, lots of questions were raised at every meeting, but I wasn't closing any out. It was not that I didn't have smart people on my team, but they were frightened about making a wrong decision. So I came up with what I called a *working decision*—a project decision based on the facts known at the time. It does not mean that we cannot reopen it again, but we have to make some decision so we can move on. I keep a separate list of working decisions, and I catalog all key decisions that have been made about the project and distribute that with my meeting package.

That brings me to another important point. A good rule is that within forty-eight hours after the project meeting is done, a project package goes out to everyone on the team. In the project package is a very brief set of meeting minutes, the updated project plan, the updated issues list, the list of working decisions, and a financial report card. Everybody has access to the same information, which increases ownership and gets everyone on the same page. Lots of project managers make the mistake of hording that information. That is a kind of power trip.

What do you do to generate excitement around projects? Is it all logic?

I believe project managers need to remember that their work isn't just about solving problems and meeting timetables. It's also about maintaining momentum and morale. I pay careful attention to project rituals. From my first days at BankAmerica, I began projects with half-day or full-day kickoff meetings. It doesn't matter how big or small the project is; I always invite (require) the sponsor of that project to attend the kickoff. This tells the team members that the person is committed to the project, and allows them in turn to ask questions and learn how this project affects the next year's operating plan, budget plan, and profit plan.

How else do you motivate your people?

I started off with the kickoffs to create enthusiasm around something that is essentially a logical process. After a while, I began throwing celebrations for the completion of projects as well. Today, fun and games are a definite part of project life at the bank. We create checkpoints along the way, and whenever we hit one, we have a celebration. If project work isn't fun, people won't want to do it.

It is also important to give everyone credit. I am always out trying to understand who is going above and beyond the call of duty. My team is usually spread out over the country, so I will wander over the telephone wires or pop in unexpectedly on conference calls. I will find a way to go out of my way to thank people for their work. It is not a huge effort; it mainly takes discipline. It is easy to get caught up in the day-in, day-out.

You can reach Chris Higgins by e-mail at <christopher.higgins@bankamerica.com>.

CHAPTER FIFTEEN

HUBERT SAINT-ONGE

DRAGON SLAYER OF
HUMAN RESOURCE MYTHS

In his landmark book, **The Practice of Management,** *published in 1954, Peter Drucker asked a very provocative question: "Is personnel management bankrupt?" Drucker saw through his consulting work with companies such as General Electric, General Motors, and Sears that few human resource (HR) managers were integrated into strategic thinking processes, and at best their opinions were merely tolerated. Drucker felt that HR people, no matter how sincere or well intended, were too often trying to drum up fanciful HR programs that would justify their existence, only to become caught up in dispensing salaries and benefits and doing token training.*

In the past decade, almost every business function, from finance to marketing, from production to customer call centers, has been reinvented and given an attitude adjustment—except human resources. Says René Jaeggi, former CEO of Adidas, "No other area of business is in so much need of a revolutionary thought leader." In 1998, I received a scratchy cell phone call from just such a person—Hubert Saint-Onge of the Mutual Group in Waterloo, Ontario, Canada, who had come across my name on the Internet: "Can you send me some of your stuff?"

We soon developed a robust relationship. To me, Saint-Onge is not only an inspired, erudite, and original thinker on human resources, knowledge management, and organizational learning, but also one of the most practical, down-to-earth implementers of such lofty concepts in the real world of organizations. For example, when he came to the Mutual Group, he put an end to the stodgy HR organization altogether and replaced it with functions called Strategic Capability and Membership Services. I knew something was afoot when I asked one of his team members where she worked and her answer was "in Capabilities."

This was just after his departure from the Canadian Imperial Bank of Commerce (CIBC), where he had been given the mandate to create a learning organization. One of his first moves at CIBC was to shut down "training" and start up "learning networks." He disassembled a 150-person training organization and set up a learning network that would spread knowledge through discussion groups, books, videos, and so on. This was part of a larger set of initiatives in which the key objective was to shift the culture from one of entitlement to one of personal responsibility.

Having changed just about every part of the people management system at CIBC, Saint-Onge convinced senior management to build a $26-million Leadership Centre. He turned this facility into the world's most advanced center for organizational learning. With an annual budget of $15 million, the center serves more than six thousand participants a year in residential programs through which they receive feedback on the effectiveness of their leadership and examine the assumptions that shape their leadership practices.

As a coach, Saint-Onge had to convince senior management that this substantial investment would have the desired impact on the business. This required strong convictions and an ability to elicit excitement at what could be accomplished, as well as the ability to connect the preoccupations of these business leaders to solutions with which they were not familiar.

Saint-Onge has a caring, elegant, unassuming style, which can sometimes unintentionally disguise the strategic thinking and deft moves of a power player. He says, "I see my role as an organizational coach whose job is to close the gap between strategy and capability." This could entail introducing provocative ideas at top management meetings, making an Internet MBA program available to everyone in the company through Athabasca University in Edmonton, or orchestrating the integration following a bold acquisition.

Dragon Slayer of HR Myths

What do you see as the changing role of leadership in corporations?

What we are seeing is a dramatic shift from what I call leadership by *direct drive* (hierarchal) to an *indirect, more partnership-based* approach. This has come about largely due to the fact that the value chain is made up not of a single organization but rather of a network of organizations. At the same time, we still need leadership to make certain that performance of the individuals, groups, or networks is maximized in a competitive business environment. Coaching is an integral part of this high-performance, more collaborative approach to leadership.

Another thing we are seeing is that the role of coach in a big organization is not necessarily attached to just the leader. It is a role that various people on the team can play, depending on the issues involved. For example, in the top management group of the Mutual Group, the CEO can act as a coach at one point, but at other times the role of coach may shift to other members.

I see my role overall as coaching the organization, especially in closing the gap between the strategy and the capability of the organization to deliver great products and services to its customers at a profit. Some people may prefer to coach the individual, others may prefer teams. As an organizational coach, I look at the organization as a system, and even though I work with people either one-to-one or on teams, I seek primarily to have an impact on how the organization performs as a whole.

What is your coachable point of view about the future of human resource management?

If you look at the role of Personnel—as it has been called over the last hundred years—its job was primarily to manage the *employment contract* with a population of employees. The basic idea was to put aside your aspirations and suppress yourself, in exchange for a guaranteed future. The primary job of the HR manager was to administrate salaries, benefits, and the pension plan. In the industrial era, what most companies needed was some warm bodies to throw at a stack of unskilled jobs to support machines.

Today, as we move further into a knowledge economy, the strategic capability of organizations is determined not only by the skill and knowledge of individuals (human capital) but also by the capabilities of the organization combining to create powerful relationships with customers. As a result, the role of HR has shifted from managing the employment contract to expanding the strategic capability of the whole organization.

The demands of the marketplace are always being raised, which tends to create a gap between the strategic goals of the organization and the capabilities it has at any given time. In this context, it makes sense to have a function called Strategic Capability whose role is to close this gap—whether it involves strengthening the structural capital of the organization, its human capital, or customer relationships.

However, I want to make clear that when I am talking about the Strategic Capability unit at the Mutual Group, I am not just talking about a more, better, or different extension of the HR department.

How did you introduce these changes to your organization?

Before I joined the company, I had discussions with the CEO in which we agreed that traditional HR was not what the company needed. He readily accepted my proposal for a whole new business function called Strategic Capability that is not HR but embraces some of its functions. You have to make it a strategic role that involves sitting at the table with the top management group as a businessperson, not a stereotypical HR person, who is focused on salary, benefits, and training. It also involves codetermining the strategy of the organization. He said, "I don't want someone who comes in and just does HR work."

I then joined the firm and became a business partner involved in strategic discussions at all levels. We have applied the *Knowledge Capital* model to the organization. This model says that there are three components to an organization as we move into the knowledge era: (1) structural capital, (2) human capital, and (3) customer capital.

I created a three-year plan that included work on alignment of core values. We identified three core values: stewardship, partnership, and innovation, which we translated into leadership principles and behaviors. This was an important exercise that has powerfully influenced the way we make many decisions, from whom we should hire as a new executive to determining principles on how we deal with people in the event of a company downsizing.

I also made it clear to the other people in the top management group that I don't think of myself as a specialist in my job. Rather, I think of myself first and foremost as a business partner, although I contribute from a capability perspective. I expressed my opinions forthrightly from the beginning, because I wanted to make it clear that I was not going to be relegated to HR matters. My role is to ensure that we take a systematic approach to the management of our tangible assets. The place I come from is the synthesis of structural, human, and customer capital with whatever issues are arising.

Focusing solely on "people" issues or organizational issues would be largely vacuous if it wasn't centered on marketplace challenges and our relationships with customers. I don't believe in the split between things, like marketing, information technology (IT), and HR. For me, it is a mistake to say, "Let's ask HR about this," or "What does marketing think about this?" or "What would IT do?" As separate entities, they are all coming at issues from a too-narrow perspective. What we need is an integrated view. I am talking about bringing together all of the capabilities of the organization to develop the best possible relationships with customers. This is the point of view I bring to the management table.

At the same time, while I act as a business player with strong views, I also play the role of coach, which means I am always dealing with some kind of dilemma. I express my views on how to deal with business challenges, such as on the importance of developing strategic alliances while looking for ways to enhance the quality of strategic dialogue in order to produce together a level of insight that is greater than the sum of the parts. Opening up new areas of conversation or breaking a log jam to look at things in a different way are interventions that can help a team make progress. The others can then legitimately reject the idea because they were rejecting my idea, not the CEO's idea. If I put something out as an idea, it is a possibility; if he puts something out, it is closer to a commitment.

I am often consulted as a coach, as a sounding board, by people at all levels of the organization. In fact, our CEO sometimes calls me the "company chaplain."

What is the difference between your Strategic Capabilities unit and an HR department?

As head of the Strategic Capabilities unit, I see the role of the team as coaching the organization to reach strategic goals by designing people management systems that allow people to be at their best. These systems are enhanced by technology and a knowledge infrastructure. As part of this team, the *individual capabilities practice leader* has overall responsibility for making sure that our individual members have whatever they need to be at their best. The organizational capabilities practice leader is responsible for ensuring that the organization evolves to work on the organizational level and changes in ways that will optimize its performance over time. And between these roles, the knowledge team leader develops the technology infrastructure and the knowledge architecture for exchanging knowledge, accelerating learning, and building capability across the firm. (See Figure 15.1 for an illustration of the departmental structure.)

As an integral part of individual capabilities, *Membership Services* provides our members with support. Our intention is to create not a traditional company but a professional services firm in which all members contribute from a strong sense of co-ownership—an enterprise in which people feel they are true partners. We have eliminated HR because the traditional employment contract tends to evolve into a mind-set that treats people as indentured servants. We are no longer into employment serfdom. We are members of a professional service firm who feel that we are actively involved in shaping the future of the company.

FIGURE 15.1 *Structure of the strategic capabilities unit*

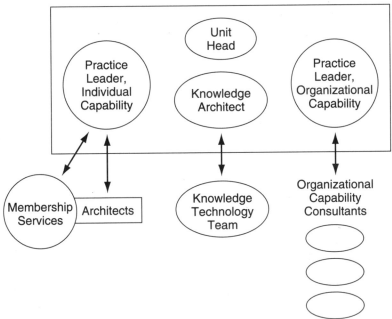

As members, we have a strong sense of ownership for our performance, for our learning, and for our careers, and we avail ourselves of all the services that are provided by the firm that allow each of us to be at our best in the organization. Our Membership Services unit allows people to avail themselves of everything they need on a self-serve basis, including career development opportunities, the chance to learn new skills and capabilities, as well as traditional HR services, such as answering salary, benefits, or pensions questions. It could also include such things as managing conflict with a manager or a sexual harassment issue.

We have found that the best way to deliver these services is either through a call center or through our intranet, where our community center site provides the information our people need. They call or go into the community center and see the offerings, such as job postings, competency maps for the kind of career track they want to have, and educational opportunities, and they do what they need to do. They do not have to go through their managers or anything like that any more. It is a true self-service approach.

Membership Services works on three levels. The first level is that a person calls or goes on the Internet to find the answers that are easy to give. The second level is when someone calls, for example, and wants a retirement calculation, or to know what the result will be if they invest their money a certain way, and it might take some time to think it through or give an answer. We will then get back to them by phone. The third level is a face-to-face interaction for more difficult situations, which need to be worked through in person, such as a conflict between two people.

There are six architects who design people management systems: (1) career development, (2) capability models, (3) compensation, (4) benefits, (5) workforce planning, and (6) organization processes.

Under Organizational Capability, we address strategic, whole-company issues. The leader of this unit works with a dozen coaches who have each been assigned to a business team. These coaches become members of the business team. Their mandate is to make sure that the business team is functioning at its best. So, now every team has a group process coach who is grounded in the real world of the business unit, whether that is sales, product development, operations, or whatever. The coaches have made huge contributions to the effectiveness of the various teams, and this idea has really caught on. No business team gets created without the question being asked, Do we need an organization capability consultant?

We have more work to do in making sure that they work against an organizationwide template. We are working with the intention that not only are the coaches part of their business teams but they are also working to develop teams in alignment with where the organization is going.

The third element is the Knowledge Teams, which have the mandate to ensure that knowledge is shared across the firm. We have trained thirty knowledge managers to form communities in which we learn together about critical and pressing business issues, and to share what they have encountered. This is not just abstract knowledge sharing; it is often job related, with very specific applications. For us, knowledge is tied to action. It is geared to enhance our agility, our capabilities, and our alignment.

For instance, when we bought the Canadian operations of Met Life, a major acquisition for us, we had to do the due diligence very fast or somebody else was going to buy it first. We formed sixteen teams with a total of 150 people, supported by our technology and knowledge infrastructure. These knowledge tools and our approach allowed us to outdistance seven or eight other bidders by a matter of weeks. With a minimum of managerial intervention, whatever issue came up was addressed and resolved immediately. Everything they encountered was put on that shared knowledge database. We were ready to negotiate on a billion-dollar-plus deal way ahead of anyone else. The investment bankers involved could not believe how fast we were moving on this.

Please share your approach to designing learning organizations.

We need to change the language of the organization and remove structural "pegs" that anchor the organization to the past. In this regard, I think the best thing that I have done at the Mutual Group is to eliminate HR and replace it with Membership Services. I think the best thing I did when I was chief learning officer at CIBC was to eliminate training and replace it with learning networks.

Many of the lessons I learned doing community development with native communities in Mexico still apply in the work I do today. First, you have to share a clear view of the future you want to create with people, but you have to work with them from where they are instead of from where you want them to be. Second, large-scale structural changes delivered through big program rollouts often fail by themselves to make a difference where it counts. The real difference they are meant to create rarely trickles down to individuals.

We often forget these two principles in the corporate world. Unfortunately, this propensity seems to be even more pronounced in HR. Not unlike the diamond cutter getting more preoccupied with his tools than with the diamond he is cutting, HR has a great tendency to get preoccupied with its tools and programs—things like 360-feedback, appraisal, and standardized curriculums.

I have discovered that you create a context for learning by paying attention to three principles: (1) linking the learning to the visions, goals, or missions that people (groups) care about passionately; (2) inviting people to be responsible for their own learning (or lack of it) and to accept the consequences of either; and (3) providing learning resources that fit each person's or group's learning style on a totally equitable basis.

It is also clear that if someone is actively involved in learning, he or she will be much more open to change [than someone who is not]. This in turn creates an organizational context that allows for a great deal of agility. This is why, for instance, we make available to our staff the opportunity to take an on-line MBA. This is costly, but we believe that the benefits are many.

If your goal is to support people in being at their best, it is important not to create a dependency relationship with them. People who are in dependency rarely are interested in learning. When I first went to CIBC, I spent two years reshaping every single people-management process to make sure it was based on personal responsibility and commitment instead of on dependence.

The first thing we did was create a job posting system in which all vacancies were to be posted by spelling out positions in terms of the kind of personal attributes that were required (being market orientated or a professional problem solver) as well as specific areas of competency, such as a discrete skill or piece of knowledge (investment management or systems integration).

We also helped people practice expressing their strengths in those values, attributes, and skills when they went on interviews. We gave them competency maps for different categories of jobs so people could say, "Well, I am not prepared for this job now, but if I take a three-year job in investment management or take these courses in systems design, I will be able to do it."

One day, after leaving the organization where I had put in place these career development and learning programs, a young woman in middle management came up to me and said, "When you first came to this organization, I thought you were totally unrealistic in what you wanted to achieve in giving us responsibility for our careers and learning. But I took full advantage of these programs as they became available. I have had three jobs since then and I am really proud of what I have achieved—and there are many more like me. I had to thank you when I saw you." I was deeply touched by this testimonial. This is the most validating statement anyone has ever made about my work.

Say more about how you transformed training into learning.

There were 150 folks in training at CIBC and what they were doing was really the antithesis of learning. All of their interest, skills, and capabilities were invested in running classes. That is what they could do. Ninety percent of what they were doing was classroom based, and they had to cart people from across the country at great cost to attend scheduled programs that usually ended up happening much before they were required, or much too late. I said we needed to move from a "just-in-case" to a "just-in-time" understanding of what people actually required in order to meet the necessary performance expectations.

Initially I had to explain to senior management that most of what was spent on training came nowhere close to producing the desired results. I spent a great deal of time explaining how the considerable amount of money spent on training was for the most part a net waste.

Essentially, I asked them two question. The first question was, What percentage of time spent in the classroom actually added to the capability of the individuals attending? In a classroom setting, the learners are all at different levels of competency on what they are meant to learn. Let's say that all of them range from 1 to 100 on a given competency scale. Most instructors will pitch their instruction at around the 30th percentile, so as not to be criticized by those who don't understand. As a result, at any given point in time, 70 percent of those in the classroom are not learning anything.

The second question I asked was, What percentage of what is learned in the classroom can actually be applied in the work context? Most of the instructors who were asked this question answered around 30 percent. If you combine the answer to these two questions, you get the following: only 30 percent of those in the classroom are learning at any one point, and of what they learn, only 30 percent can be applied on the job. This means that less than 10 percent of what is invested in training is actually contributing to enhanced performance.

When the question was asked, Why was this situation allowed to persist for so long? the answer was straightforward: no one owns the outcomes of the training—not the managers who send employees to trainings, not the instructors who respond to what is requested, and least of all not the attendees, who fail to see the relevance of the subjects taught.

Once business leaders went through this logic, they were ready for the solution: transforming training into learning. This is where individuals, instead of attending the scheduled course, are given access to the support material to learn what they need, when they need it to perform. Learning is then driven by the initiative of the learner. The time people spend learning has full impact and they acquire the capabilities they need when they are needed on the job. This is how 100 percent of the investment in learning hits the mark, as opposed to the 10 percent of training.

Once this rationale was understood by everyone and the vision of how learning was to allow everyone to meet their objectives was clearly defined, the transition took place without much difficulty. The people in the training department who had the required skills stayed to create *learning networks,* and those who could not find a place in the new structure were given the opportunity to find more worthwhile work elsewhere in the organization.

Would you get rid of classroom training altogether?

It is a matter of distinguishing what medium will work best for the learning needed. In general, classrooms should be preserved for *transformational* or double-loop learning, which requires questioning beliefs and assumptions about the business, for example, introducing a new vision or cultural change or working with people in a leadership seminar in an intense way with the idea of shifting a mind-set. In most cases, these kinds of courses are a small percentage of the training budget.

The classroom is not an effective medium for the exchange of explicit knowledge or single-loop learning—improving what we already do (like how to answer a customer call or handle questions about a product). This kind of transactional learning can best be delivered through a learning resource center with a strong Web-based training platform that results in the creation of a self-serve virtual university.

At Mutual, we are currently in the process of launching a learning center as part of our new intranet that we call Mutual Online. This virtual learning facility will guide our members on how to acquire specific competencies identified in their development plan. We even have some leadership development modules in the center; for instance, we have just completed an interactive program on change management in which a business can explore how they can be more effective at managing the change facing them.

Any closing thoughts?

It is important for me to create value in the organization where I work. And it is equally important for me to make a difference to the people in the organization who might benefit from what I have done. One of the things that I have most appreciated about working at the Mutual Group is the support I receive from the CEO and the management team to present these ideas, in written form and in various venues around the world.

Hubert Saint-Onge can be reached by e-mail at <Hubert.Saint-Onge@themutalgroup.com>.

CHAPTER SIXTEEN

JAY ABRAHAM

MARKETING GENIUS AND MONEY MAXIMIZER

Jay Abraham is an extraordinary coach. He has helped to grow ten thousand businesses in more than one hundred different industries through one-to-one and group interactions. He's been called "America's number one marketing wizard" by the **Wall Street Journal,** **USA Today,** *and others. During his twenty-five year career as a business coach and performance maximizer, he has developed a large body of principles that can be applied successfully in any business or profession.*

He is prodigious in thinking of different ways to maximize money for himself and for clients. He sometimes charges up to $2,500 an hour for a consultation, or a healthy percentage of the economic value added when he takes careful control and manages a client's hidden business assets—like the untapped market potential of a new IPO, Internet start-up, or "thirty something" privately owned company. For the rest of us, there is a wealth of supercharged marketing wisdom put out by Abraham Publishing in Rolling Hills Estates, California. Says Abraham, "I make money when my clients make money."

His clients run the gamut from companies like FedEx to veterinarians, from HBO to cosmetic surgeons, and from Shearson Lehman to Australian dentists. All rave about him and his generosity of *spirit and business impact. For example, Abraham coached one investment firm to grow from $10 million in sales annually to $500 million in sales in just a couple of years. Admittedly, the majority of his clients in the last ten years or so have been small to medium-sized business owners, but here lies opportunity in disguise.*

I found that whenever I brought up one of Abraham's ideas in client meetings with companies like Fidelity Investments, Adidas, Bell Canada, Merrill Lynch, or General Motors, it would stop the conversation and make people's heads spin. "What was that you said?" And what's more, every idea of his I tried worked. Whether you are a CEO, a division manager, or a business coach, here is a chance to sit at the feet of one of the most masterful coaches in business on the planet, as well as to learn invaluable lessons as to how to increase your deal flow, cash flow, and profits.

Marketing Genius and Money Maximizer

INTERVIEW WITH JAY ABRAHAM

How do you see who you are as a businessperson, and how is it changing?

Calling me a "marketing wizard" has a certain appeal, but in some ways that has become a limitation. What I really am is a *money maximizer.* I have the ability to recognize that almost everybody is sitting on overlooked business assets, undervalued possibilities, and underperforming opportunities. What I do every day is help people turn their untapped assets into windfall sales and profits, and then convert these into recurring streams of income.

What is your teachable point of view?

It is that whoever you are and whatever you do in your work—whether you are a Fortune 500 CEO or have division responsibility for any part of a profit-oriented business, or whether you own your own business or professional practice, or even whether you are a staff member in another's employ—you owe it to yourself, your business, your employer, your future to learn how to generate maximum return from everything you do. Let me be clear that when I say *maximizing,* I am talking about more than just getting the most profit, greatest productivity, and effectiveness from an action. It means also accomplishing maximum results with a minimum of time, effort, and risk—something most people never even think about.

I come from a viewpoint that says no individual or company purposely creates underperforming assets, doesn't take advantage of the possibilities and opportunities available to them, or operates with the intent of getting less impact from what they do. It's just that they have some blind spots that prevent them from maximizing. First, either they are not aware of what their hidden assets are, or if they are, they undervalue them. Second, they keep trying to do the same thing better (like doing the same mailings to the same people) even though it doesn't get different results, because they just don't know the superior options that are available.

For example, when companies first started making computers, the computers came with the software. Then someone recognized that this was a hidden asset, and today software sales exceed computer sales by far. Or most employees tend to follow a job description rather than asking themselves, "What are my real talents and abilities?" and then figuring out a way to maximize these for their own and their employer's benefit. Similarly, a lot of people spend a huge amount of time writing books and publishing books, and then never spend any time publicizing those books, which results in an underperforming asset.

What I do is shine a light on people's underperforming possibilities and assets that give them the essential strategies they need to optimize their business actions. This also involves getting them to recognize that their present circumstances do not represent the way it has to be. What often surprises me is the astonishing results that the people and businesses I coach get from applying just one or two of these ideas.

What were the life experiences that forged your point of view?

I have had the good fortune of looking at over four hundred different industries around the world in depth, which taught me incredibly valuable lessons. Today, most of the big four consulting companies tend to stick to one industry, which gives them a specialty. However, it also tends to leave them prone to sticking with the same severely limiting strategies that everyone else in the industry is prone to. I don't want to be disrespectful, but it can become like the blind leading the blind.

We know, as Peter Drucker has pointed out, that breakthrough innovation usually comes from snatching ideas from different industries. For example, Federal Express is successful because they borrowed an idea from banks based on the hub-and-spoke system, where checks would all be sent to one processing unit and then sent back to branches. Another example is Tom Landers, who was looking for a way to apply deodorant better and came up with an invention based on the ballpoint pen.

What I can claim that few others can, as a result of my exceedingly diverse experience, is the ability to ponder my clients' goals and challenges in a Socratic dialogue with them, to creatively calibrate across hundreds of different industries, and then to come up with a brilliant flash of the obvious that will produce a real business breakthrough.

I want to share a fascinating discovery I made years ago. If you look at a hundred different industries, you discover that each industry has pretty much depended on just one basic successful practice to generate and sustain clients: direct sales, referrals, a field sales force, the Internet, and so on. That alone is amazing, but what's more incredible is that if you look at a hundred different industries, you will see more than ninety-five totally different success practices being used. Industry A doesn't know anything about the methods of Industry B, corresponding Industry C is totally unaware of the way Industry B sells and markets, and so on. By helping people study and identify the fundamental principles that drive the successes in a hundred different industries, you will be able to choose the most powerful and effective breakthrough strategies to introduce into your company.

Let me add that my point of view has also been forged by the fact that I have worked on the front lines of capitalism, putting my observations and strategies into play, by putting a billion dollars of my own money and other people's money on the line to validate what has worked and what has not. For much of my career I have worked on the basis of getting paid for the economic value added (EVA) I brought to the table (financial performance). In other words, I make money when my clients make money.

How do you usually enroll clients in working with you as a coach—or money maximizer?

I know I talk a lot about making a profit and increasing revenues. This can sometimes be misleading in the sense that it may lead people to believe that I am someone who cares only about success. In truth, who I am is really about making the maximum contribution I can to the maximum number of people. I believe that if I do that, then success will follow. In answer to your question, what I am really saying is that a lot of people don't approach the selling process for what it really is, which is a contribution process. My philosophy is not to hold anything back, even if I give a lot away for free. The world of business today is such a dynamic process that teasing the customer with a few tidbits that show what you are going to do for them, if they buy, is really dumb.

Something I have found powerful in establishing new relationships is an attitude I try to teach everyone I ever work with. I tell the potential client that, "It's only a matter of time before you and I have an economically satisfying relationship. And if I have to wait to contribute to you because you haven't paid me yet, it is sort of stupid. Why? The reason is that, the more I can contribute to you now to enrich, solidify, and enhance the quality of your life, your business, and your performance, the better off we will both be when the transaction finally occurs." This is one of the most charming and disarmingly powerful and simple approaches to business development.

Now, there is method to my madness because from the moment I start to add value I tell my clients, "I've probably got more knowledge, more understanding, and more capacity to help your business than anybody in the world. Now, you don't see that yet, and I understand that fully, so I am not going to push you to do business with me. What I am going to do is just start adding value and let you decide for yourself." I think the smartest thing to do is to start adding value to the other side, because it is only a matter of time before it will come back to you.

I fall in love with my potential client and say, "It grieves me immensely to see you miss out on opportunities because I am not even in your life. So what I am going to do is start sharing with you the stratagems, observations, and constructive critiques and introduce you to people I think you need to know. I am going to do this knowing that it is only a matter of time before you are going to become clearly aware of the contribution I can make to you."

How do you coach people to leverage their marketing and maximize their revenue? What does the process look like?

Step 1: *Get the lay of the land.* I put my Socratic hat on—one of my favorite role models—and start interviewing the person, whether a Fortune 500 CEO, a small business owner, or a professional. I take the stance that the person has hidden assets, potentialities, opportunities that could produce a much higher yield, and knowing that, I am going to hit pay dirt.

First, I just want to get the lay of the land. What's the person's passion, the nature of his or her business, and how it works? For example, if your field is coaching, I would ask, "What does a coach basically do? Who are the biggest clients for it? Why do they seek you out? What would be the most tangible application? Who is the competition? What are the ways you traditionally market and sell your services?" I always want to observe and appreciate the whole premise on which that person's business is founded before I challenge that reality.

Step 2: *Find out the method in their madness.* Next, I start to look at the rationale behind doing something in a particular way. I question whatever they take for granted in a curious way, not in a judgmental way. Then I take each piece of their business apart and explore the method in their madness. This could include new product innovation, their usual approach to marketing, and their primary method of getting customers. I want to know in my own mind that they do it that way because they have studied fifteen other alternatives and decided it is the most viable.

Step 3: *Plant the seeds for a superior strategy.* I start to get them to question their stratagem and tactics without necessarily leading them anywhere. I plant the seeds of them needing to defend their positions. I want them to be able to defend them, because if they can't, I want them to come to their own conclusion that the basis on which they're doing something is not fundamentally sound or viable. For example, How do you run your business? Is that the most creative and effective way to run it? How do the most successful people in your industry do it? How come you don't do it that way?

Step 4: *Maximize what they are already doing well.* I try to be empathetic, knowing that they probably don't know why they are doing it that way. I let them off the hook of culpability while opening the window of a superior solution. I am not trying to win the war; I am trying to give them battle strength. I start by making suggestions about what they are doing right now that they could get much more leverage out of, whether Jay Abraham is in their lives or not. For example, let's say you have three hot products coming down the innovation pipeline, fifty salespeople in the field right now, and twenty magazine ads that you are running. I want to look at those transactions and figure out what I can do right now that can give increased boost, thrust, and performance to each one. This is a way of giving them a validation, a confirmation, a win, as I work my way toward an overall superior strategy.

Step 5: *Suggest lots of alternatives based on other industries.* I then begin suggesting lots of alternatives that they have probably never thought of. I say that here are two or three examples of where that has worked really well in other businesses outside (or inside) their industry that I have been involved with or studied. Then I look for peer confirmation by asking for examples they may know of where this same approach has worked in their own field. It gives them comfort because they know I am not asking them to do something that has never been validated before. We go through a litany of what if's, and why do's, and how would's. I am subtly introducing many provocative, superior, or comparable alternatives for them to add to, buttress, or replace what they are doing.

Step 6: *Arrive at an elegant solution.* By now I have looked at all the complexity of their business, processed it, and boiled it down to the lowest common denominator. Somewhere in this process I am going to make use of one of my greatest gifts, which is to be able to come up with an elegant solution. It may come out in a declarative way, but as it is usually a result of a long process of curious questioning on both of our parts, most of my clients are able to seize it and own it, seeing it as their idea, not mine. I like to get the "Aha!" response.

What are some of your most powerful strategies that help people and businesses find hidden gold?

There are a number of key strategies I focus on, and they can be successfully used by the Fortune 500 CEO, the small business owner, or the single employee. It starts with a basic mind-set about what it takes to grow a business. Peter Drucker said that there were two ways to grow a business exponentially: innovation and marketing. These are the areas I focus on.

Let's take innovation first, although the two are dynamically interrelated. The key is to change the rules of the game, not to play by the same rules that everyone else is playing by. Take America Online: they didn't invent the Internet, but they made it broadly available to people, which changed the way many people communicate and do business. The same with amazon.com, which made it possible for people to buy any book without leaving their home or office, even books that are out of print. No wonder their stock went up 400 percent in less than one year in 1998.

The truth is that there are not ten million really new ideas, there are only a few; so a powerful source of innovation is to find out what the customer wants and then combine ideas in an innovative way, such as borrowing ideas from different industries. Success is often a matter of learning to recognize the income-increasing connections that are all around us. Sometimes it is a matter of being able to recognize the most obvious and simple. Here are some examples:

Milton Hershey was surprisingly the first man to see that selling chocolates in huge bars was undesirable to a lot of people who really wanted just a little bite. So Hershey's Kisses changed an industry.

Perrier was the first company to apply cola and beer brand positioning techniques to sparkling water. A quart of Perrier sells for over 40 percent more than a quart of Budweiser does today.

The modern flush toilet was invented in 1775, but it wasn't until 1857 that somebody thought up toilet paper.

Ice cream was invented in 2000 B.C. Yet it was 3,900 years later before someone thought of the ice cream cone.

What are some power strategies for leveraging your marketing?

The first thing I do is give people a whole new mind-set. I show people how to work on the geometry of their business, which is a metaphor that we use to help people engineer exponential growth. How you get quantum leaps is to work simultaneously on the three ways to grow a business: (1) increase the number of customers, (2) sell more per transaction, and (3) increase the number of transactions. Let's say you have one thousand clients. They average $100 per transaction or sale, and they make two purchases a year, for a total income of $200,000. Watch what happens if you increase these numbers by only 10 percent.

$$1,000 \times \$100 \times 2 = \$200,000$$

$$1,100 \times \$110 \times 2.2 = \$266,200$$

Most companies operate like a diving board. The board is their revenue stream, which they hope to increase; the stand is the primary method the company employs to generate that revenue, for example, joint ventures and channel distributors, direct sales, a field sales force, or referrals. If anything happens to that one mechanism, the company is in danger. (See Figure 16.1.)

Now, imagine the Parthenon in Greece. It has been there for thousands of years. (See Figure 16.2.) It is strong because it has many pillars supporting it. My concept is to have pillars and pillars of revenue-generating (or assisting) activities working in conjunction to multiply and bring geometry to bear on the business.

Imagine how much your business could grow geometrically if you brought to bear additional revenue-generating pillars. More importantly, imagine that underneath each of these additional pil-

FIGURE 16.1 *The diving board method for growing a business*

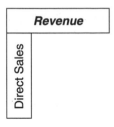

FIGURE 16.2 *The Parthenon method for growing a business*

Revenue								
Direct Sales	*Telemarketing*	*Referral System*	*Joint Ventures*	*Direct Mail*	*Advertising*	*Developing a Back End*	*Endorsements*	*Host/Benefit Relationships*

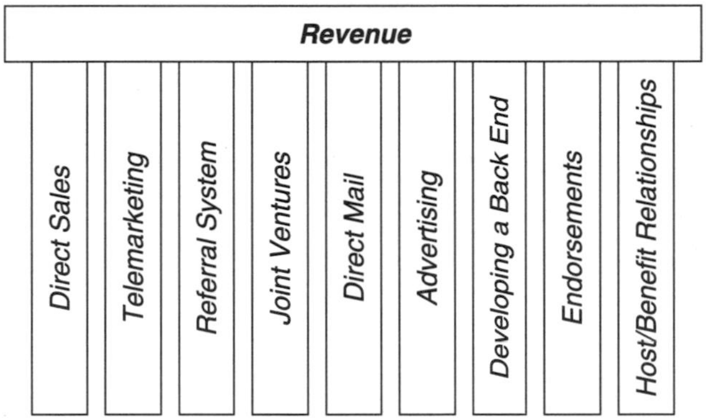

lars you engineered additional reinforcing pillars—twenty other selling approaches that vastly reinforced that approach.

For example, a company may be trying to increase revenue through advertising. I know at least fifty different ways to improve advertisements, such as getting rid of institutional ads (or tombstone ads) and replacing them with ads that lead a customer to actually carry out a money-making transaction with you. Another good example is evident with entrepreneurial firms that have a field salesforce. That group usually does just one thing: sell the product. I might know fifty different ways to use a field salesforce. Or referrals—it is amazing that companies think their business comes from their field salesforce when it actually comes from referrals. Yet they have no systematic ways of tracking and increasing the number of referrals they get.

Please share some of your favorite strategies, methods, and tools in more specific terms.

Create a unique selling proposition. Go to a cocktail party and ask people to describe what their business does that is different from all the other "me too" competitors. Sadly, most people will be at a loss to tell you. Or they will say very general things like "service," "quality," or "total solutions," which don't tell a customer exactly what they are going to do for them, like Federal Express's unique selling proposition does— "We guarantee delivery absolutely, positively in twenty-four hours." If you can't articulate why buying from your company is the only decision for your customer, then you are surrendering the business to your competition.

Test everything! A marketing genius is not someone who is always right about what the market will respond to. Rather, he or she can devise simple, powerful, cost-effective tests to find out. It is mind-boggling how many companies don't test any aspects of their marketing, such as their ads. They bet their destiny on arbitrary, subjective decisions and wild guesses. The best test for an advertisement, for example, is not to run a focus group to see what people like. Rather, it is to run two different ads that give the customer an opportunity to engage in a transaction, and then see which one brings in the most revenue.

Break even today, break the bank tomorrow. Let's face it, the place where most companies make the most profit is from repeat business. Why is it then that so many companies insist on making a big profit on the first sale? Wouldn't it make more sense to break even today and then create a relationship that would allow you to break the bank tomorrow (and the day after)? Try this experiment: Estimate how much the value of the typical good customer will be over time. Then reduce the barriers to that customer buying from you by lowering the price of the initial sale to where you break even.

Reverse the risks. Guarantee the outcome or give customers their money back. A lot of companies offer some kind of guarantee but don't push it into the heart of their selling process. I believe in "better than risk free." I send my clients audiotapes before a seminar, before they commit themselves. Then, when they sign up I send them $500 worth of materials a full week before attending. I still don't consider this a commitment. If by 2:00 P.M. on day two of my three-day program they decide not to continue, they can leave and have an immediate refund, plus keep all of the materials with no hard feelings.

Always have a back end. Many people and companies make an initial sale but don't have a back end or any add-ons to sell. Sometimes people don't do this because they feel it means applying too much pressure. I often use an analogy with people who have that issue. I say, "Pretend that you are coming to Jay Abraham's Water Emporium. You come in and are really parched and ask to buy half a glass of water. If I enthusiastically sold that to you without first trying to make sure how you would get the other seven and a half glasses you need so that your body and brain chemistry would function properly, I would be doing you a disservice. Now, at the same time as I enthusiastically sell you those glasses of water, I am both increasing the value of the transaction and your satisfaction as a client. This will directly result in an increased number of transactions."

Any final thoughts to sum up?

Simply stated, a masterful coach can use two possible strategies to increase business income and success. The first category is *maximizing what you have.* This has to do with helping people leverage their hidden business assets, as well as the best strategies they already have in place to cause customers to do business with them. Be ready to coach people on using this in conjunction with the second category of income and success strategies: *multiplying your maximum.* Create multiple sources of income. A simple analogy: If you are fishing and have one pole with one line in the water, you will be able to catch only a limited number of fish. But if you use ten poles and ten lines with ten different baits in the water at the same time, your fish-catching potential will increase significantly.

Jay Abraham can be reached at (800) 635–6298.

CHAPTER SEVENTEEN

ART WILSON

COACHING LARGE, COMPLEX, TEAM-BASED SALES ACROSS BOUNDARIES

Some time back, I was at a kickoff meeting with a senior executive of a company that is a big provider of data services. The executive was addressing a group of thirty of his people—finance people, project managers, consultants—on the issue of sales, saying, "This year we are going into the year with half our business plan unknown—without knowing where half our sales are coming from. We need to understand our clients' needs at a higher level, and to do that we need to have a higher level of consultative selling skills throughout the organization. That means each and every one of you." People looked up in disbelief.

Then Art Wilson, of Critical Path Strategies (CPS), an outfit that consults with major companies in strategic selling, walked into the room to talk in his Texan drawl about coaching on major account selling and a company culture in which "everyone is in business development." Says Wilson, "Most professionals in companies tend to view their world through a pipe. They crunch numbers, design specs, produce widgets, and service customer needs. Many don't see how what they do connects to the customer, except in a way that is abstract or three times removed from any direct contact."

According to Wilson, an ex-IBMer who for five years in a row was on their top ten list in sales and sales management, "When these professionals get involved in the selling process, they are able to come out of that pipe. It is an eye-opening experience. Not only do they see the customer's needs at a higher level, but they also begin to see how they personally and collectively add value at a level they never thought possible. This can really expand the customer's recognition of value and make the sales and profit curve jump up."

Twenty years ago, if I had been looking for a sales guru for this book, I would have called Zig Ziglar for his famous Vince Lombardi quotes; fifteen years ago, I would have called Tom Hopkins for his closing techniques; five years ago, I would have called Larry Wilson or Miller Hieman on relationship selling. Today, there is no question that Art Wilson is one of the nation's leading gurus on coaching virtual sales teams. Wilson and his colleagues at CPS are doing leading-edge work coaching virtual sales teams to achieve extraordinary goals in their large accounts in an environment shaped by global competitors, ever-increasing customer demands, dizzying technological change, boundaryless corporations, and the increasing tendency to blur the distinction between producer and consumer. In other words, reality.

Coaching Large, Complex, Team-Based Sales Across Boundaries

INTERVIEW WITH ART WILSON

Could you paint a graphic picture of today's selling versus the old way?

The old selling worked this way. Rick F., sales manager of XYZ Ball Bearing Corporation, would assign veteran salesman Bill G. to a territory or a group of major accounts, then check up on him once or twice by phone, and maybe once a year make an account visit. Bill would walk into the customer's place of business, get the order, shake hands with the customer, and walk out. The only people Bill ever talked to back at the factory were the "girls" at the order entry desk. The guys on the floor would take the order, load the goods into a big cannon, and fire it into the customer's premises. Bill would show up again in three to six months. Today, XYZ Ball Bearing is out of business.

The new major account selling usually involves a coach, who may not be the sales manager at all, and a fluid, independent group of problem solvers who are really there to service customers, to partner with them in solving business problems. But how does it work? As a participant in our seminars shouted out at me, "How do you organize these sales groups?" The answer is that they often organize themselves, but in fact there are two kinds of sales coaches—the ones who wait to have people assigned to their teams and the ones who round up the teams themselves. Guess which ones are more successful?

It works like this: Sally J., a respected data services consultant, calls you, Sam F., and says she has heard from Dave B. about your brilliant performance as a coach on the Dallas Instruments major account sale. She sees a similar opportunity with a few intriguing possibilities coming up with KL Computers, which is interested in outsourcing its data services.

Let's say you agree to sign up and get going as soon as you finish your current project. As soon as you put the phone down, you turn to the whirling Rolodex in your mind and jot down the names of seven people you would like to have on your team—maybe from three different states or three different continents. Then you start contacting these people by phone or e-mail.

"Hi, Manuel. Sally from consulting just enrolled me into coaching this major account project. Can you be available for a meeting on Tuesday (face-to-face or virtual)? It sounds really intriguing. I believe you could contribute a lot. I think you might beef up your knowledge of . . ." and so on.

In the next forty-eight hours, you successfully recruit the other members of your team. At the meeting on Tuesday, you create a breakthrough goal for the account and then develop the strategy and tactics to reach it.

Is sales management about to become part of the coaching revolution?

In many organizations, hierarchal sales management structures have been or are being replaced by self-directed selling project teams. These teams are composed of people from various places in the organization. The selling project could be a big account, a sales opportunity, or even a business partnership. The implementation of a coaching "culture" is emerging as a competitive differentiator in bringing these virtual teams together around extraordinary sales goals, enabling value recognition by the customer and profitable growth for the sellers.

The role of the coach has traditionally fallen primarily on the shoulders of the first-line sales manager, but this is changing quickly because many salespeople, and particularly the nonselling professionals who are involved in making the sale, do not report directly to the sales manager. Managing large accounts and large, complex sales opportunities is no longer the responsibility of just salespeople and their management. It is the job of everyone in the organization who interfaces with the client.

What business factors are creating a climate for coaching?

First, *the demands of the marketplace have forced companies to do complex, difficult things continually for customers in order to meet and beat the competition.* This has increased the complexity of effectively pursuing major accounts, complex sales opportunities, and key relationships.

As a result, most companies have expanded selling to major accounts from a one-person "Lone Ranger" game to a team enterprise. This has required a change from hierarchal to virtual selling organizations, as well as the expansion of selling roles to distribution and partnering organizations.

Today these selling teams are more project oriented. They can consist of a broad group of professionals, including technical specialists, operations, research and development, consultants, distribution channels, and even competitors and customers. The sales leaders must build relationships with insiders and outsiders and nonsales professionals, many of whom come from a project management or operations background.

The complexity of managing through this is often beyond the experience of most of the individuals responsible for leading the selling teams, as well as beyond the knowledge of those managers charged with directing them. We have found that instilling coaching into the selling culture provides a solution to these puzzles. It is a consistently powerful method that leads to extraordinary results.

Second, *there's now a need to outsource business functions and projects.* Reduced staffing levels and a significant increase in competitive pressures are causing customers to focus much more on ways to use outside resources to accomplish their missions. Outsourcing at the project or functional level has become a way of life for most organizations. This increases the value of selling organizations that are dedicated to meeting customer needs.

Also, the way customers buy has shifted dramatically from buying specific products or services to buying solutions that meet specific needs. This shift is creating incredible new selling opportunities for selling organizations that are customer-centric.

Most customers' executives now see tremendous value in and are very open to reducing the number of vendors and integrating the remaining key vendors into the very fabric of their organizations. Some of our clients' customers see bottom-line costs of purchased products and services reduced up to 35 percent through "sole sourcing" with trusted vendor teams.

A coach can support the sales leaders and teams to stay focused on customer needs and to stretch to ensure that efforts are directed toward accomplishing extraordinary results, not only for individual complex selling projects but also for the overall company-to-company relationships and relationships with key personnel within the customer's organization.

Third, *because of significant changes in the entire selling organization, the role of sales manager has changed significantly over the past few years.* Many nonsales managers—such as national account owners, principals in consulting organizations, and project managers—now have the role of managing the selling process. In fact, the participation of these people in our training and account strategy sessions has grown from less than 20 percent to more than 60 percent during the past six years.

As the selling situation becomes more complex and the people involved become more diverse, the role of coaching becomes critical. Targeted coaching of functional selling teams and their leaders to help all of them acquire strategic selling skills can have a dramatic impact.

Sales leaders and coaches are the key focal points for creating a high-performance selling culture. When they employ consistent coaching practices, enabled by tools and techniques, they can help transfer experience and enable these diverse professionals to get quickly "into context" with the selling situation so they can bring their expertise to bear.

What is your coachable point of view on teaching salespeople and teams?

Since 1992, at CPS we have been developing high-performance thought processes supported by a set of coaching tools that help selling teams create and manage strategies for large accounts, complex sales opportunities, and key relationships. They are centered around logical planning steps that enable the team to define an extraordinary goal, develop a strategy, execute the work plan, then review and update the work plan until its successful completion.

We have also distinguished four *habits* (steps) for coaching in the complex team-selling environment. Although there are many facets to becoming an effective coach (for individuals or for selling teams), we have observed that the leadership's incorporation of these four critical habits produces breakthrough results for selling teams. Also, within each of these four habits we have a *best practice* that we have found most useful for becoming a world-class coach.

My overall coachable point of view is to learn from the best. The subject of large-account-selling best practices has intrigued me for thirty years, ever since the day my IBM branch manager, Dick Haar, told me, to my surprise, that I was going to be a salesperson rather than a systems engineer, the job for which I had been hired. Although being in sales gave me a great deal of anxiety, it was the only option available at the time.

During the first meeting with Bill Barley, my new sales manager, he asked me how I felt about the job. I told Bill that I was excited. Actually, I was petrified about getting up in front of groups and about making sales calls. I asked for his suggestions about getting started and excelling. He suggested that I find the territory salespeople who were most successful and then identify and adopt their best practices.

What I found, over time, was that these best territory salespeople did only a few things differently but had substantially higher results. The best tended to do 50 to 100 percent more business than the average salesperson. (Later I discovered that the sales reps and selling teams who sold to large accounts produced 200 to 1,000 percent higher results than the average.)

What are the four coaching habits?

The four key coaching habits we employ encompass changing the manager's and team leader's roles with the selling team. They form a sequential process for forming and maintaining a high-value coaching relationship. The coaching habits are:

1. Establishing high-value coaching relationships

2. Identifying "coachable moments"

3. Helping teams develop extraordinary goals

4. Getting commitment to actions

How is a high-value coaching relationship established?

Whether the coaching relationship is requested by the "player" (the person being coached) or by the potential coach, it is very important that this relationship (and the act of coaching itself) be clearly separated from any other, preexisting relationship. Otherwise the conversations will quickly revert back to the previous relationship.

Also, it should be a cardinal rule of every coach to ask permission to give coaching, every single time. A player who has given permission to be coached will always be more receptive. Without permission, the coaching runs the risk of evolving into telling, directing, or preaching, as well as people resisting.

For example, recently I was meeting with a salesperson who was responsible for one of his company's largest customers. The salesperson was very emotional and was loudly complaining about the situation with his customer and asked for my advice. However, every time I tried to interject, he would complain more loudly.

I finally decided just to let him talk, and after a few minutes I asked him if he wanted me to coach him. He sat back and said yes. I then asked him a few questions. We quickly found what was missing and then developed some short-term actions that might correct the situation. Before I asked the question, I was just someone convenient to dump on. After the question, I became a partner in solving the problem.

One effective way to establish a good coaching relationship is to share your coaching philosophy with the player and be true to it. I have found it best if the coach

- *Listens hard!* Coaching is a conversation, not an interrogation.

- *Offers and suggests, rather than tells and dictates.* Mutual trust is extremely important.

- *Asks thoughtful questions.* Count to five slowly before interjecting.

- *Helps the player find out what is missing to move forward.*

What is the best practice for establishing a high-value coaching relationship?

The best practice is to establish a coaching relationship even when "it ain't easy and ain't comfortable." Focus your coaching energy on enrolling and engaging players who *need* you the most, as well as on those who *want* your coaching the most. A high percentage of clients and other players who later became some of my best friends were, in the beginning, very difficult people with whom I persistently pursued developing a coaching relationship.

Do you recommend using a coaching contract?

If the coach isn't the manager, we recommend that an actual coaching contract be set up. It should cover basic ground rules, expectations, and scheduling the coaching calls.

However, in the field of large-account sales, a coach and player may find it difficult, if not impossible, to stick to a regular schedule for coaching calls—particularly if the coach is also the manager. Things come up, the most urgent of which are customer or competitor driven. Therefore, we have found it valuable for the coach to look for "coachable moments"—moments in which the player will be particularly receptive to being coached. Looking for coachable moments is the second coaching habit.

How can a coach tell that a coachable moment may have occurred?

One signal of this may be when the player says something like any of the following: "Do you have a minute?" "There's something I would like to run by you," "What would you do in a situation like this?" or "I'm stuck." One of my favorites to look for is, "By the way. . . ."

A key to discovering coachable moments is *being there,* that is, being centered on the player, not on yourself as coach. This other-centeredness becomes a measure of the coach's maturity. Finally, the ideal signal that a player is coachable is when the player says to the coach, "I would like to request your coaching on something." The best coaching is coaching that has been requested.

What is the best practice for finding coachable moments?

Look out for those instances when large-account salespeople are planning a customer call about which they are not highly confident. This is a highly coachable moment. We have found that the following questions will typically yield several times the impact of normal call preparation. Have the players write their ideas down.

- Would you like me to help you prepare for this customer call?

- What are your most important two or three objectives for the meeting?

- What are the two or three important customer needs that we could satisfy during this meeting?

- What are the two or three questions we could ask that would have the highest impact in helping us achieve the objectives of the call?

- What would be the best two or three openings we could use that would get the call off to the best possible start?

Tell us about the third coaching habit: helping set a clear goal.

Nothing inhibits "right actions" by salespeople and team members more than not having a clear goal and a target date for completion. Without a clear goal, selling teams are destined to spend most of their time focused on the urgent rather than on the important. Without a clear goal, even the most skilled professional selling team members will wander in the desert looking for the oasis. And those selling team members who are part-time on the project will lower the priority for this project as part of their share of mind and actions.

We all know that having goals is very important, but in selling situations most professionals will avoid setting clear goals with dates. Why? In our subconscious minds we believe that if we set a clear goal and a deadline, we have set ourselves up for potential failure, whereas if we don't, there are a number of ways we can declare success. Experience shows, however, that those who set specific goals have significantly higher success rates.

The coach's role is to help players set *extraordinary* goals that are clearly stated and, even though the plan to accomplish them is not yet clear, are possible. We recommend that the coach always ask the person (or team) to state clearly and openly (penalty free) the goals to be achieved for that situation from his or her standpoint and from the standpoint of the customer.

There are three aspects to setting goals that I believe are important: (1) everyone on the team understands clearly the goal of the project and the target date for completion, (2) there are a few clearly identified milestones (with target dates) that will ensure successful completion of the project, and (3) everyone associated with the project (including the customer) understands his or her accountability to short-term actions that will accomplish the targeted milestones.

What is the best practice for setting the clear goals?

It is to think big from the customer's point of view. I have a great personal example—my first sales partner, Jeff Pace, a great coach and role model, who took a lot of interest in my success. Our major account was a large city government, and Jeff assigned me to the city hospital. At the time, computers were primarily used only for back-office accounting functions. Being anxious to succeed quickly, my obvious focus was to sell a new medium-sized system to move the processing for the back-office accounting from the city's system to the hospital.

I was very excited about this sales opportunity and asked for Jeff's advice. He got me to step back and take a longer-term look from the customer's view. He suggested that if we could get the customer to see the long-term value of automation of the whole hospital, our odds of success on the first phase would be higher, and the medium-term to long-term business would be much easier to sell.

And that is exactly what happened. The initial part of the sales process did take a couple of months longer, but in the end the client sole-sourced the business to us, the commitment was for a longer term, our revenue was five times larger and, because of the linkage to their business needs, emphasis on successful implementation was across the *entire* organization. The client's measured return showed better than a two-year payback on the entire capital investment, and my company supplied that customer with its key computer needs for over a decade—all because of a great coach!

I have personally experienced and studied the phenomenon of thinking big for almost thirty years as a player and as a coach. I know that using a coach (whether a manager, team leader, consultant, or customer) to identify an extraordinary goal increases the overall business opportunity significantly. By using a coach, you increase the value to the client, the revenue to the selling company, and the odds of winning.

What is a clear goal? Could you give some examples?

First, the specific products and services (with terms and conditions) that we would like the customer to buy from us by a specific target date; second, the "future state" of a higher value relationship that would exist from the client's and our perspective by a specific date; third, the success of a critical sales meeting and the satisfaction of potential needs of the targeted participants at the meeting from our point of view and from the client's; and fourth, having the ability to identify the best option to take in a critical situation that will satisfy the various constituents.

Tell us about the fourth coaching habit: getting commitment to action.

I have a story that illustrates this. After a number of years of success as a salesperson, I was promoted to lead a number of salespeople in a territory composed of large medical centers and hospital chains. This territory had been a sales disaster for several years. The technical support people and young salespeople who survived these difficult business times were excellent, but quite depressed.

During the first year, I took the lead in setting and managing strategies for all key accounts and for major sales opportunities, and in directing the actions of all team members. I noticed over time that although everyone agreed to my strategies during the planning sessions, people seemed to be waiting around for me to take action or to tell them what to do. And as hard as I worked, I could not handle and direct all the active strategies. As a result, the second year was one of the worst business volume years in the history of that territory.

In fact, my job was on the cutting block and I decided to get some coaching from my new sales manager, Scotty Walsh. He gave me one year to fix the business volume, and some excellent advice: "Art, you are a great salesman, but you can't do everything. You have some people working with you who have incredible potential, but they can't grow if they have to be directed by you in every strategy and action. If you don't move into more of a coaching and support role with the other account leaders, you and we won't make it." That got my attention!

Although it was still necessary to put my director's hat on from time to time, my role changed from leader to strategy facilitator and coach. I learned the value of stepping back and helping others create their extraordinary goals, customer-centric selling strategies, and work plans that consisted of a small number of milestones and short-term, written, committed actions. After that was done, it was a matter of reviewing these work plans once a month, or when coaching was requested. There was a continuous team focus on short-term actions that supported the key strategic goals for each client. As a result, for five years this team sold more business each year than had been sold in the previous five years combined!

Why is it so important for the coach to gain commitment to next actions in a team-selling environment?

Unlike normal project planning, strategies in complex selling environments are built with only limited knowledge of all the facts surrounding the account, the selling opportunity, and key relationships. These projects also tend to be much more dynamic than most other types of projects. Because of the dynamics of these situations and selling team members' work lives, we should not try to get long-term committed actions from team members. However, committed short-term, accountable actions, related to critical milestones of the extraordinary goal, hit the important, urgent category for all team members, including the customer!

What is the best practice for gaining commitment to action?

As a sales leader, the best-practice coaching habit for gaining commitment to action is to transfer, by example and mentoring, your best practices in coaching to those you coach, for in today's virtual teams, coaching the coaches is really the job of sales managers and sales leaders!

How would you sum up?

The highest-impact selling organizations of the future will be made up of relatively few selling professionals and many others who will focus on, develop, and execute customer-centric selling strategies for their major customers, complex selling opportunities, and key relationships. They will manage these strategies and the virtual teams that execute the work plans as projects.

Leadership and management will continue to be vital. But in conjunction with leadership and management, the implementation of an unencumbered coaching culture is the key to creating successful selling organizations and will be the key competitive differentiator for organizations that continue to prosper consistently.

Art Wilson can be reached at (888) 877–0801.

NOTES

CHAPTER ONE

1.   Richard Pascale, "Grassroots Leadership," *Fast Company,* Apr.–May 1998, p. 114.

2.   I am very appreciative of my conversations with Benjamin Zander. His teachable point of view and the way he coaches his students are truly an inspiration.

3.   Bill Breen, "What I Bargained for," *Fast Company,* Apr. 1998, p. 234.

4.   Pascale, 1998.

5.   Kevin Kelly, *New Rules for a New Economy* (New York: Viking Press, 1998). Copyright ©1998 by Kevin Kelly. Used by permission of Viking Penguin, a division of Penguin Putnam Inc.

6.   Pascale, 1998.

7.   The phrase "teachable point of view" was first introduced by Noel Tichy and Ram Charan in *Every Business Is a Growth Business* (New York: Times Books, 1998).

8.   Betsy Morris, "Doug Did It," *Fortune,* May 25, 1998.

9.   Gino Imperato, "How to Give Good Feedback," *Fast Company,* Sept. 1998, p. 144.

10. Victor K. McElheny, *Insisting on the Impossible: The Life of Edwin Land* (Reading, MA: Perseus Books, 1998).

11. Pascale, 1998.

12. John A. Byrne, "How Jack Welch Runs GE," *Business Week,* June 8, 1998, p. 104.

13. Peter Drucker, "New Paradigms," *Forbes,* Oct. 2, 1998.

14. I am grateful for the time spent with Tom Kaiser, president of Zurich-American's International Accounts, as he shared his secrets of success about leading a group that consistently gets extraordinary results.

15. I am indebted to Joan Holmes, executive director of the Hunger Project, for conversations during which she shared insights about collaborative leadership and the work of the Hunger Project.

16. Warren Bennis, *Organizing Genius* (Reading, MA: Addison-Wesley, 1997).

17. I am grateful for the time spent with Douglas Dayton, the Boston director of IDEOS, who introduced us to the fascinating work his group is doing.

18. Tom Peters, *Circle of Innovation* (New York: Knopf, 1997).

19. I am very grateful for many conversations with Hubert Saint-Onge, executive vice president of Strategic Capability of the Mutual Group, who shared his incredible wealth of insight. Saint-Onge is a thought leader known for his groundbreaking work in knowledge management and the positioning of human resources as strategic capability. His teachable point of view on the subject contributed greatly to this book. Chapter Fifteen contains a more extensive interview with him.

20. Peters, 1997.

21. Peters, 1997.

22. Jack Stack and Bo Burlingham, *The Great Game of Business* (New York, Currency/Doubleday, 1994).

CHAPTER TWO

1. Tom Peters, *Circle of Innovation* (New York: Knopf, 1997).
2. Bill Gates, *Business at the Speed of Thought* (New York: Warner Books, 1999).
3. Noel Tichy and Eli Cohen, *Leadership Engine* (New York: HarperCollins, 1997).
4. Tichy and Cohen, 1997.
5. John Byrne, "How Jack Welch Runs GE," *Business Week,* June 8, 1998, p. 90.
6. Warren Bennis, David A. Heenan, and David Heenan, *Co-Leadership: The Power of Great Partnership* (New York: Wiley, 1999), p. 125.
7. Noel Tichy, Christopher Derose, and reporter associate Anne Faircloth, "Roger Enrico's Master Class," *Fortune,* Nov. 25, 1997.
8. Again, I am grateful for conversations with Hubert Saint-Onge.
9. I am appreciative of the time that Bob Mason spent sharing what he does to coach people in his job as marketing manager for Poland Springs in the Boston area.
10. I am grateful for conversations with Phebe Farrow Port, vice president of Retail Sales Development of Estée Lauder Worldwide.
11. Peter M. Senge, *The Fifth Discipline* (New York: Doubleday, 1990); Peter M. Senge (ed.), *The Fifth Discipline Fieldbook: Strategies and Tools for Building a Learning Organization* (New York: Doubleday, 1994).
12. Tichy, Derose, and Faircloth, 1997.
13. I am appreciative of conversations with Juliet Neufeld, vice president of Corporate Capability Development of Zurich Financial Group, about the leading-edge work she is doing in leadership development.

CHAPTER THREE

1. I am grateful for conversations with Jay Abraham about coaching. A conversation with him is always a thought-provoking and energizing experience. See also Chapter Sixteen for a more extensive interview with Abraham.
2. I appreciate being able to tell this story about my friend René Jaeggi, former chairman of Adidas.
3. Tracy Goss, Robert Pascale, and Anthony Athos, "The Reinvention Roller Coaster," *Harvard Business Review,* Nov./Dec. 1993.
4. Goss, Pascale, and Athos, 1993, p. 46.
5. Frank McAuley of the Royal Bank in Canada gave me a powerful insight for transcending the hierarchal relationship in providing coaching and feedback—keep the coaching conversational. It also seems to work best when it is a two-way conversation and both people feel they are learning.
6. Bill Gates, *Business at the Speed of Thought* (New York: Warner Books, 1999).
7. Again, thanks to Jay Abraham.
8. The guidelines for effective groups have been developed by Roger Schwarz, *The Skilled Facilitator* (San Francisco: Jossey-Bass, 1994).
9. Gates, 1999.
10. Arun Maira, "Connecting Across Boundaries: The Fluid-Network Organization," *Prism,* First Quarter 1998.

11. I am appreciative of conversations with John Seely Brown, chief scientist at Xerox's Palo Alto research and development center (PARC) in 1998 about his insight into a collaborative approach.

12. Again, thanks to Phebe Farrow Port of Estée Lauder for sharing aspects of her work.

13. Andrew Grove, *Only the Paranoid Survive* (New York: Bantam Books, 1999).

CHAPTER FOUR

1. Jack Nicklaus and Ken Bowden, *Golf My Way* (New York: Fireside, 1998).

2. Polly LaBarre, "Leadership—Ben Zander," *Fast Company,* Dec. 1998.

3. Again, appreciation to Tom Kaiser, president of Zurich-American's International Accounts.

4. Daniel P. Goleman coined the phrase *emotional intelligence;* see his book *Emotional Intelligence* (New York: Bantam Books, 1997).

5. Tom Peters, *Pursuit of Wow!* (New York: Vintage Books, 1994).

6. Chris Argyris, "Good Communication That Blocks Learning," *Harvard Business Review,* July/Aug. 1994.

7. I am grateful to Susan Fletcher for the use of this example of coaching.

8. The Left-Hand Column Exercise was created by Chris Argyris of Harvard University. Argyris has contributed much to the work of organizational learning; he has written numerous books, among them, *Overcoming Organizational Defenses* (Needham Heights, MA: Allyn and Bacon, 1990); *Strategy, Change, and Defensive Routines* (Boston: Pitman, 1985); and *Knowledge for Action* (San Francisco: Jossey-Bass, 1993).

9. LaBarre, 1998.

10. I am extremely grateful to my close friend and colleague Michel Renaud for our conversations on coaching. Renaud is the founder of Renaud Pemberton Consulting in Montreal, Canada.

CHAPTER FIVE

1. Lou Holtz, *Winning Everyday* (New York: HarperCollins, 1998).

2. Bill Bradley, *Values of the Game* (Wheaton, IL: Artisan Books, 1998).

3. This exercise is from Tracy Goss, *The Last Word on Power: Executive Re-Invention for Leaders Who Must Make the Impossible Happen* (New York: A Currency Book published by Doubleday, 1996).

4. Tracy Goss, Robert Pascale, and Anthony Athos, "The Reinvention Roller Coaster," *Harvard Business Review,* Nov./Dec. 1993.

5. Again, special thanks for conversations with John Seely Brown, chief scientist of Xerox's PARC.

6. I am appreciative of conversations with Bob Meekin, director of Organization Effectiveness at Becton Dickinson for this exercise on coaching people to see their growth spots.

7. Michael Schrage, *No More Teams!* (New York: Doubleday, 1989).

8. John William Gardner, *On Leadership* (New York: Free Press, 1998).

9. Chogyam Trungpa, *Shambhala: Sacred Path of the Warrior* (Boulder, CO: Shambala, 1968).

10. This story is from Ikujiro Nonaka in a *Harvard Business Review* article published in Robert Howard, *The Learning Imperative: Managing People for Continuous Innovation* (Boston: Harvard Business School Press, 1993).

PART II

1. *Masterful Coaching—The Method™,* a five-step model, is reprinted with the permission of Robert Hargrove Consulting.

CHAPTER SIX

1. Richard Teitelbaum, "My Airport, My Palace," *Fortune,* July 22, 1996.
2. Betsy Morris, "Doug Did It," *Fortune,* May 25, 1998; "Betsy Morris, Robert Goizueta, and Jack Welch: The Wealth Builders," *Fortune,* Feb. 5, 1996.
3. Again, I am appreciative of conversations with Joan Holmes, executive director of the Hunger Project.
4. Andrew Grove, *Only the Paranoid Survive* (New York: Bantam Books, 1999).
5. Bill Bradley, *Values of the Game* (Wheaton, IL: Artisan Books, 1998).
6. Portions of this story about Chris Galvin and Motorola were in the May 23, 1998, *Wall Street Journal.*
7. I am grateful to Gary Peck, executive vice president of Adidas, USA, for sharing his teachable point of view.
8. Peter M. Senge, *The Fifth Discipline* (New York: Doubleday, 1990); Peter M. Senge (ed.), *The Fifth Discipline Fieldbook* (New York: Doubleday, 1994).
9. I am grateful for conversations with Douglas Dayton, director of IDEOS in Lexington, Massachusetts.
10. James Kouzes and Barry Posner, *The Leadership Challenge* (San Francisco: Jossey-Bass, 1987).
11. Tom Peters, *In Search of Excellence* (New York: Warner Books, 1988).

CHAPTER SEVEN

1. I am appreciative of conversations with George Vanderheiden, fund manager at Fidelity Investments.
2. Kevin Kelly, *New Rules for a New Economy* (New York: Viking Press, 1998). Copyright ©1998 by Kevin Kelly. Used by permission of Viking Penguin, a division of Penguin Putnam Inc.
3. Kelly, 1998. Copyright ©1998 by Kevin Kelly. Used by permission of Viking Penguin, a division of Penguin Putnam Inc.
4. Michael Schrage, *No More Teams!* (New York: Currency Doubleday, 1989).
5. I am especially appreciative of my numerous conversations with Tom Sudman, founder of Digital AV, on the leading-edge work he is doing on bringing virtual teams together in "Knowledge Rooms" to create extraordinary results. Chapter Thirteen contains a more extensive interview with him.
6. I am thankful for conversations with Eric Wilson, founder of Cogos Consulting, Inc., in Cambridge, Massachusetts.
7. Again, a special thanks to Joan Holmes of the Hunger Project.
8. Again, thanks to Eric Wilson.
9. James Kouzes and Barry Posner, *Encouraging the Heart* (San Francisco: Jossey-Bass, 1999).
10. John Sculley and John Byrne, *Odyssey: Pepsi to Apple* (New York: HarperCollins, 1987).
11. A special thanks to Dr. Rob Manning, chief engineer of the NASA Mars project, for conversations about how the group worked together collaboratively to put the Rover on Mars on July 4, 1997.
12. Rick Pitino and Bill Reynolds, *Success Is a Choice* (New York: Bantam Doubleday, 1998).

13. Katharine Mieszkowski, "Radical Mentoring," *Fast Company*, Sept. 1998, p. 104.

14. Thanks again for conversations with Hubert Saint-Onge.

15. I am appreciative of a conversation with Jodi Uecker-Rust about the coaching culture at Great Plains Software company in Fargo, North Dakota.

16. The guidelines for effective groups have been developed by Roger Schwarz, *The Skilled Facilitator* (San Francisco: Jossey-Bass, 1994).

CHAPTER EIGHT

1. James Kouzes and Barry Posner, *Encouraging the Heart* (San Francisco: Jossey-Bass, 1999).

2. Eric Ransdell, "Redesigning the Design Business," *Fast Company*, Aug. 1998, pp. 36–37.

3. I am grateful for the time Joan Holmes spent with me in conversation about the work she is doing to end hunger with the Hunger Project.

4. Again, thanks to Bob Mason of Poland Springs for his stories of coaching.

5. I am truly grateful for conversations with Michel Renaud of Renaud Pemberton Consulting in Montreal, Quebec, Canada, about coaching an individual using strategic planning in action.

6. Thanks to Joan Holmes for highlighting the importance of a *convener*.

7. I am appreciative of the conversations with John Coonrad, second in command at the Hunger Project.

8. Thanks to Peter Jackson, director of marketing for Royal Insurance, for his metaphor of "orienteering" for strategic planning.

CHAPTER NINE

1. Again, a very special thanks to Michel Renaud, Renaud Pemberton Consulting.

2. I am grateful to Robert Schaffer for sharing his ideas and expertise on developing high-performance teams using the Breakthrough Strategy, which we have called here the Breakthrough Technique. See Robert Schaffer, *The Breakthrough Strategy* (New York: Ballingcr, 1988).

3. Again, special appreciation to Tom Kaiser, president of Zurich Insurance.

4. I appreciate conversations with John Reingold, general manager for project management software business at Microsoft, who was in charge of creating the new version of Microsoft Project.

CHAPTER TEN

1. This story of Ted Williams and coaching is part of Boston sports lore.

2. Again, I really appreciate being able to observe Benjamin Zander in a coaching situation at his music classes, and I appreciate being able to tell a little about how he coaches his students for breakthrough results.

3. Again, appreciation to my friend René Jaeggi for this story.

4. A special appreciation to Richard Perry of the Peregrine Design Group for sharing this great example of coaching people in action.

5. Again, thanks to Michel Renaud for this example of coaching.

6. Sidney Lumet, *Making Movies* (New York: Knopf, 1995).

7. The three ground rules for coaching communication were developed by Chris Argyris and Donald Shón, who did groundbreaking work in developing tools that help groups be effective; see Chris Argyris, *Overcoming Organizational Defenses* (Needham Heights, MA: Allyn and Bacon, 1990); Chris Argyris, *Strategy, Change, and Defensive Routines* (Boston: Pitman, 1985); and Chris Argyris, *Knowledge for Action* (San Francisco: Jossey-Bass, 1993).

8. Gina Imperato, "How to Give Good Feedback," *Fast Company,* Sept. 1998, p. 144.

9. Thanks again to Tom Kaiser, Zurich Financial's International Accounts.

CHAPTER ELEVEN

1. Stuart Wells, *Choosing the Future: The Power of Strategic Thinking* (Woburn, MA: Butterworth-Heinemann, 1998).

2. Jerry Hirshberg, *The Creative Priority* (New York: HarperCollins, 1998).

3. Peter Drucker, *The Effective Executive* (New York: HarperCollins, 1985).

4. Alfred North Whitehead, *The Aims of Education* (New York: Macmillian, 1929).

5. Edgar Schein, *Process Consultation* (Vol. 2) (Reading, MA: Addison-Wesley, 1987), p. 6.

6. James March, *The Technology of Foolishness* (Oslo, Norway: Universitetsforlaget Oslo, 1976).

ACTIVITIES
& Assignments

CHAPTER FIVE

CHAPTER SIX

CHAPTER TEN

THE AUTHOR

Robert Hargrove is the founder of Robert Hargrove Consulting, Brookline, Massachusetts. He has worked with more than thirty thousand people in transformational coaching programs that shift thinking and attitudes. He expands the capacity of people in groups to produce the results they truly desire. He is the author of **Masterful Coaching: Extraordinary Results by Impacting People and the Way They Think and Work Together** *and* **Mastering the Art of Creative Collaboration.**

Hargrove is a sought-after inspirational and thought-provoking speaker. He is an executive coach and collaborative consultant to organizations in government, business, and education in the United States, Canada, and Europe. Program topics include lateral leadership, strategic planning in action, creating a collaborative organization, masterful coaching with a results orientation, and coaching virtual teams.

Hargrove and his group have extensive experience in consulting to large organizations as well as to midsize and entrepreneurial companies. His clients include Adidas, Fidelity Investments, Ciba Geigy, Royal Bank of Scotland, AT&T, and Genetics Institute. His humanitarian interests include work with the United Nations Commission on Refugees and dispute resolution in South Africa.

For more information, call (617) 739-3300 or e-mail robert.hargrove@masterfulcoaching.com.

ROBERT HARGROVE CONSULTING

Robert Hargrove Consulting can help you grow your business exponentially, multiply your profit, win the talent war.

If you have a leadership supply gap that is preventing you from building your business, we can work with you to design an approach that will allow you to fill it. If you need to foster strategic collaboration between different people or groups so that you can develop new products, distribute and see them, we can provide you with the necessary wherewithal. If you want to create coaches and a culture of coaching, we have decades of resident expertise.

We accomplish this work by being master architects for today's leading companies in building performance and capability. We work in a collaborative way with clients to come up with the best possible design solutions. We work from a coaching paradigm that is grounded in producing extraordinary and tangible results in your business with colleagues, not a training paradigm that is merely transactional in nature.

- Leadership Development

- Collab Labs—*Accelerated Solutions Environment*

- Virtual Teams

- The Pathfinder Project Process

Our client list includes Motorola, Zurich Financial Services, Fidelity Investments, NUMMI, Adidas, Novartis, Estée Lauder, Genetics Institute, National Security Agency, National Education Association, National League of Urban Cities. Contact Robert Hargrove Consulting at 1689 Beacon Street, Brookline, Massachusetts 02445 (617) 739–3300; fax at (617) 738–9149; or see our Web site at *www.masterfulcoaching.com,* or e-mail at *robert.hargrove@masterfulcoaching.com.*

THE MASTERFUL COACHING GROUP

Wanted: A Small Consortium of Companies
Committed to the Coaching Revolution

The Masterful Coaching Group is a consortium of leading firms of all sizes that are committed to making the shift from traditional management to coaching and that work closely with Robert Hargrove over time. Here are some of the benefits of membership that are made with special arrangement:

- *Keynote Presentations.* Robert Hargrove and his colleagues throughout the world do keynote talks to large groups and mini-workshops for selected groups .

- *Masterful Coaching Summits.* We engage you in a dialogue about the business case for coaching and creating a climate of coaching in their company.

- *Coaching site visits that allow sponsors to push the envelope.* Robert Hargrove will personally visit the site of the member one to four times a year for 1:1 coaching, dialogue with selected groups, and to present special workshops.

- *Coaching Forums for best practices, videos, newsletter.* You will share with colleagues in other businesses and industries key learnings about coaching.

- *Masterful Coaching Seminars.* We have developed a number of coaching seminars based on *Masterful Coaching, The Method*™. These are highly interactive in nature and each participant is asked to come with a recent coachable moment. We offer a packaged program co-published with Jossey Bass.

To learn more call (617) 739–3300, or visit our Web site at *www.rhargrove.com*. You may email Robert Hargrove at robert.hargrove@masterfulcoaching.com.

INDEX

General Electric, 20, 33, 34, 59, 65, 289. *See also* Welch, Jack

General Motors, 59, 71, 289

Generalists, coaches as, 80

Generosity of spirit, as qualification of coaches, 81

Gerstner, Lou, 53

Give Me a Moment and I'll Change Your Life (Lakein), 254–255

Gladstone, William, 123

Goals: clear, 321–323; collaborative planning of, 134, 136, 185–216; defining, 12; focusing on, 209; at Ford Motor Company, 259; shared, 58, 73; strategic planning in action and, 189–197; stretch, 189; thinking partner approach to, 187–188

Goizueta, Roberto, 10, 142–143

Goleman, Daniel, *Emotional Intelligence,* 97

Great Plains Software Company, 179–180

Grout, Jack, 77

Grove, Andy, 6, 34, 70; *Only the Paranoid Survive,* 145

H

Hernandez, Arthur, 31

Hershey, Milton, 307

Hieman, Miller, 314

Higgins, Chris, 241, 279–288

Hightower, Sallie, 232

Hiring: assessing talent when, 118; current climate for, 6–7

Hirshberg, Jerry, *The Creative Priority,* 247

Holmes, Joan, 23, 169, 188, 193

Holtz, Lou, 107

Holzman, Red, 146

Honda, 124

Hopkins, Tom, 314

Hot Seat activity, 225–226

Human resources: reinvention of, 289–300; strategic capability unit replacing, 291–292, 293–296

Humor: "crazy," 90; used in coaching, 250–251

Hunger Project, 193–195. *See also* Holmes, Joan

I

In Search of Excellence (Peters), 157

Innovation: coaching for, 250; in design, 257–265; expected of employees, 69; growing business through, 307–308; ideas from other industries as, 303–304, 306–307

Intel, 31, 33, 34, 70. *See also* Grove, Andy

Interaction, 11. *See also* Coaching conversations

International Paper, 273

Internet, business transactions via, 70

Ivester, Doug, 10

J

Jackson, Peter, 195–196

Jackson, Phil, 146

Jaeggi, René, 55, 120, 224, 289

James, William, 2

Jimenez, Tony, 240, 243–255

Jobs, Steve, 107, 155, 174

Jones, Richard Perry, 258

Jones, Steve, 108

Jordan, Michael, 108, 146

Journal writing, 95–96

K

Kaiser, Tom, 21, 80, 207–208, 234

Kaplan, Abraham, 253

Kelly, Kevin, 7, 164, 165, 166; *The New Strategic Rules,* 97

Kentucky Fried Chicken, 43

King, Martin Luther, 83

Knowledge capital model, 292

Knowledge rooms, 166, 267, 268; advantages of, 269–270; coaching in, 270–271, 272–274, 275–277; components of, 271–272, 274–275, 277

Knowledge workers, 21; higher-level thinking tasks for, 64–65; increasing productivity of, 78

Korkosz, Dave, 84

Kotter, John, 42

Kouzes, James, 186; *Encouraging the Heart,* 174

L

Lafebvre, Paul, 105

Lakein, Alan, *Give Me a Moment and I'll Change Your Life,* 254–255

Landers, Tom, 304

Language of Change, The (Watzlawick), 253

Lauder, Leonard, 6, 38, 39

Leaders coaching leaders, 249

Leadership: agility in, 24; change in nature of, 291; coaching as responsibility of, 34–35; coaching and teaching as, 5–6, 8–9; creating collaboration as, 23–24; project, 279–288

Leadership development: in coaching contract, 59; coaching through stages of, 235–237; customized experiences promoting, 229–233; focusing on, 40–44; PULL approach to, 46–50; PUSH approach to, 45, 46; as role for coaches, 18–19

Leadership Engine, The (Tichy), 249

Learning: something new, 100–102; training transformed into, 296–300; transformational, 89–90; triple loop model of, 22, 134; while working, 40, 228–229. *See also* Providing feedback and learning

Learning organizations, 296–298

Left-Hand Column Exercise, 93–94

Leonard, George, *Mastery,* 100

Life experiences, translated into teachable insights, 144–147

Line leaders, coaching responsibilities of, 15–16

Listening: before giving advice, 118; committed, 109, 110–111; importance of, 319; metaphors to describe, 251; by project managers, 282, 283–284; "to" versus "for," 111

Lumet, Sydney, *Making Movies,* 233

Lynch, Peter, 163, 164

M

Making Movies (Lumet), 233

Mamet, David, 233

Management: coaching as, x, 271; coaching responsibilities of, 15–16; coaching senior, 243–255. *See also* Leadership

Manning, Rob, 174–175

March, James, *The Technology of Foolishness,* 252

Marketing, coaching emphasizing, 301–311

Marks, Bill, 137

Mars project, 105, 174–175

Marshall, Sir Colin, 56, 117

Mashburn, Jamal, 175

Mason, Bob, 35–36, 188

Masterful Coaching—The Method™: model of, 132–136; Web site, xi. *See also* Coaching

Mastermind groups, 65–66

Mastery (Leonard), 100

Mays, J., 240, 257–265

McCall, John, 230

McKinsey and Company, 6

McLaughlin, Bill, 43

Media, using multiple, 12, 62

Meekin, Bob, 118

Meetings, 73; encouraging participation in, 35–36; ground rules for, 180–181

Mental morsels, 247

Mentoring: of coaches, 87; connected to award system, 179–180; radical, 175

Metaphors: to communicate teachable point of view, 155; to draw people out, 124; for strategic planning, 195–196

Microsoft, 59, 208–209

237; coaching caps for, 218; in coaching contract, 58; courage and compassion in, 219–223; customized experiences for, 229–233; framing feedback in, 223–228; guidelines on, 234, 237–238; steps in, 218; timing of, 228–229. *See also* Feedback; Learning

PULL approach to leadership development, 46–50

PUSH approach to leadership development, 45, 46

Q

Quaker Oats, 155

Qualifications, of coaches, 78–82, 102, 158–159

Questions: value of, 246–247, 319; for weekly coaching sessions, 213–216

R

Radical mentoring, 175

Recognition: in coaching contract, 59–60; providing, as coaching activity, 13; thank-you as, 39

Redstone, Sumner, 145

Reengineering, 71

Reflection: in action, 232–233; on coaching abilities, 158–159; on coaching mission, 148–149; on life experiences, 144–147

Reflection assignments, 96

Reframing: in coaching conversations, 114, 125–127; to focus on similarities, 281; in interactions with coachees, 253

Reframing Cap, 114, 125–127

Reingold, John, 208–209

Relationships, 163–184; building, with employees, 35; coaching contracts in, 181–183; coaching conversations in, 177–181; deciding which to invest in, 168–172; design as creating, 265; engaging people in, 172–173; enrolling people for, 174–177; formal versus informal, 178–179; investing in, 133–134, 135, 167; orientation toward, 165–167; willing partners in, 164–165

Renaud, Michel, 100–102, 189, 191–192, 202–203, 209, 214

Responsibilities: of coaches, 15–16; coaching, as belonging to leadership, 34–35

Results: orientation toward, 79–80. *See also* Goals

Rewards: in coaching contract, 59–60; connected to mentoring, 179–180; providing, 13

Rodman, Dennis, 146

Roles: clarifying, 11; of coaches, 16–24, 174

Roosevelt, Theodore, 83

Royal Dutch Shell, 7, 18–19. *See also* Miller, Steve

Royal Tire of England, 152–153, 200

Russell, Paul, 42

S

Sacherman, Jim, 185–186

Saint-Onge, Hubert, 16, 26, 34, 179, 241, 289–300

Sales: coaching in, 313–324; project team approach to, 315–316

Savkar, Vikram, 221

Schein, Edgar, *Process Consultation,* 248, 252

Schrage, Michael, *No More Teams,* 119, 166

Schwab, 69

Schwarz, Roger, *The Skilled Facilitator,* 66, 180

Sculley, John, 174

Sears, 289

Self-image, altering your, 13–14

Senge, Peter, 154; *Fifth Discipline,* 40, 229

Shell Oil Company. *See* Royal Dutch Shell

Shogun (Clavell), 97

Six-Cap Coaching System, coaching conversations and, 112–115. *See also individual caps*

Skilled Facilitator, The (Schwarz), 66, 180

Smith, Dean, 108

Soleri, Paolo, 83

Speaking, committed, 108–109, 110

Specialists, coaches as, 80, 239–241

Spring training, observing, 97